A Many Colored Kingdom

A Many Colored Kingdom

Multicultural Dynamics for Spiritual Formation

Elizabeth Conde-Frazier, S. Steve Kang,
and Gary A. Parrett

B
Baker Academic
Grand Rapids, Michigan

© 2004 by Elizabeth Conde-Frazier, S. Steve Kang, and Gary A. Parrett

Published by Baker Academic
a division of Baker Publishing Group
P.O. Box 6287, Grand Rapids, MI 49516-6287
www.bakeracademic.com

Printed in the United States of America

Library of Congress Cataloging-in-Publication Data
Conde-Frazier, Elizabeth.
    A many colored kingdom : multicultural dynamics for spiritual formation / Elizabeth Conde-Frazier, S. Steve Kang, and Gary A. Parrett.
        p.   cm.
    Includes bibliographical references and index.
    ISBN 10: 0-8010-2743-8 (pbk.)
    ISBN 978-0-8010-2743-7 (pbk.)
    1. Christian education. 2. Multiculturalism—Religious aspects—Christianity.
    I. Kang, S. Steve. II. Parrett, Gary A., 1957– III. Title.
    BV1471.3.C66 2004
    268—dc22   2003052382

Contents

Introduction

An Exploration and an Experiment

ELIZABETH CONDE-FRAZIER, S. STEVE KANG,
AND GARY A. PARRETT

Probing Critical Issues

This book is both an exploration and an experiment. In terms of its subject matter, this book is an exploration of how ethnic and cultural diversity, and our interactions with such diversity, affect the dynamics of Christian spiritual formation. The conviction set forth in these pages is that when authentic relationships are built that embrace diverse backgrounds, tremendously positive growth in Christlikeness can occur. In terms of its format, this book is an experiment within that very exploration, for it is the work of three persons who, writing from diverse ethnic, cultural, and personal backgrounds, have been seeking to build such relationships. Further, each of us is actively engaged in facilitating such spiritual formation and relationships in both academic and church contexts.

Elizabeth Conde-Frazier, a Puerto Rican-American, teaches courses in religious education at Claremont School of Theology. S. Steve Kang is a Korean-American who teaches in the department of Christian formation and ministry at Wheaton College. Gary A. Parrett, a white American, teaches in the area of educational ministries at Gordon-Conwell Theological Seminary. The unique perspective each of us brings

7

involves not only different cultural and ethnic experiences but other differences as well. For example, each of us is from a different denominational tradition and teaches in an academic setting with its own unique cultural realities. We have been cultivating personal and professional relationships with one another since 1996. This book represents some of the fruit of our friendships, as well as our common passion for the ministry of Christian formation and an appreciation of the ethnic diversity of the church, which, we believe, is a critical part of God's design for the health and wholeness of the body of Christ.

It is our intention to stimulate the understanding, conversation, and practices of the local church in light of the wondrous realities of the global church of Jesus Christ. It is our hope that the local church can rediscover its unique responsibility as a subculture of the global kingdom culture, that is, the kingdom of God. It is hoped, further, that the ideas in this book will provide resources for Christian educators in academic settings and will encourage each reader toward personal growth in kingdom consciousness and obedience. Indeed, we desire to come alongside each reader—through the medium of this book—to seek an encounter *together* with the truth, taking aim to perceive it more clearly, consider it more critically, embrace it more passionately, obey it more faithfully, and embody it with greater integrity.[1] Specifically, this book examines the implications of the Great Commission to make disciples of all nations (*panta ta ethnē;* Matt. 28:19) and the great commandment's requirement of each of us: "Love your neighbor as yourself" (Mark 12:31).

There is much to suggest that evangelical churches in America are often out of alignment with God's heart and purposes regarding ethnic diversity. In their challenging book, *Divided by Faith,*[2] Michael Emerson and Christian Smith investigate the attitudes of contemporary American evangelicals toward issues of race and ethnicity. The picture sketched through their significant research and analysis is not a pretty one. The United States, the authors charge, continues to be a "racialized society."

---

1. This line is based on the following definition of Christian teaching by Gary A. Parrett: "To teach is to come alongside another, in the power of the Holy Spirit, to seek an encounter together with the Truth; taking aim to perceive it more clearly (perception), consider it more critically (cognition), embrace it more passionately (affection), obey it more faithfully (behavior), and embody it with greater integrity."

2. Michael O. Emerson and Christian Smith, *Divided by Faith: Evangelical Religion and the Problem of Race in America* (New York: Oxford University Press, 2000). In a recently published companion volume, *United by Faith: The Multicultural Congregation as an Answer to the Problem of Race* (New York: Oxford University Press, 2003), Curtis Paul DeYoung, Michael O. Emerson, George Yancy, and Karen Chai Kim argue that the best antidote to the national and evangelical struggles over racial and ethnic issues is to build multiracial congregations whenever this is possible.

By this they mean "a society wherein race matters profoundly for differences in life experiences, life opportunities, and social relationships."[3] The evangelical church community, far from being exempt from such things, is, according to their findings, even more prone to divisions based on race. Citing a 1998 study, they note that "more than 90% of American congregations are made up of at least 90% of people of the same race."[4]

Factors that contribute to this partition along racial lines, in the view of Emerson and Smith, are many and varied. They point out that blacks and whites view the sources of racial tensions very differently, with whites tending to look at the problems as individualistic and blacks tending to see structural issues as the primary source.[5] In the interviews they conducted, the authors found that whites were particularly irritated when suggestions were made that anything other than individual responsibility was to blame for the plight of poor blacks. In fact, whites seemed more irritated by the thought that inequities between whites and blacks might be due to structural issues than they were by the inequities themselves.[6] The white evangelicals that Emerson and Smith studied also tended to dismiss the notion that historical factors were significant in shaping present understandings of and responses to contemporary racial issues. Further, white evangelicals denied that they had any connection to the sins of injustice committed by whites against blacks during the history of the country.[7] Emerson and Smith paid special attention to the role that "marketing religion" plays in keeping the church in America divided. As churches heed the "wisdom" of church growth leaders, they carve out a "market niche" for their church planting and evangelistic efforts. Typically, the niche that is sought is intentionally homogeneous. It is often by design, then, that America's evangelical churches are largely mono-ethnic.

Certainly, arguments can be made, especially those with an evangelistic thrust, for targeting particular audiences. But what happens if such methods are successful in bringing large numbers into the church? What kind of church will that be? What kind of Christians will such a church form? If a homogeneous church is planted in a community that is truly heterogeneous, how will members defend its shape in light of the biblical teaching that the cross destroyed the barriers that separated us not only from God but also from one another? What will members say to the watching world, who, according to

3. Ibid., 7.
4. Ibid., 136.
5. Ibid. This is probed throughout the book. Pages 94–96 are an example.
6. Ibid., 101, 110.
7. Ibid., 81–82.

Jesus, will believe that God sent his Son when they behold the unity of Christ's followers (John 17:23)? Is such a church simply a way station for people until they are ready to move on to more mature experiences of biblical *koinōnia?* The reality is that such questions raise complex issues. The reality is, further, that there are no easy solutions to these issues. Tragically, however, many Christians seem uninterested in seriously engaging the questions at all. It should be expected that believers would disagree on how to answer such questions (after all, we manage to disagree on just about everything else); to simply ignore these matters, on the other hand, is indefensible.

Some may suggest that there is an easy answer: do away with all the "hyphenated American" congregations (such as African-American, Cuban-American, Taiwanese-American). Then we can all just be Americans and worship together. Often, when people set forth such a plan, however, they do not offer to leave their churches to join those hyphenated Americans in worship. They simply suppose that "they can join us. After all, we're 'just American.'" The further supposition may be that when they join us, they can simply check their "hyphenatedness" at the front door, and we will all get along just fine.

Miroslav Volf, reflecting on Paul's teachings about the church, argues that the Bible points us in another direction: "Baptism into Christ creates a people as the differentiated body of Christ. Bodily inscribed differences are brought together, not removed. . . . The Pauline move is not from the particularity of the body to the universality of the spirit, but from separated bodies to the community of interrelated bodies— the one *body in the Spirit* with many *discrete members.*"[8] For Volf, it is imperative that all of us *give ourselves to others and 'welcome' them, to readjust our identities to make space for them.*"[9]

The reality in far too many cases is that "churches, the presumed agents of reconciliation, are at best impotent and at worst accomplices in the strife."[10] Volf drives this point home when, citing Peter Berger, he notes that even today "many black Baptists or Methodists feel closer to black Muslims than to their white fellow Christians." Ultimately, Volf calls believers back to the way of Jesus, who embraced all, even his enemies, through a powerful act of "self-donation" at the cross. To those who will not follow, Volf offers this rebuke: "To claim the comfort of the Crucified while rejecting his way is to advocate not only cheap grace but a deceitful ideology."[11]

---

8. Miroslav Volf, *Exclusion and Embrace: A Theological Exploration of Identity, Otherness, and Reconciliation* (Nashville: Abingdon, 1996), 48.

9. Ibid., 29, italics in original.

10. Ibid., 36.

11. Ibid., 24.

Facing Our Ambivalent Selves

In many respects, it seems that the experiences of evangelical churches in America simply mirror the enduring national struggles surrounding these issues. The diversity of cultures and the worlds they represent have long been coming into contact with one another, especially in urban areas but even in places not once seen as diverse. Anthropologist Renato Rosaldo speaks of this dynamic as one in which a person is continuously encountering persons from different races, ethnicities, and classes.[12] The United States is becoming increasingly multicultural. Indeed, the U.S. Census Bureau projects that by the year 2060, there will be no clear majority population. The majority will be a multicultural, multiethnic people.[13]

We have responded to this growing trend in different ways throughout our history as a nation. In the nineteenth and earlier twentieth centuries, we responded to immigrant groups by advocating assimilationist policies that forced them to give up their native languages, cultural practices, and, at times, even their names in order to join the "melting pot" of American culture. This worked for those whose appearances permitted them to blend into the accepted majority of the United States. Groups such as the Chinese and the Japanese, however, as well as those who were considered black, did not have this option, given their physical features.[14]

An understanding that differs from that of the melting pot has evolved since the 1960s and 1970s, when persons belonging to cultural and linguistic groups considered minorities made efforts to reclaim their ethnic histories, languages, and cultural practices. This image is the "salad bowl." According to this image, persons and groups are in the same bowl yet maintain their uniqueness.

In the 1980s and 1990s, the largest influx of immigrants to the United States in any twenty-year period took place.[15] In the book *Death of the Church*, Mike Regele asserts that the church is being left behind by the

12. See Renato Rosaldo, *Culture and Truth: The Remaking of Social Analysis* (Boston: Beacon Press, 1989).

13. See www.census.gov/population/projections/nation/summary/np-t5-g.txt. The projection is that by 2060, the percentage of U.S. citizens who are "white, non-Hispanic" will drop below 50 percent.

14. For a history of Asian-Americans and the issues pertaining to the immigration and acculturation process at different times in the history of the United States, see Ronald Takaki, *Strangers from Another Shore: A History of Asian Americans* (Boston: Back Bay Books, 1998). For a broad understanding of the issues of immigration in the United States, see Alejandro Portes and Rubén G. Rumbaut, *Immigrant America: A Portrait* (Berkeley: University of California Press, 1990).

15. Mike Regele with Mark Schulz, *Death of the Church* (Grand Rapids: Zondervan, 1995), 104.

change in neighborhoods that is being created by these ethnic changes in population.[16] Our neighborhoods are changing not only due to immigration but also because of economic necessity. The gap between rich and poor is increasing in our nation indiscriminate of race or ethnicity. This has two important results in relation to growing multiculturalism. First, the rich are no longer from just one ethnic group. Wealthy neighborhoods can be multicultural. Second, the number of the poor is increasing, and there is less ability to choose one's living space based on factors such as race or ethnicity, leaving one to choose primarily on the basis of affordability. It no longer makes sense, then, to construct ministry on the basis of ethnicity if the surrounding community is not divided in that way.[17]

Diversity is increased by economic and power disparities that create inequalities and injustices at every level. Such inequalities and injustices increase the possibilities of conflict. Yet even within diversity there exist numerous creative possibilities for carving out a common ground. In a diverse world, the discovery of mutuality and the exploration of common ground are necessary.[18] The wisdom of bicultural peoples can be helpful in learning to create such a space.

Recently, the Partners in Urban Transformation in California met with pastors of multicultural congregations, denominational leaders, and scholars in theological education to discuss these issues. Their dialogue explored the issue of power in the structure of these congregations. They identified space, time, resources—including financial resources—leadership style, theology, and identity as the places of power in the church. Space involved the use of facilities, and time had to do with whether suffi-

---

16. Ibid., 106.

17. Brian Parcel, "Called to Be Multicultural," New Testament and Religious Education Perspectives to Develop Multicultural Churches, DMIN Project, Claremont School of Theology, Claremont, Calif., 2002.

18. Hispanic/Latina theologians name this common ground the borderland. Those who compose the borderland are *mestizos/as*. A *mestizo* does not fit into the categories of either of the parent groups. A *mestizo* is both an insider and an outsider, understanding both while having a closeness and a distance at the same time with both. For further reading, see Virgilio Elizondo, "Mestizaje as a Locus of Theological Reflection," in *Frontiers of Hispanic Theology in the United States*, ed. Allan Figueroa Deck (Maryknoll, N.Y.: Orbis, 1992), 104–23. Also see Gloria Anzaldúa, *Borderlands/La Frontera: The New Mestiza* (San Francisco: Aunt Lute Books, 1999). For alternative terms such as *mulatez* and *sato*, see Loida I. Martell-Otero, "Of Satos and Saints: Salvation from the Periphery," *Perspectivas* (summer 2001): 8–9. Asian theologian Jung Young Lee speaks of this space as the place of marginalization where there is no center but only marginalizations, making those at the center and those at the margins equal. He calls it an "in-between" and an "in-both" space. These are spaces where we transcend dualistic modes of thinking and understand how opposing ideas and knowledge can interact with one another. See his book *Marginality: The Key to Multicultural Theology* (Minneapolis: Fortress, 1995).

cient time is given to each group for worship and other programs. The differences in how each culture understands time were also discussed.

Leadership style dealt with the image of the pastor held by the congregation and the pastor. Does the pastor function as a chaplain or as an equipper and organizer? Identity referred to the issues faced by a first-generation church.[19] The ability to maintain cultural identity and language empowers the first generation while also helping members deal with the sense of loss of their country of origin. It helps them create a safe space.

Theological issues had a historical root that went back to the missionary legacy of the twentieth century. Theology was at times used as a way of Americanizing people both in their countries of origin, where missionaries served, and when they came as immigrants to the United States. Theology was used as "power over." Some missionary literature used "to evangelize" and "to Americanize" interchangeably, as if there were no difference between them. Values and behavioral changes were linked to this understanding that to be Christian meant embracing the values of the United States. At times, this Americanization led to redeemed lives while on other occasions it led to the stripping of one's culture and thus separation from families and cultural groups.

Cultural differences also fashion spiritual practices such as prayer and how we engage Scripture. Are we contemplative or discursive? How is power shaped when we speak the truth in love? For example, can a member of a congregation that is sharing a facility with a congregation of a different cultural group dare to name the discrimination with which his congregation is treated. In this discussion, styles of confrontation, respect, and voice were addressed.

The group found that narrative frameworks are helpful when coming to understand and practice being the people of God as a diverse community. Narrative not only asks "Who am I?" but "Who is God?" and "Who are we in God?" Narrative looks at the biblical, the autobiographical, and the communal stories. The communal story is the interweaving of our story with God's epic metanarrative.

For these and other reasons, narrative plays a key part in the present book. We each tell something of our own personal story to illustrate our own formation and struggles with the complex issues of multiethnicity and cultural diversity. We also examine God's unfolding drama as it relates to all the peoples of the earth and consider who believers are called to be as they take up their parts within that drama.

Put briefly, for now, we are persuaded that God's unfolding drama embraces people from every nation, tribe, and tongue as he establishes

---

19. A first-generation church is a congregation formed by persons who have immigrated to the United States from a variety of countries of origin.

and extends his glorious and eternal kingdom. To be faithful to this kingdom vision, we, the followers of Jesus Christ, must seek to align ourselves with God's purposes and to do so with all that we are and all that we have, thus engaging ourselves in the world as kingdom citizens. Obedience to God's heart and will must characterize our responses as individuals, as congregations, as Christian centers of learning, and as the church universal. As we seek such obedience, we will grow in conformity to the likeness of Jesus Christ. If we turn aside from God's way, our own spiritual formation—and the formation of those we serve in our families, churches, and schools—will surely be hindered.

Answering Objections

Before proceeding further, however, it is important to acknowledge that reasonable matters of concern have been raised about the idea of multiculturalism. For example, it is one thing to suggest, as we do in this book, that God values people from all cultures and ethnic groups. It is another to suggest, as we do *not* do in this book, that all cultures and lifestyles ought to be equally valued, and therefore, no approach to life should be judged as better or more just than another.

Another concern expressed by some is that paying too much attention to the ethnic diversity of America will invariably be divisive. Arthur Schlesinger Jr., who was an advisor to President John F. Kennedy, sounded such an alarm in his 1992 book, *The Disuniting of America: Reflections on a Multicultural Society.* The author argues that the ethnicity obsession will divert attention from real needs and likely lead to "a society fragmented into separate ethnic communities. The cult of ethnicity exaggerates differences, intensifies resentments and antagonisms, drives ever deeper the awful wedges between races and nationalities. The endgame is self-pity and self-ghettoization."[20]

20. Arthur Schlesinger Jr., *The Disuniting of America: Reflections on a Multicultural Society* (New York: W. W. Norton, 1992), 102. Schlesinger is especially concerned about the rise of "Afrocentricity." He does acknowledge that African-Americans, in particular, have been victims of horrific racism in this country. But he does not, it seems to me (Gary), deal adequately with how the enduring plague of racism makes impossible the realization of his vision for America—a country in which "individuals from all nations are melted into a new race of men" (Schlesinger uses this line, a quote from Hector St. John de Crevecoeur, a Frenchman who immigrated to the American colonies in 1759, in the book's foreword and again in its closing paragraph). I would argue that the same kind of problem exists in many of our churches today. Our racist attitudes and practices prevent fulfillment of the vision many churches profess to have for a truly multiethnic community.

Schlesinger notes that "the eruption of ethnicity" in the American consciousness "had many good consequences."[21] Yet the growth of "the cult of ethnicity" and its accoutrements—cultural pluralism and the rejection of a unifying American vision—concern him. But such things need not be part of acknowledging and speaking openly and honestly about ethnic differences among Americans. Quickly glossing over these differences in the name of national unity, on the other hand, will result in a melting pot in which some experience more melting than others. Referring to the national slogan, *E pluribus unum* ("out of many, one"), Schlesinger argues that ethnocentrism glorifies *pluribus* and belittles *unum*.[22] We would argue, to the contrary, that if due attention is not paid to *pluribus*, the concept of *unum* is missed, for the unity envisioned in the national slogan implies, even requires, the reality of diversity. When genuine diversity is either ignored or disallowed, the result is uniformity, not unity.[23]

Lawrence E. Adams, in his 2002 work, *Going Public: Christian Responsibility in a Divided America*, encourages Christians to respond faithfully to the divisions they see around them. The book offers thoughtful insights into the political and moral divisions in the country and challenges believers to take up the responsibilities of citizenship. But Adams pays only scant attention to the factors of race and ethnicity in detailing the national divide. He cites the 2000 presidential election as a timely example of how deep the national divide runs and notes the "cleavage of voter support largely along racial and moral cultural lines."[24] Adams, however, fails to probe further into possible racial aspects of the "cleavage," apparently opting instead to focus entirely on the "moral cultural lines." Speaking later in the book about issues of race, he concludes that "Americans in general do not seem to see race or sex as very significant factors in political life. Nor is this the case with ethnic identity or age. . . . Americans claim that individual identity overrides any of these external characteristics."[25] Very little data is offered in support of such conclusions. The survey data that is offered is not convincing and seems only marginally related to the issue about which Adams reaches the conclusion noted above.

21. Ibid., 15.
22. Ibid., 17.
23. The same is true of the biblical concept of "unity" (see chapter 3 for a fuller discussion of this).
24. Lawrence E. Adams, *Going Public: Christian Responsibility in a Divided America* (Grand Rapids: Brazos Press, 2002), 12–13.
25. Ibid., 95.

The fact of the racial divide in the 2000 election cannot be, it seems to us, so easily dismissed. In fact, a 2002 study conducted by the Joint Center for Political and Economic Studies concluded that the divide had widened during the two years following the election. In 2000, 56 percent of African-Americans and 57 percent of whites, according to the Center's National Opinion Poll, expressed belief that the country was moving in the right direction. By 2002, the numbers had substantially shifted. While 40.6 percent of whites surveyed still held that view, only 23.9 percent of blacks agreed. Views about what issues are most important for the nation also differed significantly for whites and blacks.[26]

Throughout his book, Adams's investigation clearly runs along "moral cultural" rather than racial lines. His otherwise helpful review of historical factors that have brought the country to its current condition does not include the history of race relations in the nation. Given his subject matter, this is a glaring omission. It is not altogether surprising, however, in light of the fact that many Christian authors before him also overlooked or downplayed the role of race in their analyses of the American landscape.

There are, of course, people from all racial backgrounds who prefer to downplay the importance of race in discussing national concerns. Chinese-American Eric Liu writes of "a fear of ethnosclerosis: the hardening of the walls between the races." Still, he confesses that "race matters . . . mainly because *race matters*. It's undeniable, in other words, that society is still ordered by the random bundle of traits we call 'race'—and that benefits and penalties are often assigned accordingly. But it is this persistent social fact, more than any intrinsic worth, that makes racial identity deserving of our moral attention." Liu wonders if his worries "belong to a time that is already passing. Perhaps over the horizon, beyond multiculturalism, awaits the cosmopolitan realm that David Hollinger calls 'postethnic America.'"[27]

Although Liu's own skepticism concerning such prospects seems evident in his remarks, it may in fact be easier for someone like him, who as a young man has admittedly enjoyed tremendous educational and professional opportunities, to dream of such a society than it is for those Americans who have not known such things. His apparent ambivalence about how much attention matters of race and ethnicity deserve may be a reflection of the fact that his American experience has been a

26. DeWayne Wickham, "Racial, Ideological Issues Split Black, White Voters," *USA Today*, 5 November 2002, 15A.

27. Eric Liu, *The Accidental Asian: Notes of a Native Speaker* (New York: Random House, 1998), 65.

mixture of prosperity and pain. Others—who have known far more pain than prosperity—may not be as ambivalent.

Such concerns notwithstanding, we believe that serious attention must be paid by all persons, but especially those in the church of Jesus Christ, to issues of race, ethnicity, and culture. We affirm, with Volf, that

> in order to keep our allegiance to Jesus Christ pure, we need to nurture commitment to the multicultural community of Christian churches. We need to see ourselves and our own understanding of God's future with the eyes of Christians from other cultures, listen to voices of Christians from other cultures so as to make sure that the voice of our culture has not drowned out the voice of Jesus Christ, "the one Word of God."[28]

Defining Key Terms

It will be useful to offer at least a few thoughts about a number of key concepts dealt with in this book. Each of these words is difficult to define and somewhat "loaded." Hence, attempting to define them can be a perilous venture. What follows, therefore, are suggested definitions or, perhaps, descriptions of some of these terms. Figure 1 reminds us of the complexity of the interaction between these concepts and other formative forces constantly at work in our lives.

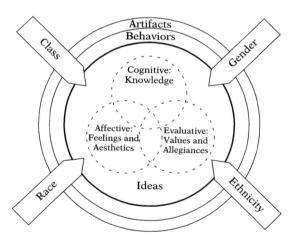

Fig. 1. Culture: Interaction of Formative Forces in Our Lives

28. Volf, *Exclusion and Embrace*, 53–54. Volf lifts the phrase "the one Word of God" from the Barmen Declaration, affirmed by those confessing Christians who sought to stand against the national idolatry fostered by the Nazi regime.

Culture

Culture can be described as an integrated system of ideas, feelings, and values and their associated patterns of behavior and products (i.e., learned behaviors, beliefs, attitudes, values, and ideals) shared by a group of people (i.e., a particular society or population). Culture organizes and regulates what the group thinks, feels, and does.

Human social life involves ceaseless interactions between beliefs and behavior. In this continuous and complex process of dialogical interaction, not only do beliefs guide behavior, but the reverse is also true, especially in the long run. Behavior "shapes, orients, uproots, tears down, and raises up a nexus of cognitive features that accompany and guide behavior in the long run."[29] In short, human social life shapes culture and is profoundly shaped by culture.

Race

Using various biological criteria to locate the concept of race in disciplines of sciences—for example, focusing on blood groups, skin color, cranial and skeletal features, and DNA—has not yielded a coherent definition of race. The resulting typologies based on the use of different classificatory criteria can only be construed as arbitrary demarcations that lack biological significance and integrity.[30]

Nonetheless, race or racial differentiation is commonly understood as physical differences based on inherited biological materials and has had profound implications in how human beings function in society. It is not uncommon for members of society to rank themselves based on race, which was all too common during the European colonization of Africa and the period of slavery in the United States. In terms of designating racial identity, society has often used arbitrary rules of descent in classifying individuals. For instance, in the United States, the "one drop of blood" rule still exists. According to this rule, a single ancestor of a darker, thus the "other," race is sufficient to establish one's racial identity. In other words, if one parent is Latino or black and the other white, their children are considered Latino or black, respectively.[31]

29. Marvin Harris, *Theories of Culture in Postmodern Times* (Walnut Creek, Calif.: Alta Mira, 1999), 28.

30. See discussions on race in William Outhwaite and Tom Bottomore, eds., *The Blackwell Dictionary of Twentieth-Century Social Thought* (Oxford: Blackwell, 1994), 536–38; Stephan Jay Gould, *The Mismeasure of Man* (New York: W. W. Norton, 1996); and David Unander and John M. Perkins, *Shattering the Myth of Race: Genetic Realities and Biblical Truths* (Valley Forge, Pa.: Judson, 2000).

31. Harris, *Theories of Culture in Postmodern Times*, 67–77.

Often groups who have enjoyed and seek to maintain their privileged status utilize such arbitrary rules to justify the status quo or racial "harmony" in society and thus their domination of others.

Race, then, should be construed as a social construct. The term *social race* is perhaps more appropriate when acknowledging certain physical differences. Moreover, social race highlights the profound socioculturally constructive implications the notion of race has had and continues to have on the human race, which is one species with great phylogenetic variability.

Ethnicity

Anthropologists and sociocultural theorists have battled one another in explaining cultural differences and similarities. Those who view ethnicity as a largely biological phenomenon point to a set of common hereditary, racial, genetic, and geographic factors in explicating the formation of ethnic groups. They believe that ethnic groups result from subtle differentiations within a race. Cultural theorists, however, look to the influence of environment. Among cultural theorists, for instance, instrumentalists see ethnicity as a political instrument utilized by a certain group of people in pragmatic pursuit of their own interests, and constructivists emphasize the contingency and fluidity of ethnic identity, treating it as something that is constructed in specific sociohistorical contexts.[32]

Ethnicity embraces all the above perspectives. While ethnicity and social race overlap in terms of common descent or physical appearance, a greater emphasis is given to sociocultural commonalities in describing ethnicity. Perhaps the single most salient cultural source of ethnic demarcation is the possession of a common language or dialect through which life is arranged and culture is negotiated. Ethnicity, then, is associated with "distinctive cuisines, holidays, religious beliefs, dances, folklore, dress, and other traditions."[33] Ethnicity, however, can be misappropriated to promote a group's interests. For instance, the Jews, who were an ethnic group with a distinctive religion- and language-based culture, were represented as a race by Nazi ideologists and were subjected to persecution of an epic proportion.[34]

Class

Class refers to a large segment of people that is generally demarcated by the nature and consequences of the distribution of economic

---

32. Alan Barnard and Jonathan Spencer, eds., *Encyclopedia of Social and Cultural Anthropology* (London: Routledge, 1996), 190–93.

33. Harris, *Theories of Culture in Postmodern Times*, 114.

34. Outhwaite and Bottomore, *Twentieth-Century Social Thought*, 204.

goods in society. Functionalists such as Max Weber, on the one hand, understand class as a taxonomy or relationships based on the economic role or function of segments of people who are engaged in common economic activities in society. Conflict theorists such as Karl Marx, on the other hand, define classes as segments of people who are in conflict as a direct result of the unequal distribution of economic goods. Conflict theorists have been much more explicit about class formation being a result of the preferential division of political prerogatives and the discriminatory differentiation of cultural values and *habitus*. They criticize that such a *habitus* stems from the confluence of economic exploitation, political oppression, and cultural domination.[35]

Gender

Gender generally encompasses the traits that are culturally attributed to women and men, while sex refers to the physical characteristics that make human beings biologically women and men. In the second half of the twentieth century, the traditional understanding of gender was questioned by theorists who asserted that the perceptions of biology, nature, or sex are formed only within language, culture, and history. For instance, Judith Butler argues that gender should not be construed as a given symbolic or biological identity but as a *practice* that is historically constructed and produces gender identities.[36] These theorists are concerned about the hierarchy that is implicit in gender binarism in which masculine authority and feminine subservience have shaped and continue to shape sociocultural practices and identity formation.[37]

The Plan of the Book

Following the introduction, this book turns to our own stories and then proceeds to a survey of God's unfolding drama of reconciling all things to himself and establishing his eternal kingdom. The remainder of the book is a combination of biblical and theological reflection, educational theory, and pedagogical suggestions for the church and the classroom. Readers will notice differences in each of our styles and approaches;

35. Michael Payne, *A Dictionary of Cultural and Critical Theory* (Oxford: Blackwell, 1997), 105–7; and Outhwaite and Bottomore, *Twentieth-Century Social Thought*, 80–84.
36. Judith Butler, *Gender Trouble: Feminism and the Subversion of Identity* (New York: Routledge, 1990).
37. Payne, *Dictionary of Cultural and Critical Theory*, 217–18.

this is by design. We hope that even these differences will be appreciated. As the tags that are sometimes attached to silk garments say, "Irregularities in this garment are a mark of its authenticity and enhance the natural beauty of the fabric." For anything beautiful or praiseworthy found in this work, may all glory go to the Lord of the nations.

1

Three Stories

Elizabeth Conde-Frazier, S. Steve Kang, and Gary A. Parrett

Elizabeth's Story: Two Vignettes

What brings me to the task of writing about multicultural Christian education? Perhaps I can best describe it with two vignettes. The first is one in which I am in a nondominant position. The second is one in which as a Protestant Christian I have power because I represent the dominant religious view. Eric H. F. Law speaks of how in different situations we are in positions of power or powerlessness.[1] As a teacher, I am in a position of power over my students, but as a person who is labeled a minority in this country, I have experienced powerlessness through disenfranchisement and discrimination. Both of these experiences have taught me valuable lessons about ministry in a multicultural world. Each one is an expression of the passions that bring me to the work of this writing.

Powerlessness as Invisibility

It was a cold January day in New York City. The ice-covered streets were treacherous, but the funeral home was full, and more people kept

---

1. See Eric H. F. Law, *The Wolf Shall Dwell with the Lamb: A Spirituality for Leadership in a Multicultural Community* (St. Louis: Chalice Press, 1993).

coming. The ministers stood together in the front. They were there from every Hispanic Baptist church in the city. A taxi rolled into the parking lot. The door opened and a frail, older woman emerged with a walker. She was helped up the few stairs into the building and began looking for a chair in the already too crowded room. Patiently, she looked down every row in the dimly lit room.

My father saw her, and they exchanged words of greeting, she in her soft quivering voice and he in broken English. He quickly made room for her at the end of our row, where the family was seated. She, a stranger, sat next to me. The service began. It was my mother's funeral service.

In 1959, my mother had gone back to work to help with the family income. The first day of her new job she was excited and nervous but happy to be working for the Lord. She was to be the secretary in the office of the Spanish department of the denomination.

That same night as we ate dinner my mother cried as she ate. She told my father in whispers that the women where she worked had treated her poorly. They had not spoken to her. She had been surprised and deeply disappointed by the discrimination and prejudice evident even in the church. My father could not believe it. "But, honey, how can this be? This is the church!" His confusion and disbelief questioned the credibility of my mother's observations, her interpretation of the events of her first day at work.

Future dinner conversations revolved around the continuing story of my mother and the women she worked with. They would not speak *to* her, but they spoke *about* her while she was present. They said things that hurt her, called her names, and made accusations about things she had not done.

Now, fifteen years later I was at her funeral. During the service, a difficult moment made my tears well up, and they flowed on to my lap. Silently, a white, wrinkled hand slipped over mine. It felt soft yet firm with strength, and with it she carried me through that moment. It was difficult to receive this strength, for I was trying to be strong on my own, but I appreciated it. She quietly reclaimed her hand as she felt me grow calm.

At the end of the service she said, "I had to come. I could not stay away. I had to pay my respects." She sat down again to regain her own strength. I sat with her. She then told me her story. "When your mother came to work for the Spanish department, her office space was adjacent to mine. I and the other women who worked there were insulted by the fact that she worked alongside us as if she were like us. We did cruel things. We blamed her when the community kitchen was left dirty, and we called her names that I do not wish to repeat, for they are lies. We never spoke to her, and we used notes to communicate only what was work related. It must have been very difficult to work with us. She, in turn, started to leave our favorite pastries on the right-hand corner of our desks every morning. She used the prison of silence we created for her to listen to our needs and wants. She got to know us very well. She gave us birthday cards and holiday cards. She cleaned and decorated the kitchen all the time. We were relentless in our campaign to keep her in her place lest she believe she could be like us. The truth was that she was faster at the typewriter, never making mistakes. She took short-hand and could do accounting. Everything she did was done perfectly, and we became even angrier. How could a spic be so smart?" She puck-ered her lips and looked into a corner of the room where soggy umbrel-las stood draining into the thin, soiled carpet.

"After the first year, she started to write us notes with prayers every morning. Sometimes a Scripture verse accompanied them; other times they contained a short meditation that she had copied. Each one was different, custom-made to our needs. Then I remember a fierce winter. It snowed and became icy, much worse than today. Dorothy had prob-lems with her legs, and we had to walk up a hill from the subway sta-tion. She complained about it one day, and would you believe it? Your mother was there waiting for Dorothy the very next morning. Dorothy said your mother offered her arm to support her and walked with her all the way without one single word. She did that every day until the snow and ice melted. Who could resist her?"

My storyteller companion was Mrs. Campbell, a woman who had worked with my mother for nine years. She was living in Poughkeepsie, New York, and had come all the way in a taxi that was waiting to take her back. A pretty penny that must have cost her.

She continued her account of recollections. "All we knew were the habits and patterns of our prejudices, but slowly she taught us new pat-terns of compassion. She broke the power of our habits and led us into new ways. At first, we could not understand, but we followed and began to see with her eyes the love of Christ. The new habits emptied us of our prejudices, our fears. We made room for all of us." Mrs. Campbell got up slowly and walked over to the casket. She touched my mother's hand, and I saw her mouth some words. Then she turned and left.

I understood my mother's story, but I had lived it differently. It is the story of invisibility. Invisibility means not being seen, to be indistin-guishable. It is to be too small to be seen, like a germ. This was what I learned in elementary school. Teachers affirmed white students, seemed able to hear them when they spoke, but the rest of us went unnoticed.

We needed to be taught, controlled. I kept wondering how to be pleasing, how to earn the right to be like the others. I hated school, but I loved to learn. School made me feel ill and afraid. I can say now what I could not say as a child. I did not feel safe. I hurt inside every day as I came home from school.

We were drilled into reading the words that told of Dick and Jane. We were drilled into understanding that our worlds were not good enough. It is difficult to start the day and spend six hours of it somehow knowing in your bones that you are not good enough. Such lessons taught us to be silent lest we be seen as unpleasant. Learn more words, more rules for spelling those words, more about how to say those words, how they work. We went home to very different words and sounds of words. Home was where we felt safe once more.

Church, the Hispanic Protestant Church, was where we could express ourselves in art, music, drama, words, poems, jokes, laughter. It was okay with God to be who we were. God was accepting and celebrated everything with us. We were free to be real, to exist, to break out of our prison of silence. There we were visible people. God is the God who sees us.

Invisibility means not being comprehended. In high school, nothing I said in class seemed to make sense. I always felt as though I were speaking about a different subject. I was sharing about my world—one not apparent or evident but invisible. Invisibility makes others blind, unable to see, to trace, to perceive. It leaves them without knowledge, without the power to understand or judge. Prejudices blind us. Blindness means there is no opening. Openness to my person, to my world, was unimaginable. There was no openness when the counselor at my high school saw my fine grades but refused to provide information about colleges or even the process for applying to college. I was the first in my family to go to college. I knew nothing about the process.

Even if I speak English, when I am invisible, there is no sense to what I say, no knowledge of me, no perception of my person, and therefore no receptors to my presence. Others cannot know my warmth or their own incompleteness without me. Their faculties are not fully developed. There is no understanding, no appreciation, no esteem, and no sense of meaning. I make no sense. "This essay makes no sense. The reader does not know what you are talking about." I had drawn parallels between the experiences of the author of the short story and my own experiences, but the teacher had no way of relating to my experiences. My grade in that class reflected this "no sense," this having no faculties, no organs for perception, no good judgment, no experience. I was relegated to continue to be invisible, nonexistent. Nonexistence is to have no being. One is not real, has no life, no presence. One has not occurred. I haven't taken place. I have no past, present, or future. It's as if God had never said, "Let there be Elizabeth."

I was given the classical canons of education. I accepted the offer. I appreciated the gift of Shakespeare, the history of the Western world, industrialization, capitalism, democracy, Locke and Hume, Martin Luther and Calvin. I learned to be, to become according to the becoming standards of others.

In seminary, I was told to keep my hand movements during the sermon in an imaginary box in front of me. If I preached that way in my church, people would wonder if I had an impairment that inhibited my movement. I was to preach for no more than twenty minutes. That would mean I hadn't prayed and therefore didn't have much of a word from God to share with others. In all of my classes, I kept two sets of notes. One contained the linear thoughts that would get me an A on the exam. The other set contained the integration of one subject with another such as church history with theology or ethics with urban ministry. These interdisciplinary discussions never took place in class. We separated everything into sacred little boxes: two ways of looking at life, two sets of notes to keep my lives flowing alongside each other.

Now I had presence. I was in plain sight, no longer alone but in the company of others. I was perceived as clothed and in my right mind. But I still had no being, for I still spoke of things with the nuances and from the perspective of a world unknown, a reality still not evident. I was still outside the plan of intention of the institutions that taught me.

I decided to declare that my world was and is. It represents a reality. Others merely had not been taught to perceive it. I wanted to make my world present and not absent. Being absent is to be away from one another, distant and out of sight. It is to be lacking. I lack you, and you lack me. Through my words here I want to present, to acquaint you with, another world. This is a world that is not mine or yours alone but a world that is ours. I want to become a gift, an offering to be seen. I want to give myself to you. I will bring before your mind, offer for your consideration, a journey that takes us from the habit of being absent from one another, lacking an awareness of and having an inability to pay attention to one another, to the habit of presence or being.

God presented himself to Moses as "I AM." "To be" is a verb used to express future time. Presence is "I amness." I am in Jesus as Jesus is in God, and we are in Christ a new creation brought together in him. This is our future. I wish for my words on these following pages to be a presentation. Presentation is a word used to describe the position taken by a fetus during labor. My hope is that we will create a labor room where we might be born to one another.

Power as Kenōsis

In August of 2001, my daughter was getting ready to go off to college, and at the same time she was celebrating her eighteenth birthday. Her friends were at the house. I always admired how she managed to bring such a diverse group of people together through friendship. They were Korean, Tongan, Pakistani, Mex-Vietnamese, English, Afro-Mexican, Colombian, Jewish, Christian, Buddhist, Muslim. They played the piano and sang show tunes from their chorus repertoire. They ate hot dogs and chips and salsa.

After several hours the room began to empty, and countless hugs and good-byes took place. I stationed myself at the door as a hospitable host, thanking them all for coming and wishing them well on their own journeys. And then Salma came into my home to pick up her son. She is Pakistani and Muslim and wore a full hijab. Before she left my home I said to her, "I must go to the mosque with you," and she cheerfully invited me to come with her.

Why had I asked Salma this? For the past two years I had been led by the Spirit to read about Islam and the countries that are predominantly Muslim. My heritage does not consider learning complete until the experiential dimension is included. It was necessary for me to attend the mosque if I was to learn, to understand a world that seemed so different from mine.

Salma became my broker into that world. She is a natural teacher and can tell when something is not comprehensible to someone seeing it for the first time. She would often lean in my direction and explain things in whispers. After my visits, she would extend her hospitality, and we would sit while she explained much to me. She has invited me to many community events and always interprets her world for me. This is a labor of love, and I have done the same for those who wish to understand my Latino world. What have I wished of those who enter? What has been insulting and what has been appreciated? I worked hard to remember so that I would be both appreciative and respectful of Salma.

She meets me at the entrance, introduces me, and secures a safe place for me as a stranger. But she does more. She uses her own place in her world to open up to me my own place there, access to all that I wish. She has gone out of her way to make sure that I talk with those who have much knowledge to impart. She facilitates dialogue between our two worlds, an exchange of ideas and visions for living together in a world in which we build walls by offering false characterizations of one another.

Salma set one rule for our coming together. "I am not going to convert you, and you are not going to convert me." This was a good rule. It set parameters that eliminated any fears concerning that which was sacred for both of us, our faith. Besides, the Holy Spirit alone converts. I am only a witness. My actions of love would be a witness. Sometimes, we need to till the land before planting seeds in it. She had known Christianity as imposition. This had made the ground hard and unreceiving to the seed of the gospel. Respect would in turn till the ground. After setting her ground rule, Salma gave me the freedom to ask questions. Asking lets others speak first, to tell how they feel, what they believe. This taught me to accept. I was not sure what my prejudices were, but I knew enough to know that they had to be lurking somewhere.

Listening followed asking. Salma poured out her life, and that was like giving me something worth much more than gold. Her faith is so vital, and she lives it as intensely as I live mine. Her relationship to Allah is so real. I focused on what she shared, and I saw the September 11 events through the eyes of a praying community of Muslims who love and preach of loving one's neighbor. I saw the discriminations against their lives. I listened to the news with new ears and new questions.

One day I saw my own prejudices rush forth within me over the rights of women. I felt the blood rush to my head, my passion. I had to work hard to silence myself and to listen. I listened so hard that day, fighting my "yes, buts," and I forced myself to see what she was seeing. It was the first time that I realized what it meant to empty oneself of presuppositions. I realized that I could not assume that the words and behaviors of persons meant what I thought they meant. I had to hear them from inside their world. I learned to let go of my guard and to throw off my biases. To do this I let Salma's world engulf me and enter me and influence me deeply and fully. I was afraid of losing myself, of accepting too quickly and uncritically. I learned to spend much time reflecting, seeing the similarities and differences, the points of intersection between beliefs and expressions of our beliefs. I compared the behavior patterns that were fashioned by our beliefs. I examined my own world from the standpoint of hers and saw how my thinking and expressions had been conditioned by my previous experiences. This allowed me to see the limitations of my own world as well as its gifts and then to appreciate the insights from Salma's world. We are both free to be ourselves, free to continue to ask and to listen. We can each bear witness to who we are and where we stand without arrogance or a sense of superiority so that neither one imposes but rather offers with humility and openness.

Never have I been so enriched, so challenged to do theological reflection, to search out the meaning of the *kenōsis* passage in Philippians: "Let the same mind be in you that was in Christ Jesus" (2:5 NRSV). I have had to identify my own cultural filters and to learn the meaning of respect. Salma and I have made meanings together with integrity and faithfulness to our faiths. They are meanings in a world that names us enemies instead of neighbors. She has taught me the meaning of prayer to her and has asked me what the cross means to me. We have sought out together the meaning of peace, justice, and hope in this time. Together we have found strength in our faiths to seek shalom.

Steve's Story: Still an Alien

In a quiet, western Chicago suburb called Wheaton, you will find a school called Wheaton College with the motto "For Christ and His Kingdom." A leading Christian liberal arts college, boasting 140 years of history, the school has produced quality Christian leaders who have left a deep impact on the world, a legacy fitting of the college's motto. Here, in this place, a boy who used to traverse the streets of a small township in Seoul, Korea, with his rascal friends finds himself trying to teach a few things to the largely mainstream American students whose childhood and adolescent years bear little similarity to those of their professor.

I am that boy, and I teach what for most of my students is their first class with a non-European-American instructor, especially in the non-science disciplines. Students desperately try to respect me as a professor, one who speaks English with an accent and engages in nonlinear patterns of thinking. I repeatedly reassure my students how fortunate they are to have a teacher like me. They will learn more because they will have to try harder to understand my teaching. Some students believe that having such a teacher is a blessing in disguise because I can expand their horizons in ways they never thought possible. Then, too, there are the casualties of my teaching, those who clam up and merely try to extract the best possible grade without engaging fully with what I have to offer. Instead of being surprised by those who cannot or refuse to connect with me, I am constantly surprised at how God works through me to bring transformation in the lives of students.

From Korea to New York

As a 1.5 generation Korean, I came to the United States at the age of thirteen with my parents, an older sister, and an older brother. Many years ago, I never would have guessed I would be walking the path I am on.

When my family landed in Anchorage, Alaska, of all places, we were called "permanent residents" of the United States and were instructed to carry two pieces of identification: a social security card and an alien registration card. I carried these two cards until ten years ago, when I succumbed to my wife's pressure to become a naturalized citizen. My wife wanted my daughter to have a naturalized citizen for her father. I guess I am no longer an "alien" in this country; I am supposed to act "natural."

Yet I remain an alien—with a name like S. and later Steve, just imagine the kind of experience I have had in America. People say I am neither a first- nor a second-generation Korean-American. I ask them, "Then what am I?" They say, "You are a 1.5 generation Korean-American." I am not even given an integer (a whole number) to define myself. No wonder I don't feel whole. I am caught between two cultures and languages. People sometimes ask me what kind of food we eat at home and what language I think in, Korean or English. I reply, "I don't know. Don't ask me such hard questions." I eat and think a mixture of the two; therefore, I am one confused 1.5 generation Korean-American.

Both of my parents grew up in Korea during a period of much strife and turmoil. Their childhood years were marked by the Japanese occupation of Korea and the Korean War. Both grew up in family contexts marked by either alcoholism and adultery or poverty. They learned early on that if they were to get anywhere in life, they would have to do it without their parents' help. They proved themselves through their achievements, particularly in education.

After getting married and having three children, they started having concerns about the uncertain future of their children. They were troubled by the fact that, in Korea, the rich got richer and the powerful got more powerful by exploiting the common, hard-working people who tried to make an honest living. They believed that the United States offered an opportunity for diligent people to succeed and make something of themselves through education or work, and they eventually made the agonizing decision to leave behind the fruit of their hard work and to come to the States.

When my family came to the States, we soon learned that living here was not what we had imagined it would be. We all experienced some form of racism and prejudice during the difficult settling-in period. My parents became even more convinced that education was the only way to become successful in this nation, which was hostile to racial minorities. They also saw education as a way to earn the respect of the dominant society and their own people (Korean-Americans) and to help fellow Korean-Americans.

I grew up in the neighborhood of Flushing, New York (the unofficial capital of Korea America on the East Coast), and graduated from my high school with grades that made my parents proud. I went on to an Ivy League school where I followed in the footsteps of my father (organic chemistry), my sister (biochemistry), and my brother (inorganic chemistry) by pursuing studies in chemistry and preparing for some sort of professional school. Yet despite the smooth transition from high school to college, a successful academic career, and good friends, I experienced a deep spiritual crisis at the midpoint of my college career that no academic success or merit could resolve. Subsequently, I fell into depression and earnestly pondered the meaning of life. Nothing could ease the deserted feeling I had, like I was falling deeper into quicksand.

A turning point came as I stood on the bridge on campus that students called "Suicide Bridge." For some reason, I thought committing suicide would be the most beautiful thing I could do for myself. But I couldn't do it. I just couldn't. I was overcome by fear and hopelessness, and that's when I started to pray to God. "God, I know that you love me, but I have been running away from you. I need to be found in you!"

From Undergraduate School to Seminary

That was the starting point of the process of discovering God's will for my life. I was convinced that God wanted me to go to a seminary or a Bible college. However, the road was not without obstacles. It was difficult to convince my parents to give me their blessing to pursue full-time ministry as a career. They wanted me to stay in school and finish my chemistry studies and then go to medical school, as my siblings had done.

I waited while praying that God would change my parents' hearts. I prayed, "Lord, I need to obey. How can I obey you when I can't even obey my parents?" God faithfully answered my prayer, and they finally consented. They had two conditions. First, they wanted me to go to an Ivy League school's seminary, and, second, they wanted me to become a professor. I was overjoyed regardless of the conditions.

However, I later found myself led by the Lord to attend a leading evangelical theological institution in the Midwest, which did not fit my parents' Ivy League expectations. My mentor, a former faculty member at the seminary, influenced my decision. By God's grace, my parents granted me their approval for this step.

At the seminary, I was exposed for the first time to the phenomenon called American evangelicalism. This was the first time I not only systematically reflected on my faith in Jesus Christ but did so outside the context of the Korean-American church. I was able to drink at the well of "the professors who write books," as the school's self-description promised that I would. Evangelical theology and ethos were combined to shape the lives of students at the institution, and I was eager to give full allegiance to the tenets and trajectory of American evangelicalism.

Prejudice in an Unexpected Place

Why was I so eager to give my full allegiance to a movement I knew so little about? Simply put, I wanted to shed the cultural encumbrances that I thought the Korean-American church brought with it. For instance, during my formative years in the Korean-American church, I was thrust into the issue of women's roles in the church, which changed the spiritual climate of my family forever. Throughout Korean history, Korean women were strongly discouraged from engaging in anything in society other than serving the men of the house. Although women were not forbidden to pursue an education, the societal pressure against such a pursuit was enormous. My mother's parents shared this societal value and had wanted her to marry a man from a wealthy family.

My mother's growing-up years were difficult. My grandfather was a high-ranking police officer who also happened to be an alcoholic. He beat up my grandmother every time he drank, and in his stupor, he would throw his family out of the house. He also fooled around with other women and yelled at my mom every time she asked for tuition money and bus fare to go to school. He was very chauvinistic and believed that a woman should stay home, cook, raise children, and be absolutely obedient to her husband. Yet Mom persisted because she was convinced that education was the only way to escape from the vicious cycle in which wives were abused and women were continually denied opportunities to become who they wanted to be in a male-dominated society. Despite all that was going on at home, she excelled in school; she got the best education possible in Korea from the most prestigious schools. She proved her parents wrong when she achieved something that most men could not achieve in terms of social status. During those years, the Korean church, by and large, was silent about the plight of women, the poor, and the downtrodden.

Many years later, in America, I saw my mother stop going to church because of the prejudice she faced in her Korean-American church for being a female pastor. Although she had much education, many gifts, and much ministry experience, Mom was treated poorly both financially and professionally in comparison with male pastors in the church. Moreover, she faced much opposition when she tried to bring troubled, at-risk, inner-city teenagers to the church. As a pastor, she worked hard at nurturing people both inside and outside the church. However, the parents of teenagers in the church, who were usually more acculturated into American culture, were opposed to bringing in and nurturing recently immigrated, at-risk teens. The parents were afraid of potentially negative influences and were concerned about what the Korean-American community would think of their children for associating with the recently immigrated teens.

Although all the members of the church were once immigrants, those who had lived in the States longer treated the recent immigrants with harshness and prejudice. Seeing such acts, coupled with my mom's experiences in the church, made me yearn to understand the complex nature and outworking of prejudices, whether subtle or overt, even within ethnic/racial minority groups, due to socioeconomic and gender differences. Thus, I was eager to jump ship and become part of mainstream American evangelicalism, in pursuit of the pure gospel, understood and lived out in perfect harmony.

Seminary to Ministry and Back to Seminary

During my seminary years, I found my passion in studying the traditional curriculum, namely, biblical studies, theological studies, church history, and practical theology. For the first time, I felt that what I was learning about God was legitimate, wholesome, untainted by the cultural baggage that entangled me in the Korean-American church. As graduation approached, my professors, the school's placement office, my white seminary friends, and my Korean-American seminary friends expected me to take a pastorate in a Korean-American church. I was somewhat surprised by their expectation of me, but I went ahead and found a place of ministry in a Korean-American church.

Upon entering ministry in a Korean-American church, I was overwhelmed by the needs of the congregation's youth and adults, and I found that serving in a Korean-American church could be a very lonely business. I was asked to do many things for various groups, which were clearly demarcated in terms of gender, generation, language, socioeconomic status, and years of residence in America. However, at the end of the day, I didn't feel I belonged to any of the groups. In spite of my desire to build leadership and facilitate a vision for the church, I found that people were caught up in the everyday struggle of life as immigrants or as second-generation Koreans who were trying to fit into mainstream America. I felt like a failure. On the one hand, I felt ill-equipped to serve multigenerational Korean-Americans with various needs. On the other hand, I felt engulfed in doubts about my calling to minister in a mono-ethnic church. I eventually decided to return to my studies, looking for more adequate ministry preparation and ways to deal with the intersection of the gospel, ethnicity, and culture. So I began my second master's program at the seminary where I had received my first master's degree, which eventually led to a doctorate program.

Awakening to Issues of Justice and Equality at the Seminary

My teaching career started when I received an offer from the seminary where I was studying to supervise the Korean-American seminarians who were involved in internships at local Korean-American churches. Additional doors opened when I was hired as a part-time adjunct instructor while working on my doctorate. During this period, I experienced a severe reaction against the institution, which I deemed to be racist toward Americans of ethnic minority descent and paternalistic toward international students. My anger and frustration extended to American evangelicalism as a whole. While I don't believe my reaction was necessarily against evangelical theology, it was definitely against the evangelical culture and ethos that were predominantly Western, triumphalistic, paternalistic, and modernistic. I was ready to give up my evangelical theological commitments because, in my view, the theology and the culture were inseparable. I began to understand what it meant to be an alien in a foreign land, especially as a Korean-American Christian in a white, American, evangelical institution.

I was disillusioned by the subtle yet systematic prejudice that was pervasive throughout the institutional commitment and curriculum, which was designed by and for mainstream American evangelicals. The seminary had only a few professors with cross-cultural experience and only one instructor of color. As I looked at the meeting minutes of a certain department at the seminary, I discovered the department had decided to hire an African-American instructor. When I asked what had happened with the search, I was told, "We couldn't find anyone who was qualified." I was troubled by the lack of understanding and vision for serving God's global kingdom. I was concerned as I watched American students of minority backgrounds and international students being trained for suburban, politically conser-

vative, white, middle-class evangelical churches. My previous exposure to racial/cultural issues at an institutional level had been minimal, and having been a graduate of that very seminary, I wasn't
equipped to articulate my concerns or even to get a good handle on
these issues for myself.

Looking back on my days as a student and employee of the seminary, I can still say that I am grateful for its uncompromising commitment to the Bible as the Word of God, among other commitments. Yet evangelical institutions, such as the seminary I attended,
have put an inordinate emphasis on teaching the Christian faith as a
set of propositional truths.[2] This evangelical tendency can be traced
back to the Enlightenment, particularly to a rationalistic approach
to theological inquiry and biblical interpretation.[3] American evangelicals have often neglected to ponder theology as a second-order
reflection (i.e., the task of interpreting various church dogmas and
practices). Instead, the task of theology has by and large been construed as deducing the truths of the ancient biblical text into the
contemporary affirmation of doctrine and labeling the truths as
"self-evident."[4] In the process, the evangelical faith tradition has experienced three unfortunate bifurcations: between the text, the Bible,
and context; between theology and spirituality; and between faith
and learning.[5]

In the midst of my rebellion against what the seminary and American
evangelicalism had to offer, I began to realize that more might be involved than merely my reaction to the school. My well-meaning friends
and professors tried to convince me to finish my doctoral studies there,
but I felt they were dismissing my concerns and questions. That is when
I realized I no longer belonged there. With the encouragement I received from my wife and close friends, I quit my job and took a leave of
absence from the doctorate program at the school. Since then, I am
happy to say that the school has made some progress in rectifying its
institutional priorities.

2. Walter Liefeld and Linda Cannell, "The Contemporary Context of Theological Education: A Consideration of the Multiple Demands on Theological Educators," *Crux* 27,
no. 4 (1991): 19–27.

3. George M. Marsden, *Fundamentalism and American Culture: The Shaping of Twentieth-Century Evangelicalism, 1870–1925* (New York: Oxford University Press, 1980); and
Mark A. Noll, *The Scandal of the Evangelical Mind* (Grand Rapids: Eerdmans, 1994), 83–
98.

4. Stanley Grenz and John Franke, *Beyond Foundationalism: Shaping Theology in a
Postmodern Context* (Louisville: Westminster John Knox, 2001), 13.

5. S. Steve Kang, "The Church, Spiritual Formation, and the Kingdom of God: A Case
for Canonical-Communion Reading of the Bible," *Ex Auditu* 18 (2003): 137–51.

Finding the Grace of God in an Unexpected Place

The grace of God shined in a powerful manner in an unexpected place—in the midst of my struggle to think through the intersections of theology, culture, ethnicity, and justice. I was referred by a good friend to a doctorate program at a major university in the Midwest where I could do interdisciplinary work that combined the above disciplines and issues.

At this "secular" and "liberal" university, I saw God's hand at work in my life. Through my professors and colleagues there who represented a variety of backgrounds, traditions, and commitments, I not only came to realize my sense of calling but also experienced healing. Through one of my professors at the school, an African-American woman who was a former nun, I was able to visualize what God's grace could make of me. Moreover, I experienced God's grace as I befriended those whom evangelicals would call the sinners of sinners. As I spent time with them, God gave me a growing compassion for them. All the liberal commitments and agendas in the world could not detract from the generosity and kindness of their hearts. I soon realized what God wished to do through me—to embody a small piece of God's shalom in any place God might have me be.

A Pan Asian-American Church

Around this time, I became one of the founding pastors of a pan Asian-American church along with two pastor friends. The church was to be open to becoming a multiethnic community church. As we worked together with leaders of different ethnic and cultural backgrounds, we quickly realized that the gospel was not just a ticket to heaven; it was the message of holistic reconciliation in and through Jesus Christ. I came to appreciate how God brings people together from different cultural backgrounds so that they can worship and live life together as Christ's community. I definitely caught a glimpse of what God's kingdom is like.

At Wheaton College

I have hope for the future of American evangelicalism. I am not so naïve as to think that the movement is thriving. I witness regularly confirmation of the criticisms of Christian scholarship offered by my mentor, Mark A. Noll, in his *Scandal of the Evangelical Mind*, and of the evangelical church offered by David Wells.[6] However, I do have hope in

---

6. Noll, *Scandal of the Evangelical Mind*; David Wells, *No Place for Truth or Whatever Happened to Evangelical Theology?* (Grand Rapids: Eerdmans, 1993); and idem, *God in the Wasteland: The Reality of Truth in a World of Fading Dreams* (Grand Rapids: Eerdmans, 1994).

many college students, such as those I work with at Wheaton College. Over the past six years of teaching at the college, I have had to, sometimes reluctantly, let go of my prejudices against Christians from mainstream evangelicalism. I have realized that not all whites are alike. There are those committed and bright students who have had much experience in crossing borders that they don't have to. Many of my heroes spend two years preparing to go overseas to spend six-month internships in remote parts of the world, serving in Christian development organizations. Others spend a semester in Chicago, involved in Christian development and social justice organizations. Then there are those who volunteer throughout their entire four years to work with homeless shelters, tutoring programs, refugee settlement, and peacemaking ministries.

Many of them excel in their studies and are willing to learn about God's heart for the church and the world. They are self-reflexive yet eager to make a difference. They constantly expose themselves to different cultures and build lasting relationships. They are willing to tackle some taboo issues in evangelicalism, such as racism, capitalism, and individualism. They long to see the kingdom of God become the reigning paradigm in not only their lives but also the church and society.

Have I been becoming color-blind or honorary white at the school? Do I think I have fully assimilated into mainstream white culture and American evangelicalism? Only God knows how much I still struggle with American evangelicalism and mainstream white culture! I have been called a Hong Kong pastor by my colleagues, despite my repeated reminders that I am a Korean-American. Some see my primary responsibility at the college as teaching and shepherding Asian-American students, although I have taught two courses on Asian-American experience at the college for the past six years. I still remember vividly what one colleague told me when I was interviewing at the college six years ago. He said, "We like you a lot for being a Korean-American, but can you do a sex change?" I suppose I was a token but one that still does not fit all the minor categories. We Christians are all well-meaning people. We are all sanctified sinners who have long journeys ahead of us. If we can only learn to be on the journey together, committing ourselves to our God, who showers us with more than we are able to imagine.

Living in the Present as a Foreigner and an Alien

Twenty-six days into my life in America, on August 27, 1977, my family was walking to the I.S. 237 Rachel Carson Junior High School in Flushing, New York, so that I could register for the eighth grade. My brother got showered with spit from the balcony of a fourth-floor apartment. My father, with a very limited and broken English vocabulary (he still can't carry a sentence in English to this day), blurted out something to the two teenagers up on the fourth floor. Immediately, they threw a bottle of ketchup at us, shattering glass pieces and splashing ketchup around us. I knew then that my life would never be the same.

Once an alien, I will always know what it means to be an alien. When reading in Genesis 23 about Abraham being a stranger and an alien, I know what it means. And I have always been comforted by 1 Peter, where the apostle Peter declares that Christians are to live as aliens and strangers in the world.

Each day, I find myself sitting in my office in the Billy Graham Center at Wheaton College asking God what I should be doing. God reminds me that I am to be an instrument of his shalom in my cross-cultural teaching and ministry encounters with students who, while sharing one faith in Jesus Christ, come from many walks of life. I am to convince them that we are to be engulfed, as kingdom citizens, in the kingdom reality and to live as strangers and aliens in this world.

Gary's Story: Cracks in My Universe

> I reel in confusion; I don't understand what I see. With the naked eye I can see two million light-years to the Andromeda galaxy. Often I slop some creek water in a jar and when I get home I dump it in a white china bowl. After the silt settles I return and see tracings of minute snails on the bottom, a planarian or two winding round the rim of water, roundworms shimmying frantically, and finally, when my eyes have adjusted to these dimensions, amoebae. At first the amoebae look like muscae volitantes, those curled moving spots you seem to see in your eyes when you stare at a distant wall. Then I see the amoebae as drops of water congealed, bluish, translucent, like chips of sky in the bowl. At length I choose one individual and give myself over to its idea of an evening. I see it dribble a grainy foot before it on its wet, unfathomable way. Do its unedited sense impressions include the fierce focus of my eyes? Shall I take it outside and show it Andromeda, and blow its little endoplasm? I stir the water with my finger, in case it's running out of oxygen. Maybe I should get a tropical aquarium with motorized bubblers and lights, and keep this one for a pet. Yes, it would tell its fissioned descendants, the universe is two feet by five, and if you listen closely you can hear the buzzing music of the spheres.[7]

I have come to believe that sins of prejudice are among the last to be uprooted from redeemed hearts. This conclusion is consistent with

---

7. Annie Dillard, *Pilgrim at Tinker Creek* (New York: Harper & Row, 1974), 24.

what I have observed during many years of ministry in the parish and in the academy, and it resonates with the experiences that have marked my personal and family life. Some of these experiences I will now relate in the space of the next several pages. As I began to consider the contours of my own journey toward cultural sensitivity, I recalled the passage above, taken from Annie Dillard's *Pilgrim at Tinker Creek*. I see myself as the pet amoeba, growing up in a universe that "is two feet by five." But I have come to discover that there are cracks in my universe.

Adolescence

The Wonder Years was a popular television sitcom in the 1980s that featured the adolescent experiences of Kevin Arnold. Kevin was born in the 1950s, and his screen life and my own childhood often seemed to run on parallel tracks. In fact, a number of times, as I watched an episode, I quietly wondered if the screenplay had been written by an old schoolmate of mine who was dedicated to producing laughs by exposing my childhood on-screen.

In one episode, Kevin is moved by the experience of watching his Jewish friend, Paul, prepare for and participate in his bar mitzvah. Kevin is struck by the religiosity of the event, but he is equally curious about the ethnic and cultural nature of the celebration. His curiosity prompts him to ask his mom about his own ethnic background: "Mom," he asks, "what are *we*?" As his mom launches into a lengthy, complicated tale of twisted branches on both sides of the family tree, her voice fades into the background. It is replaced by Kevin's own voice as he, thinking out loud for the television audience, announces, "That's when it hit me—I'm a mutt!" Rolling with laughter at his words, I identified immediately with the protagonist.

Ethnically speaking, I, like Kevin Arnold, am a "mutt." Growing up in suburban America during the 1960s and 1970s, I was far from alone in this identity. In my neighborhood and schools, it was the rare child whom we could easily label ethnically or culturally. I had a few Jewish friends as a child, a couple of African-American friends, and knew only a handful of Asian and Hispanic children. Most of my friends were, as I considered myself to be, simply "American." That is to say, we were "normal." Although I do not recall ever saying it quite this way, I surely *believed* that to be an ordinary American was to be white and Protestant.

My view of reality was reinforced in my small world in ways subtle and not so subtle. There were occasional remarks and recurring terms and jokes that kept matters clear. I learned to call Brazil nuts "nigger toes." I learned to say "Yowsir, yowsir, three bags full" when reciting the popular rhyme "Baa, baa, black sheep." I learned to laugh at jokes about blacks, Jews, Asians, and Native Americans. I watched friends throw rocks at the kids coming home from the Catholic schools in their slacks and sweaters. All of this must have seemed a bit incongruous to me, given the love that had always marked my home and a growing reality in my life: As I moved through junior and senior high school, I began to have a number of friends, classmates, and teammates who were black, Asian, and Jewish. Still, I never lost any sleep over the matter, and from time to time I caught myself parroting those things I had "caught" or been taught—even in the presence of those I was offending.

One day, a bunch of us gathered in the yard of a friend's house to walk to school together. As we were leaving the yard, I followed a black friend in climbing over the fence. He was either being playful in getting over or was having some trouble negotiating the maneuver. "Come on, man, climb over that fence like a white man," I joked with him. No sooner had the words left my mouth than I realized what I had said. My friend never said a word, and I dared not look in his eyes. Our friendship continued for some time, but we never spoke about the incident. That became my pattern. If and when I did have a slip of the tongue, I pretended that nothing had happened.

It was with that incident, I believe, that something new began to work in me. Perhaps for the first time I sensed that there was something wrong with the language and the worldview I had inherited. Not long after this episode I watched the television movie *Brian's Song*. The film told the story of the untimely death of the professional football player Brian Piccolo. It also told the story of the unlikely, deep friendship between Piccolo and his teammate, football legend Gayle Sayers. I was drawn to the film by my love of sport, but I was transformed by the film's portrayal of the relationship between these two men—one white, the other black. Although I was not yet a Christian, I had been raised to believe in God and to believe in right over wrong. Many themes were becoming important to me in my pre-conversion high school days. Among those at the top of the list was a growing concern about reconciliation, especially between whites and blacks.

When I became a Christian during my junior year of high school, my interest in reconciliation deepened. During my senior year, my home church—which I loved deeply—split over issues related to the charismatic movement. From that time on, I have been marked by a desire to seek and promote unity in the church. It began to occur to me that there were two main fronts in the battle: working against divisions based on secondary theological issues and differences of worship styles and working against divisions based on race and ethnicity. The former was predominant in my thinking, for I had experienced firsthand the devastation that such divisions can cause. These many years later, my heart still breaks over such matters, and I remain dedicated to church unity based on the historic theological verities that have marked the one, holy, apostolic, and catholic church for two millennia.

If divisions over worship styles were notable in the '60s and '70s, divisions based on race and ethnicity were even more striking. As Billy Graham put it in a 1960 article in *Reader's Digest*, "The most segregated hour in America is still eleven o'clock, Sunday morning."[8] Had you asked me, in those days, how I would respond to these issues, I would not have been able to articulate a clear answer. Perhaps I would have spoken about the need for all Christians to become "color-blind" and to get out of their comfort zones. Today, I understand that being color-blind is neither possible nor desirable—a point I will address more fully later. I have come to understand also that there are profound sociocultural realities that contribute to the segregation we still face on Sunday mornings and that no easy answers to this dilemma are available to us. All my thoughts on this matter remained untested, however, until I was forever changed through the gift of marriage.

Marriage and Family

In 1977, I was joined in marriage to a young woman who had moved to the United States from Korea three years earlier. I cannot recall having known any person from Korea before I met her. For more than twenty-five years now, we have been learning to live together and to raise our daughter in ways that are God honoring and mutually encouraging. Both in marriage and in parenting, issues of race, ethnicity, and culture have proven to be significant for our family. Through the years, I have learned and am still learning a great deal. And the learning has never been easy.

With my wife, I began to feel for the first time the stinging pain of discrimination based on skin color and other physical features. As a "mixed couple," we have turned many heads through the years, particularly when we have lived in areas where there were few other such couples. When our daughter was born and we began to go about as a trio, the head turning became even more commonplace. Whatever I have personally felt, however, has been trivial compared with what I have

8. Quoted in Norman Anthony Peart, *Separate No More* (Grand Rapids: Baker, 2000), 73. Peart goes on to note the close relationship that developed between Graham and Martin Luther King Jr., who often forcefully drove home the same point.

watched my wife and countless other non-white Americans endure. A brief example may be helpful to illustrate.

During the days of my seminary studies in Vancouver, British Columbia, in the early 1980s, my wife and I had to cross the border between the United States and Canada frequently. We soon discovered that the journey into the States was almost always a painful one for us. By this time my wife was a naturalized citizen of the United States, and therefore we both answered "U.S." to the question of citizenship when we crossed the border. But on nearly every occasion, the customs agent would look at my wife, seated in the passenger's seat, and inquire of her, "Where were you born, ma'am?" The conversations that followed were always brief, and agents were always satisfied with our answers. But my wife began to be very irritated with the ritual. For some time, I tried to be defensive (what I was defending, I am not quite sure) and suggested that my wife was reading too much into all this. Finally, however, I had to acknowledge the obvious fact that she was being discriminated against because of her appearance. Never once was I—a white man—ever asked about the place of my birth. Apparently, the agents were oblivious to the fact that many Asian-Americans are third- or fourth-generation Americans or that many white persons traveling into the States are not native-born Americans. On the one occasion when we did finally confront an agent about these things, we incurred his ire and were detained at the border for some time, apparently for trying to cause trouble.[9]

Such incidents may seem minor and insignificant to some, but I am sure they are not insignificant to the countless people who face them day in and day out. And, of course, many regularly face far more painful outrages. Without question, ours is a race-conscious society, and there is no sign of this letting up any time soon. Incidences of racial profiling among police and other security officials continue to be daily fare in the news.

Out of My Comfort Zone

For the first twenty-five years of my life, my journeying in the world had been restricted to three of the country's fifty states and one Canadian province. In 1983, soon after graduating from seminary, I took

---

9. Some readers may think the customs officers' questions were understandable, particularly in light of the recent flood of Asian immigrants into the greater Vancouver area. That stream was not quite in full force in the early 1980s, however. Even if it had been, I would still charge that there was plainly a racist edge involved in singling out one person for such a basic question simply because of her physical appearance.

my first airplane flight. My wife and I traveled to Korea for a month of visiting friends, family, and churches, and then to Japan for two weeks of the same and several weeks more of short-term mission work. To this underexposed young man, the travels were eye-opening in many respects.

In Korea, I found that I was a source of entertainment for many children and even some adults. I did not enjoy the attention. Frequently, I was taunted by children in the neighborhoods where we were staying. My wife was verbally assaulted by taxi drivers and other strangers who took exception to her being partnered with an American man. These experiences were, for me, always unpleasant, and they would be repeated many times over during subsequent visits to Korea.

Most striking to me on that first trip, however, was how the church operated in Korea. I knew the nation had undergone an amazing explosion of church growth in previous decades, and I had the opportunity to witness some of the fruit. Churches were everywhere. We visited several, and they all seemed large, busy, and vibrant. We sat with thousands of believers for one of the daily prayer meetings held all over the country each morning at dawn. One Sunday, I sat with others wearing headphones for spontaneous English translation of the sermon in a church that boasted eighty thousand members. I met missionaries and many national pastors and lay Christian leaders.

As impressive as all this was, however, something deeply disturbed me. I became convinced that many of the church practices in Korea were not biblical or Christian. On occasion, I found myself blurting out to my wife that something we had seen done in a church was "not Christianity." I asserted, "That's simply Korean culture masquerading as Christianity." By the time we were ready to leave the country, I was actually angry with the Korean churches. I wanted to write and publish a pamphlet on the errors of Korean Christianity. My wife, ever wiser than I, assured me that I would do no such thing.

When we traveled to Japan, I was amazed to see how different Christianity looked to me in that nation. The churches we visited there were very small, and compared with the overly emotional expressions of faith I saw in Korea, the churches we visited in Japan seemed unhealthily non-expressive. In fact, they reminded me of business meetings. Soon, thoughts were being formed in my mind again: "This is not Christianity. This is Japanese business efficiency disguised as Christianity." Although in Japan, as in Korea, I had a number of wonderful encounters with people who plainly loved the Lord, I was largely skeptical and critical of what I saw in the churches. By the time we returned to the

States, I was genuinely grieved at how twisted the faith had become in these Asian nations.

Thankfully, it was not long after my return to America that I became aware of the depths of my ignorance and arrogance. Having seen, for the first time, expressions of the faith in other cultures, I began to see how the faith had taken root in my own cultural context. My home church was made up of people who were white, suburban or rural Americans, and, almost uniformly, politically conservative. On most Sundays, my wife was one of only two or three non-whites present in a congregation of more than two hundred people. Many of the members were active politically in support of Republican candidates and causes. Members lived comfortably, many on large plots of land that ensured plenty of space and privacy. Church was run very democratically. Devotion to family was consistently cited as the reason why people could not commit themselves to being more involved in church gatherings or community outreach. This is how things had always been in my church. But I now began to suspect that we had, as a community, assumed that God was one of us. He too was white, English-speaking, American, evangelical, and Republican. We had wrapped him up in the red, white, and blue and weekly served him up with a slice of mom's apple pie.

My wife joined a women's intercessory prayer group at the church that met weekly. The concerns of the group often reached overseas. My wife found herself among a large group of women praying for justice and righteousness around the globe. And she began to notice something: Members of the group assumed that wherever the United States was involved around the globe, it was always and invariably in the right. Its interests were, apparently, always noble and pure. Americans could be sure that God is on our side. My wife began to grow uneasy with what seemed to her to be an uncritical equation of the nation's interests with the cause of Christ. On one occasion, she expressed her concerns to the group. The leader responded by suggesting that perhaps my wife was not yet ready for intercessory prayer.

We stayed in this church for some time. We enjoyed the fellowship and ministry opportunities we had there. Our best friends and many of my family members were involved, and we honestly loved the community. But we began to feel uneasy about the prospects of long-term involvement there. Our marriage had involved a good deal of cultural discomfort, of learning and stretching. We began to sense that God was calling us away from this familiar and comfortable church home. This sense of what was coming was soon confirmed.

In 1985, my wife and I accepted an invitation to serve the youth group of a large Korean-American church in New York City. Our acceptance surprised us. We had envisioned ourselves going overseas to serve as missionaries, but a call to a Korean-American church had not crossed our minds. If such a thought had entered our thinking, it would not have included the idea of working with teenagers—something for which neither of us felt gifted. And New York City would have been one of the last places on earth we could have envisioned ourselves living and serving. But convinced that this was of God, we soon found ourselves immersed in a whole new world.

There were many points of pain and difficulty in our adjustment to this new community. New York represented a huge cultural challenge to us. Working in a very large and very busy church was also challenging. Becoming the only white member on a staff of fifteen full-time pastors was very stretching for me. Portions of our meetings were translated into English for my sake. Other portions were not. But most of our time and energy was spent learning how to minister to more than two hundred young people, almost all of them Korean-Americans. This experience, while extremely taxing, became life giving and future shaping for us.

Our students were at a number of places in terms of their own cultural identities. Most spoke English well enough for it to be the official language of our youth ministry, although a steady stream of new immigrant families in the church meant that we always maintained some level of Korean language ministry as well. Some of the teens had been born in the United States. These were second-generation Korean-Americans. Others had come to the States very recently. Typically, these first-generation immigrants, like their parents, regarded themselves simply as Koreans. I learned that others, mostly those who had come to the States during early adolescence, were described as the 1.5 generation. These young persons were usually bilingual and bicultural. There were also significant differences in acculturation levels based on precisely where in the greater New York area these students were living. Those who lived in Queens, for example, tended to retain Korean language and cultural self-identity far more than those who grew up in suburban Long Island.

Even as we were struggling to understand these sheep that had been placed in our charge, we were beginning to understand more about ourselves. We saw that most of these young people were caught between two cultures. As we ministered to them, we realized that we, too, had been caught between the same two cultures. In our marriage, we had been trying to negotiate a sense of cultural self-identity, just as surely as these students were. During the process of giving ourselves to love and serve them, we were finding ourselves as well.

Over the course of the next dozen years, we, in a very real sense, grew with those we were serving. Although we moved to other Korean-American churches, there was a sense of constancy to the journey. As the youth became collegians, we became college pastors. When they became young adults, we became young adult ministers. When the young married couples began to have children, we had a daughter of our own. And all the while we felt that we were at "home" with these friends. On a personal level, I came to identify myself, culturally, as Korean-American. I still see myself this way. Through deep, enduring relationships—with my wife and her family, with church members and friends, and with a bicultural daughter—I have been profoundly and irrevocably changed.

One year, in the midst of our pastoral journey with Korean-Americans, we spent eight months living and serving in Korea. There we spent considerable time with my wife's family and friends. My wife was engaged in music ministry and recording. I helped a large church begin an English-language service of worship. I also pursued formal study of the Korean language at a university. As expected, gaining familiarity with the language only deepened my grip on the culture and its grip on me. On the whole, our time in Korea was busy and profitable. It was also painful.

Each day as I left our home and boarded the bus that would take me to school or as I went to the market with my wife, I had to steel myself against the fact that I would face the glances and stares of the curious and the prejudiced. Each day, without fail, these apprehensions were confirmed. For the first time in my life, I began to suffer from depression. I was with people who looked very familiar to me, who looked like my family, my friends, my church members. I felt as though it should have been natural for me to fit in among them. But to most of my new neighbors, I was a stranger, a foreigner, an American. For the vast majority of them, I am sure, it never crossed their minds that I should be invited into their lives. Realizing this depressed me.

In time, however, I began to see that this slight measure of pain was critically important for me. I knew there were others in Korea, such as my African-American classmate, who had it far worse than I did. I knew, further, that this season of discomfort had a terminus—I would be returning to the States in a few months. But most important, I was gaining insight into the lives and experience of those I had been ministering to back in the States. I had heard their stories of facing prejudice daily, of enduring stares and racist remarks. My own wife had shared her experiences with me as well, and I had tried to be sympathetic. It is one thing to hear a person's testimony, however. It is quite another thing to have a taste—even a small one—of what someone is actually experiencing.

This little bout of pain, then, became a teacher for me. I became more compassionate toward the sheep I had been called to shepherd. I realized that most of them were facing racism daily without the prospect of escaping it by going "home." For my students, America *was* home. Many of them were born in the United States. Most of them were United States citizens. Even so, they were viewed by many as strangers, as foreigners, as something other than Americans. I began to think also of what the experience of other non-whites might be like in the States. Finally, I found comfort in the realization that Jesus had come "to that which was his own, but his own did not receive him" (John 1:11). He had known rejection consistently and at deeply profound levels. My pain was not, after all, so great in the overall scheme of things.

In the Academy

Another key fruit of our time in Korea was that I had the opportunity to consider future direction. I began to discern a call to teach at the college or seminary level. This was confirmed by many people and in many ways. Soon after returning to New York, I began doctoral studies in education. For several years, even as I continued to pastor, my studies proceeded. In 1996, after completing my doctorate, I assumed my first teaching position. For the past seven years I have taught in the areas of youth ministry and Christian education. But while I have become an educator of educators, my own education, especially in all things cultural, has continued and deepened.

First, life in the academy has allowed me to move backward, from the practical to the theoretical. As a full-time pastor, the demands of ministry kept me busily engaged in work. Time for serious study and reflection was difficult to find. It has been a joy to be able to take such time as part of my work as a professor. In my subsequent chapters—on theology and praxis—I will share some of the fruits of that study.

A second way in which my education has progressed is that I have intentionally tried to stretch myself culturally. Not participating in full-time ministry in the Korean-American world has allowed me to accept invitations to minister in other contexts. During the past six years, I have preached and lectured in a wide variety of ethnic settings—among Greek-Americans, Cambodian-Americans, Taiwanese-Americans, Chinese-Americans, and in the island nation of Sri Lanka. The most culturally stretching experience for me, however, has been ministering among white New Englanders. Having been raised in the Pacific Northwest and then having become culturally self-identified as

Korean-American, I have found ministry in the suburban New England world to be challenging indeed.

The third way in which my cultural education has continued has been in the classroom. I have learned by teaching on issues of culture. In most of my classes, various aspects of race, ethnicity, and culture are discussed. One of my classes deals almost exclusively with these issues. The majority of my students are white North Americans, but among them are significant numbers of non-white Americans and international students. These interactions, both with the subject matter and with my students, have been very instructive. In many ways, I have been greatly encouraged by the receptiveness of students to the kind of materials I will be presenting in this book. A good number of students are ready to learn and grow. But there are others, thankfully few, who will nod their heads in agreement for only so long. Then their struggle with these issues becomes visible—the set of the jaw, the clenching of the fist. They reach a point beyond healthy discomfort and draw a line in the sand.

After some of my courses, I have thought that perhaps it is better not to raise issues of race, ethnicity, and culture with students who are in my life for such a brief period of time and in such a formal setting. Some seem to walk away from a class congratulating themselves on how open-minded and understanding they are. But it seems evident that they are neither. Others seem to conclude that any talk of "multiculturalism" is unbiblical and unwise. I wonder if they will go forth as staunch defenders of the status quo in their churches and communities. Yet I continue the risk taking, always hoping that I will find a better, more effective way to engage such conversations. I also know that the "watering" I do today may be unwelcome to some, but it may yet contribute to a fruitful harvest later.

Ongoing Education

My education in things ethnic and cultural is certainly incomplete. In my relationship with my Korean-American wife, I continually stumble upon new insights (*stumble* being the operative word). Together with her I watch and wonder as our daughter grows up in an overwhelmingly white, upper-middle-class, suburban community. How will she come to understand herself in terms of ethnicity and culture? As a fifth grader, my daughter took a state-required exam with her classmates. The teacher, while giving instructions about how to fill in the bubbles for the preliminary questions, told the students, "You can all just fill in the bubble marked 'white' for that question." Then, taking another peak around the room, she spotted our daughter and corrected herself: "Most of you, I mean." That evening, my daughter wept as she recalled the incident. Her parents joined her.

I also continue to learn from my participation in a church that is struggling to be a multiethnic and multicultural community. Only a few years into its existence, this church of 150-plus members has made some strides in these areas. The church began as a predominately Korean-American community. As I write, nearly half of its members are from other ethnic backgrounds. Most of the growth in diversity, however, has been limited to people from other Asian backgrounds or to white Americans. Church leaders actually think that other cultural factors play a greater role in defining inclusion and exclusion in this community: The vast majority of members, regardless of their ethnicity, are highly educated and on impressive professional and career tracks. It is also interesting to note that the major divisions within the community seem to concern age and marital status, not ethnic backgrounds. As they seek to apply God's Word, church leaders must also, of course, confront such powerfully formative influences as the media, postmodern thought, and much more.

These things testify to the complexity of cultural issues that may be at work in any given church setting. We must not fall into the temptation of concluding, however, that because culture is multilayered we need not attend to issues of ethnicity. It is easy to ignore issues we do not understand and attend to those with which we are more comfortable. Many educators and ministers have acted in a manner like this. Youth ministers have concluded that "the youth culture" is the key cultural influence of significance for their work. Pastors have painted their congregations with broad brushstrokes: "We're a 'Gen X' church."[10] Such approaches, however, miss the mark. *All* the cultural factors of significance to those we are ministering to must also be significant to us as we serve, including issues of race and ethnicity.

Even as my education continues, I remain convinced that among the last sins uprooted from the redeemed heart are sins of prejudice. Such sins easily remain undetected. If they are detected, most of us are quick to absolve ourselves of crimes of failing to love our neighbors. Perhaps it is too large a task to try to move mountains such as these, mountains that have stood so tall and for so long in the evangelical world. But I know I have no choice in the matter, for the testimony of Scripture on these matters is clear and inescapable. To that testimony, we must now turn our attention.

10. For a fuller treatment of my discomfort with terms such as these, see chapter 6.

2

Lord of the Nations

GARY A. PARRETT AND S. STEVE KANG

After this I looked and there before me was a great multitude that no one could count, from every nation, tribe, people and language, standing before the throne and in front of the Lamb. They were wearing white robes and were holding palm branches in their hands. And they cried out in a loud voice: "Salvation belongs to our God, who sits on the throne, and to the Lamb."

Revelation 7:9–10

Personal experience may play a key part in forming convictions and commitments regarding issues of culture and ethnicity. Far more significant, however, must be a reading of Scripture. The overwhelming weight of the biblical data persuades us that the church must acknowledge and confront racism, that seminaries must train future church leaders to be culturally sensitive, and that individual believers and congregations must intentionally seek to stretch themselves through significant and ongoing relationships at home and abroad. Scripture drives our thinking on these and other such issues; our experiences, and those of others, provide corroborating testimony.

From cover to cover, the Bible testifies that God's heart is inclined toward people from every nation, tribe, and tongue on earth. Let us survey, briefly, the evidence for this.

The Beginnings of Culture

On the sixth day of creation, "God created man in his own image, in the image of God he created him; male and female he created them" (Gen. 1:27). Christian theology consistently affirms that all humans, male and female, were created to bear God's image on the earth. Just as this applies to both genders, it applies also to people of all nations, tribes, and tongues. All people bear the image of God. God's intentions for these, his image bearers, include the command to cultivate the creation. In Genesis 1 and 2, God gives humans what has been called a "cultural mandate." Indeed, the word *culture* derives from the Latin *colere*, which means "to cultivate." Therefore, although culture is a human enterprise, it began as an act of obedience to the command of God. At the beginning of the human story, then, male and female humans made in God's likeness are busy with the various tasks of cultural development. At this point, there is but one "race" of humans,[1] and there are no nations or ethnic groups.

Genesis 3 contains the tragic story of the so-called fall of humankind. The woman and her husband reject God through defiance and disobedience. The results for them, and for all their descendents, are tragic. Sin, sickness, suffering, and death enter the human drama. Once, all relationships—between people, between people and creation, and between people and their Creator—had been characterized by harmony. Now, enmity dominates in each of these spheres. By Genesis 4, the hostility is so great that we read of the first murder, and that between two brothers! In chapter 5, when we read of the birth of Seth, we learn that he is born after the image and likeness of his father, Adam. Adam, however, is different from the person he once had been. He still retains the image of God, and this is passed to Seth, but he now bears another mark as well. Adam is fallen. He is sinful, and all of his children, from then until now, are likewise tainted.

Traditionally, Christian theology affirms that although the image of God was profoundly marred with the fall into sin, it was not eradicated. All of us are henceforth a strange mix of the very best and the very worst. In human behavior today, we can witness clear reflections of the divine; we can also witness the most despicable and galling displays of evil. In the same way, the work of culture continued after the fall, for to

1. Although "race" has been used to divide people into categories, often for exploitive and sinful purposes, the biblical emphasis is that all humans share a common origin. Paul's use of Adam as both our spiritual (as in Rom. 5:12f.) and our natural (as in Acts 17:26–28) forefather illustrates the point. See also the discussion on the terms *race, culture,* and *ethnicity* in the introduction.

be a human being is to be a cultural being. But culture, too, bears two images. As one evangelical thinker has put it, "Culture is never neutral, it is always a strange complex of truth and error, beauty and ugliness, good and evil, seeking God and rebelling against him."[2]

Beginning with the descendents of Cain, the human family spreads out, although it is impossible to determine the extent of pre-flood migrations. The first signs of distinct people groups can perhaps be traced to this time. The development of distinctive physical characteristics would be the natural product of such migrations and family groupings. Although sin is clearly a part of the landscape now, it cannot be argued that the formation of distinct groups of people is itself sinful, for God himself had commanded before the fall that humans fill the earth (Gen. 1:28). Further, such movement would have, or at least should have, occurred in any event. By Genesis 5, there appear to be two emerging classes of people: those who essentially ignore God and those who call on him.

Genesis 6 through 9 tells of Noah, his family, and the ark he builds at God's command. The overwhelming majority of people and communities had turned their backs on God, and the resulting evil had incurred his wrath and judgment. But Noah had found favor in God's sight. When the flood destroys all that lives on the earth except those kept safe in the ark, humanity, as it were, experiences a rebirth. Again, Noah, his sons, and their families are commanded to cultivate and fill the earth. But it appears that the descendents of Noah come, in time, to have other ideas. Rather than disperse themselves over the earth, as God commanded, they build a tower to the heavens to make their own mark in their own way. God intervenes again, this time forcing the dispersion by confusing the languages of the people.

Dispersal and Distinctions

The story of Babel merits closer examination. Humankind gathered itself in the land of Shinar, saying in Genesis 11:4, "Come, let us build ourselves a city, with a tower that reaches to the heavens, so that we may make a name for ourselves and not be scattered over the face of the whole earth." This was plainly contrary to God's revealed will that they go forth and fill the earth. In response to their actions, God confuses

2. Bruce J. Nicholls, "Toward a Theology of Gospel and Culture," in *Down to Earth: Studies in Christianity and Culture*, ed. John R. W. Stott and Robert Coote (Grand Rapids: Eerdmans, 1980), 56.

their language, and as a result, the people are scattered "from there over all the earth, and they stopped building the city" (Gen. 11:8).

Most evangelicals are familiar with the story from childhood. But is our understanding of the story correct? Typically, the perception is that God confused the languages as a judgment for the people's sin and that the enduring strife among different people—continuing throughout the ages to the present day—is the tragic result. But the story can be read quite differently, in light of the creation mandate, as an act of divine intervention through which God restored his own, original intentions for humankind. God's kingdom would extend to the ends of the earth, and human disobedience would not triumph over his will.

Biblical commentators, past and present, have supported such a view of the passage. John Chrysostom, the fourth-century bishop of Antioch, says, "He [God] put a stop to the impulse of their wickedness through creating differences in language. 'Let us confuse their speech,' he says, 'so that they will be unable to understand one another's language.' His purpose was that, just as similarity of language allowed their living together, so difference in language might cause dispersal among them."[3] Likewise, St. Jerome, the great thinker and translator, wrote, "Indeed, when the tower was being built up against God, those who were building it were disbanded for their own welfare. The conspiracy was evil. The dispersion was of TRUE BENEFIT even to those who were dispersed."[4] South African theologians and other biblical scholars have also been reconsidering the interpretation of the text as it relates to Acts 2.[5]

Genesis 10 records the so-called table of nations. Here we read of the scattering of the sons of Noah—Shem, Ham, and Japheth. Many Old Testament scholars believe the chapters were arranged logically so that the description of the people's movements follows the record of their emergence from the ark. Chapter 11 actually occurred first, chronologically speaking, and it is this event that explains how and why the dispersion of Noah's progeny occurred.

This separation and dispersion of families to different areas of the earth likely resulted in the emergence of distinct people groups and what would later be called different "races."[6] Physical differences be-

3. John Chrysostom, Homilies on Genesis 30.13, FC 82:229, in Andrew Louth, *Genesis 1–11: Ancient Christian Commentary on Scripture* (Downers Grove, Ill.: InterVarsity, 2001), 168–69.

4. Jerome, Homilies 21, FC 48:170, in Louth, *Genesis 1–11*, 169.

5. G. D. Cloete and D. J. Smit, "Its Name Was Called Babel," *Journal of Theology for Southern Africa* 86 (1994): 81–87.

6. Regarding the use of the term *race*, see footnote 1 above and the fuller discussion in the introduction.

came more marked with the passage of time. It is critical to note again that these physical differences, and many significant cultural differences, would have and should have occurred regardless, for God had commanded, not once but twice, that people "fill the earth." The sinful use of the Noah story to promote racism—by suggesting that Ham's descendents were cursed with dark skin as they moved southward toward Africa—is unworthy of serious discussion.[7]

As we leave the pre-patriarchal portions of Genesis, then, we find multiple groups of people spreading out upon the face of the earth. Nations are being formed. These groups are increasingly distinct from one another in terms of language, culture, and physical characteristics. Yet they remain fundamentally similar to one another. They are all part of the one race of humans (see Acts 17:26). They are all cultural beings, bearing both the image of God, with all its accompanying prospects of good, and the image of fallen Adam, with all its prospects of evil.

The story takes a major turn in Genesis 12 with the call of Abram, a descendent of Eber (from whose name, it is widely believed, the term *Hebrew* is derived). God makes a covenant with Abram, and this covenant includes the formation of one great nation—Israel—and the blessing of many nations. Indeed, Abram's name, which means "exalted father," is changed to Abraham, meaning "father of multitudes," for through this one, "all peoples on earth will be blessed" (Gen. 12:3). It is apparent, then, that even in choosing one nation to be uniquely his, God's heart is unwaveringly concerned with all the nations and peoples of the earth. God formed the one nation in order to bless the many.

God's heart for all the nations remains on display throughout the remainder of the Hebrew Scriptures. Throughout the Old Testament, as God's people continually go astray, he continues to remind them of his vision for his eternal and universal kingdom, for which the Davidic kingdom was to function as a sacramental example. In the Book of Psalms, we read of God's repeated claims upon the nations (e.g., Pss. 24:1; 33:8; 46:10). Both the Torah and the prophetic literature reveal God's concern for the aliens who live in the midst of the Israelites (e.g., Jer. 22:3; Ezek. 47:21–23). The prophets also declare the good news about God's grace extending to the Gentiles (e.g., Isa. 9:1–2). The Book

---

7. One example of this use of the story is found in the notes of Finis Jennings Dake's Annotated Reference Bible. The commentary by Dake on Genesis 9:18–27 includes the following remarks: "All colors and types of men came into existence after the flood. All men were white up to this point, for there was only one family line—that of Noah who was white and in the line of Christ." Gary's attention was drawn to this passage by Cain Hope Felder, *Race, Racism, and the Biblical Narratives* (Minneapolis: Fortress, 2002), 7–8.

of Isaiah, especially, repeatedly witnesses to God's vision of the eternal kingdom, where all nations and tongues will come together. For instance, in Isaiah 66:18–19, God says, "I am coming to gather all nations and tongues; and they shall come and shall see my glory, and I will set a sign among them" (NRSV). And verse 20 says, "They shall bring all your kindred from all the nations as an offering to the LORD" (NRSV). We read, as well, of God's concern even for the peoples and nations upon whom he pronounced judgment (e.g., Jonah 4:1–3, 10–11, concerning Nineveh).

The Light of All the World

In the fullness of time, God sends his Son, Jesus Christ, as the Messiah of Israel and the Savior of the world. His coming is the climactic moment in the biblical drama of God's reconciling all things to himself. From Genesis 3 onward, God has been about the task of bringing all creation back into alignment with his purposes. To this end, he chose Israel, that she might be a light to the nations. To this same end, he sent forth prophets to speak his word. To this end, finally, God became incarnate in Christ. God's global vision is clearly seen in the incarnation. It is for love of the entire world that God sends his Son (John 3:16). He is "a light for revelation to the Gentiles" as well as "glory to [God's] people Israel" (Luke 2:32 NRSV). Even in recording the royal lineage, Matthew reminds us that Gentiles (two, at least: Rahab and Ruth) have a place in the genealogy of Israel's Messiah. Christ comes to seek and save the lost (Luke 19:10). Through his life, death, and resurrection, "God was reconciling the world to himself" (2 Cor. 5:19).

It is critical to note that this reconciling work of Jesus affects both the vertical plane and the horizontal plane. The cross not only accomplishes reconciliation between sinners and their God but also destroys the dividing wall of hostility that had separated Jew and Gentile (Ephesians 2). In all of this, we see that Christ came also to introduce his eternal, universal kingdom. While mortals through the ages have tirelessly sought to build their own kingdoms, Jesus Christ, the Son of God, took on flesh and bone, walked and died among us, and was raised again in order to inaugurate his kingdom. His reconciling work is also kingdom-building work.

This reconciling work will go forward until the end of history. Only then—after death, the final enemy, has been destroyed—will the Son present his fully accomplished work to the Father (1 Cor. 15:24–28). In the meantime, between the first and second advents of the Lord, the ministry of reconciliation is carried on through the church. We are Christ's body on earth today, sent forth to preach good news, to do the good works God has prepared for us (Eph. 2:10), and to make disciples of all nations (Matt. 28:19).

When Christ commissions the apostles to make disciples of all nations, he affirms what was already evident in the Old Testament. As we have seen, God's heart has ever been toward all the families of the earth. Therefore, Jesus tells the apostles that they will be his witnesses "in Jerusalem, and in all Judea and Samaria, and to the ends of the earth" (Acts 1:8). This verse is soon symbolically realized when the Spirit of God is poured out upon the believers in Acts 2 and the gospel is proclaimed in the languages of many nations.

On the day of Pentecost, God graciously and powerfully demonstrates his desire to bring to himself people from every corner of the earth. In Jerusalem on that day there occurs a complete reversal of humanity's disobedience at the tower of Babel. Thus, God sanctifies cultures and redeems his people through this Pentecostal plurality. New Testament scholar James Scott, noted missiologist Stephen Neill, and others have argued that on the day of Pentecost, Jews of the diaspora traveled to Jerusalem from regions that coincided with the table of nations in Genesis 10, suggesting that, indeed, the Holy Spirit came on the day of Pentecost to advance further God's eternal purpose.[8]

In the weeks and months following the Holy Spirit's outpouring upon the infant church, increasing numbers of Christians settled in Jerusalem instead of expanding their witness from Jerusalem to all Judea and Samaria and to the ends of the earth (Acts 1:8). However, after Stephen's death, "a great persecution broke out against the church at Jerusalem, and all except the apostles were scattered throughout Judea and Samaria" (Acts 8:1). This is again reminiscent of the tower of Babel. God, in his sovereign will, dispersed his people throughout the world in order that they might live both as his kingdom dwellers and as aliens and strangers in this world.

There are three widely acknowledged, essential components of nationhood: people, language, and land. Jesus Christ, in inaugurating his kingdom, mysteriously multiplies these three elements and transforms them. He brings people from all the nations for his kingdom. He brings profound textures through many languages, the most crucial precursor

---

8. James M. Scott, "Acts 2:9–11 as an Anticipation of the Mission to the Nations," in *Mission of the Early Church to Jews and Gentiles*, ed. Jostein Adna and Hans Kvalbein (Tübingen: Mohr Siebeck, 2000), 87–123; and Stephen C. Neill, *Call to Mission* (Philadelphia: Fortress, 1970).

to culture. He constructs a heavenly "land" that defies human imagination. This is the inaugurated kingdom of God that the church is called to live out here and now.

As the account in Acts continues, the gospel breaks forth beyond the borders of national and ethnic Israel. As it does, members of the infant church begin the age-long struggle of learning to live together as the reconciled people of God. The first signs of cultural tension among this growing community are evident by Acts 6. As the Hebraic Jews and the Hellenistic Jews experience life together in Jerusalem, inequities appear. The widows among the Hellenistic Jews are being neglected in the distribution of food supports. The apostles, upon hearing the complaint, instruct the people to choose leaders from among themselves to address the issues. Seven men are nominated to provide leadership in the area. Significantly, all seven nominees have Greek names. The very people who had felt marginalized are invested with authority to respond to the needs. One of the seven, Nicolas from Antioch, is a Gentile convert to Judaism. Through careful and thoughtful listening to one another, the church negotiates its way through what could have been a crisis unto division. Another of the seven, Philip, is used by God to bring the gospel to the Samaritans, as the command and promise of Acts 1:8 now accelerate toward fulfillment.

Raised Saul of Tarsus, the apostle Paul becomes a central player in God's unfolding global work. It is evident that God had prepared this man for the role of "apostle to the Gentiles" even before his famous encounter with the risen Christ on the road to Damascus (Acts 9). As a diaspora Jew, Saul grew up in a multicultural and multilingual world. Born in Tarsus, he enjoyed Roman citizenship and the privileges it afforded. His pre-Christian life was marked by an intense hatred for the followers of the Way, and Saul was a fierce persecutor of the church. This, too, Paul understood later, would be used by God for the advance of the gospel of grace (1 Tim. 1:16).

The apostle Peter, although an "apostle to the circumcision," is surprised by God, who directs him to share the gospel with the household of the Gentile Cornelius (Acts 10). After hearing that God had clearly prepared Cornelius's heart to receive God's good news, Peter declares that he has come to understand that God does not show partiality[9] but instead freely accepts from every nation those who fear him and do

---

9. It seems that Peter, like the rest of us, has to relearn such lessons, however. According to Galatians 2:11–21, Peter later stumbles in regard to these issues and receives a public rebuke from Paul.

what is right (Acts 10:34–35). As the story continues, Peter witnesses God's Spirit being poured out on Gentiles.[10]

After a season of critical preparation for ministry, Saul of Tarsus becomes one of the five key leaders of the church at Antioch. The others are Barnabas, from Jerusalem; Simeon, called Niger, meaning "black" or "dark-complexioned"; Lucius of Cyrene, the capital city of Libya in northern Africa; and Manaean, who had been brought up with Herod Antipas. It is significant that this group of leaders is a diverse one in terms of both national origins and cultural and ethnic identities. As these leaders worship the Lord together, the Holy Spirit directs them to send forth Saul and Barnabas on a mission that will extend the gospel deep into Gentile communities and hearts. Once again we see the power of listening in advancing the cause of Christ.

In Acts 15, after that first missionary outreach to the Gentiles has borne much fruit, the church confronts an even greater challenge. What is to be done with these aliens who are taking hold of the kingdom? The Judaizing party argues that if Gentiles are to become a part of the church, they must first become a part of Israel by being circumcised and submitting to the law of Moses. After much discussion and debate—that is, once again, after much listening—church leaders reject this approach. It is not necessary for Gentiles to become Jews in order to become Christians. Ironically, and tragically, the tables are soon turned. Within the first few centuries of the young church's history, as Gentiles become predominate in the church, the Jews become the ones on the defensive. They are commanded to forsake their Jewish practices to remain in good standing in the church, effectively being forced to become Gentiles.[11]

Centuries of hostility and suspicion between Jew and Gentile are not quickly worked out in the church. The apostle Peter struggles greatly to affirm what God is doing (Acts 10; Gal. 2:11–14), and the issues are plainly confronted by Paul in many of his letters. It can be argued that even the epistle to the Romans was penned, in large part, because Jews and Gentiles were at odds with one another in the Roman church. This is clearly a focal point in chapters 14 and 15 of that epistle. Quite possibly, the earlier portions of this letter are intended to provide the theo-

---

10. Many New Testament scholars recognize this as the third stage or episode of the Pentecost blessing—a "Jewish Pentecost" in Acts 2, a "Samaritan Pentecost" in Acts 8, and now a "Gentile Pentecost" in Acts 10. See, for example, Frederick Dale Bruner, *A Theology of the Holy Spirit* (Grand Rapids: Eerdmans, 1970).

11. An overview of this development can be found in Marvin R. Wilson, *Our Father Abraham: Jewish Roots of the Christian Faith* (Grand Rapids: Eerdmans, 1989), chaps. 6–7.

logical basis for the practical appeals that appear toward the letter's end.

The issue is also on Paul's mind in his letter to the Ephesians. The cross of Jesus Christ has, Paul argues, destroyed the wall of hostility that stood between Jews and Gentiles. God builds "one new man" where once there were two (Eph. 2:15). With this truth in view, Paul offers the majestic prayer of 3:14–21. Later, with the same truth in view, Paul appeals for both the preservation of the church's essential unity and the building up of that church through the full exercise of the diverse gifts given to members (Eph. 4:1–16).

One in Christ Jesus

Because of what Christ has accomplished, Paul writes elsewhere that "there is neither Jew nor Greek, slave nor free, male nor female, for you are all one in Christ Jesus" (Gal. 3:28; see also Col. 3:11). It is important to note what Paul does *not* mean here. As he writes, the categories of slave and free, male and female had certainly not ceased to exist. Neither had the ethnic and cultural differences between Jews and Gentiles disappeared. To be one in Christ is not to cease having distinct cultural identities, any more than it means ceasing to be male or female. Paul is declaring, rather, that Christ has leveled the ground. The unbelieving world may rank and categorize people, assigning greater value to one and lesser value to another. But Paul does not regard anyone from such a worldly point of view (see 2 Cor. 5:16) because the work of Christ has brought to light God's verdict on these matters. In God's eyes, male and female—though distinct—are equals; slave and free are equals; Jew and Gentile are equals. Paul's words become seeds that later bear fruit among those who rise up to challenge the inequities of slavery, of sexism, and of racism.

Miroslav Volf, reflecting on such matters, notes that "the Spirit does not erase bodily inscribed differences, but allows access into the one body of Christ to the people with such differences on the same terms. What the Spirit does erase (or at least loosen) is a stable and socially constructed correlation between differences and social roles."[12] While Christians need not lose their cultural identities to become one in Christ, "no culture can retain its own deities. . . . Paul deprived each cul-

---

12. Miroslav Volf, *Exclusion and Embrace: A Theological Exploration of Identity, Otherness, and Reconciliation* (Nashville: Abingdon, 1996), 48.

ture of ultimacy in order to give them all legitimacy in the wider family of cultures."[13]

As we reach the close of the canon, God's eternal intentions shine with great clarity. "The kingdom of the world has become the kingdom of our Lord and of his Christ, and he will reign for ever and ever" (Rev. 11:15). "All nations will come and worship" the Lord God Almighty (15:4). Christ will be forever joined with his glorious bride (19:7), the church. In the saints' new, eternal home, "the nations" will walk in the light of the Lamb (21:24) and will experience the healing power of the tree of life (22:2). God has purchased for himself, at the price of his only Son's blood, people "from every tribe and language and people and nation" (5:9). And these, despite their varied backgrounds, will declare with one loud voice, "Salvation belongs to our God, who sits on the throne, and to the Lamb" (7:10).

The last chapter of the Bible records these words: "The angel said to me, 'These words are trustworthy and true. The Lord, the God of the spirits of the prophets, sent his angel to show his servants the things that must soon take place'" (Rev. 22:6). The Lord God sent his Old and New Testament prophets, "especially those through whom God left an inscripturated record,"[14] to call Christians of all ages[15] to come to the eternal kingdom of God, which will be inaugurated on earth through the life, death, and resurrection of Jesus Christ. With such an understanding, we are taught to pray, "Amen. Come, Lord Jesus" (Rev. 22:20) and "Your kingdom come, your will be done on earth as it is in heaven" (Matt. 6:10). So let us pray. So let us also live.

---

13. Ibid., 49.

14. Greg Beale, *The Book of Revelation*, The New International Greek Testament Commentary (Grand Rapids: Eerdmans, 1999), 1124.

15. Ibid., 1125.

3

The Wondrous Cross
and the Broken Wall

GARY A. PARRETT

The wondrous cross brought down the wall,
Vanquishing strife between us all.
Now from all flesh, Gentile and Jew,
God forms one body from the two.

Though we are many, we are one,
Each part reflecting God's great Son.
Female and male, servant and free,
Bound in one Spirit's unity.

Across the earth, the Church expands.
Saints lift God's praise in distant lands,
While others weep and suffer loss,
Still clinging to the wondrous cross.

Forgive us, Lord, the harm we do
When we refuse to follow you.
Forsaking love, we grasp at pow'r.
Come, heal our sickness in this hour.

O, Love amazing, Love divine,
Transform our hearts (Lord, start with mine).
As we've received, teach us to give:
Born in your love, in love to live.[1]

1. Gary A. Parrett, "The Wondrous Cross Brought Down the Wall" (2003). To be sung
to the hymn tune HAMBURG.

In view of the obvious and overwhelming testimony of Scripture, God's heart for the nations cannot be denied. With this as a backdrop, we now consider several key themes and passages in more depth. These further illuminate the obligations incumbent upon the church today.

"Go, Therefore, and Make Disciples of All Nations"

Most evangelical Christians take their "marching orders" from the Great Commission of Matthew 28:18–20. Here, Jesus commands his apostles to make disciples of all nations, baptizing people in the triune name of God and teaching them to obey all Jesus commanded. Similar instructions are recorded at the close of the other Gospels (Mark 16:15; Luke 24:45–48; John 20:21–23) and at the opening of the Book of Acts (1:6–8). On a number of levels, these texts are pertinent to an investigation of God's heart for the nations. The Matthew text, for example, reveals several implications.

First, as already noted, Christ commissions his followers to minister to the whole world. Although the Twelve are, like Jesus himself, Jewish, their mission is not thus restricted. God's purposes for Israel had always included blessing all the nations, and this purpose now embraces the followers of Jesus. The Greek word for "nations" is *ethne,* a plural form of *ethnos,* from which we derive the terms *ethnic* and *ethnicity.* In other words, the Matthew passage applies not so much to political entities as to distinct groupings of people. All such groups are included in God's redemptive plan. This is consistent, of course, with such passages as John 3:16: "For God so loved the world . . ."

We are concerned, however, not only with the scope of the commission but also with its essential purpose. The church is to invest itself in making disciples for Jesus Christ. Christians are to go, baptize, and teach so that people become like Jesus Christ. This is likely so familiar to us that we do not take the time to wrestle with its actual meaning. What does it mean to be like Jesus? Some evangelicals may be quick to answer in terms of personal piety: It is to be holy, righteous, morally upright, and obedient to God. But it also means being compassionate toward and caring for others. In other words, to be like Christ is to love God and one's neighbor. To be a disciple is to follow Jesus in the way he responded to his neighbors. We must ask ourselves, then, How did Jesus respond to "sinners," to women, to children, to Samaritans, to Gentiles, to his enemies?

This leads to a third implication of the Great Commission. Jesus instructed his followers not only in the scope and purpose of their mission but also in the content of their teaching. Note what he does *not* say. He does not instruct them to "teach everything I taught you." He speaks specifically of his commands, not of his teaching in general. But neither does he say merely, "Teach them everything I commanded you." Rather, he says, "Teach them *to obey* everything I commanded you." What *did* Jesus command? Although space does not allow us to probe this fully here, the evidence directs us again to the two greatest commandments: "Love the Lord your God with all your heart and with all your soul and with all your mind and with all your strength" and "love your neighbor as yourself" (see Mark 12:28–34). The meaning of these commands is considered below, but for now note that it is the *doing* of the Word, not merely the *hearing* of it, that marks a disciple of Jesus.

Here is yet another implication of the Great Commission: The work of making disciples requires going. The Matthean commission has one imperative—"make disciples"—but this is unpacked through three participles: going, baptizing, and teaching. The first of these, going, also relates to the expansive and embracing nature of God's mission, for every act of disciple making requires that we go, at least in some sense of the word. We may go across the seas; we may go across the street. But there will always be a going—a setting forth from our own place, from our own sphere of comfort—to extend kingdom love to another. The chief model in this is Jesus himself, who left the glory of heaven to bring the good news of the kingdom to us.

"You Shall Love Your Neighbor as Yourself"

Jesus, on several occasions, engaged in conversations about what constituted the greatest commandment. In each instance, he affirmed that love of God and love of neighbor are the most basic of God's requirements for humans. Scripture consistently testifies that these two commandments are inexorably connected to each other. What is love for God? John answers by saying, "This is love for God: to obey his commands" (1 John 5:3). And what has God commanded? "He has given us this command," writes John, that "whoever loves God must also love his brother" (1 John 4:21). Indeed, if anyone claims to love God and yet at the same time hates his brother, that person is a liar (1 John 4:20). This line of thinking is in keeping with Jesus' teaching to the Twelve: "If you obey my commands, you will remain in my love. . . . My command is this: Love each other as I have loved you" (John 15:10, 12). Clearly, whatever else is involved in loving God, the following is certain: One cannot love God, who is invisible, without at the same time loving persons—those who are made in the image of God (1 John 4:20).

Love of neighbor involves loving fellow believers, as the use of "brother" and "each other" suggests in the texts above, but it does not end there. In fact, Jesus' handling of this great commandment makes it clear that obedience to this Word is costly and demanding. In the Sermon on the Mount, Jesus deals with the command by dismissing the notion that one can love a neighbor but hate an enemy. Kingdom persons will love even their enemies, and in this way they will be true children of their heavenly Father. "If you love those who love you, what reward will you get? . . . If you greet only your brothers, what are you doing more than others?" (Matt. 5:46–47). The spirit of the great commandment is that we must love beyond our natural inclinations.

Jesus drives this point home with peculiar force when, on another occasion, he is questioned about the greatest commandment. Jesus agrees with the scribe that the familiar formula is the right one: God requires, above all, love of God and love of neighbor. But the scribe wants to justify himself, and so he asks, "And who is my neighbor?" Jesus does not answer him directly. Instead, he tells a story, asks a question, and gives a command. The story is what we now call the parable of the good Samaritan. Jesus clearly uses the story to demonstrate that the command "love your neighbor as yourself" pushes us beyond simple, comfortable obedience. Our neighbor is any and every person, especially the one who is in need.

In the story, a Jewish traveler is in desperate need of help. A Jewish priest and a Levite pass by without offering aid. It is a despised Samaritan[2] who, without asking any questions and at great personal cost to himself, loves this fallen stranger. The story is followed with a simple question: "Which of these three do you think was a neighbor?" The answer is clear: "The one who had mercy on him."[3] Then follows this command: "Go and do likewise" (Luke 10:36–37).

It is the "do likewise" that is at the heart of the command. Love of neighbor is doing unto others as we would have them do unto us. Such love does not pause to pepper the needy with qualifying questions: "Where are you from?" or "What manner of life have you lived?" or "What is your religion?" or "Are you one of us?" or even "How did you get into this mess?" Neither does it require an answer to the philosophical query "Who is my neighbor?" for that is entirely the wrong ques-

---

2. The original hearers would certainly have been shocked that a Samaritan would be the story's hero. Jews and Samaritans had a long history of mutual hostility.

3. Notice that the scribe apparently cannot bring himself to say, simply, "the Samaritan."

tion. The right question is "Will I obey God's clear command by *being* a neighbor to others?"

Certainly, those who love their neighbors do not behave like the villains of the story—the priest and the Levite—who somehow find ways to justify ignoring the one who is their neighbor. Yet this is precisely what we often do. Miroslav Volf uses this parable to illustrate what he means by the phrase "exclusion as *abandonment*," a form of excluding others that is

> becoming increasingly prevalent not only in the way the rich West and North relate to the poor of the Third World . . . but also in the manner in which suburbs relate to inner cities, or the jet-setting "creators of high value" to the rabble beneath them. It is exclusion by *abandonment*. Like the priest and the Levite . . . we simply cross to the other side and pass by, minding our own business (Luke 10:31).[4]

Reflecting on the phenomenon of "white flight" that Volf alludes to here, Parker Palmer notes that those who have fled "changing neighborhoods" once or twice "know, deep inside, that there is nowhere left to run, that they must somehow learn to live with diversity."[5]

As we consider the parable of the good Samaritan and its application to us today, we are forced to ask questions not only of the text but of ourselves:

> Why would Jesus make the hero of the story a Samaritan? Why would the one who illustrates obedience to this great commandment be one who was willing to love across cultures, willing to love a stranger? Why would those who claimed to know the Word, but who failed to do it, be cast as the villains? Who would fill the roles in the story if Jesus were telling it today? What does it mean for us . . . to be confronted with the full force of this word, "Love your neighbor as you love yourself"?[6]

"I Was a Stranger, and You Welcomed Me In"

The idea of loving beyond one's comfort zone is further explicated by Jesus in the familiar text Matthew 25:31–46. Jesus teaches that when we

4. Miroslav Volf, *Exclusion and Embrace: A Theological Exploration of Identity, Otherness, and Reconciliation* (Nashville: Abingdon, 1996), 75.

5. Parker J. Palmer, *The Company of Strangers: Christians and the Renewal of America's Public Life* (New York: Crossroad, 1990), 63.

6. Gary A. Parrett, "Ministering in the Real World: A Multicultural Perspective," *Christian Education Journal* 3, no. 2 (spring 1999): 38.

have ministered to the hungry, the thirsty, the naked, or the prisoner, we have in fact ministered to him. Among these ministries of love is this: "I was a stranger and you invited me in" (Matt. 25:35). The Greek word rendered here as "stranger" is *xenos*. From this we derive the English words *xenon* and *xenophobia*. A *xenos* is a stranger, a foreigner, an alien. To love such a neighbor is to love Jesus. The specific type of love that is called for in this case is hospitality, inviting the *xenos* into our homes and lives.

Care and concern for strangers is a consistent biblical theme. Throughout the Old Testament, Israel is commanded to treat the aliens in its midst with justice and mercy (see, for example, Jer. 22:3; Ezek. 47:21–23). Israel is to be mindful of and motivated by its own experiences as aliens: "You are to love those who are aliens, for you yourselves were aliens in Egypt" (Deut. 10:19). There are severe warnings against neglecting these obligations: "Cursed is the man who withholds justice from the alien" (Deut. 27:19). Jesus' teaching is thus built upon the clear and consistent pattern of the Hebrew Scriptures. The New Testament writers, likewise, join their voices to the chorus: "Practice hospitality" (Rom. 12:13); "do not forget to entertain strangers" (Heb. 13:2). The word rendered "practice hospitality" in Romans and "entertain strangers" in Hebrews is the Greek *philoxenia*. Literally, it means "love of strangers," a mind-set that is effectively the opposite of that which is, sadly, alive and well in the church today: xenophobia.

We must allow the weight of Jesus' words to hit us afresh with their full impact. Are we, individually and as church communities, characterized by *philoxenia* or by xenophobia? Who are the *xenoi* in our lives? What will it mean to invite such people in, to love them in deed and truth? Palmer is persuaded that each of us desperately needs the stranger: "Through the stranger our view of self, of world, of God is deepened and expanded. Through the stranger we are given a chance to find ourselves. And through the stranger, God finds us and offers us the gift of wholeness in the midst of our estranged lives, a gift of God and of the public life."[7]

"And Gave Us the Ministry of Reconciliation"

As noted earlier, God, since the events of Genesis 3, has been engaged in the work of reconciling all things to himself. For this cause, Jesus took on human flesh and lived a truly human life. With his physical

---

7. Palmer, *Company of Strangers*, 70.

body, he modeled for us the life of one who is reconciled to God and to neighbor. He engaged in acts of reconciliation by word and deed. With the same body, he bore our sins on the cross, thus reconciling the sinful world to God. This reconciling work continues even now and will do so until every foe of God is vanquished. Today, Christ still works through a body, but it is his *spiritual* body, the church. Paul's continual appeals for unity in the church are not merely for the purposes of our experiencing the joys of harmony within our communities. The real purpose is so that we can be the healthy, fully functioning body we are designed to be, submitted to Christ, our head (1 Corinthians 12–14; Ephesians 4; etc.). Having been reconciled to God, we are now called to join Christ in this very work (2 Cor. 5:20).

God, through Christ, is reconciling *all things* to himself, and this work involves people being reconciled not only to God but also to one another and to the rest of creation. What does it mean to be ministers of reconciliation today? The world is ablaze with ethnic and national strife. Europe is abuzz, yet again, with the shrill cries of xenophobia. The United States continues to be a racially charged society that seems largely unwilling to face both its history and its present realities.[8] Does the church have a part to play in addressing such issues? If so, what does that role look like? How much of an impact can the church make in these areas when the same issues are burning in our own communities? Tragically, it seems that churches themselves have too often been under prophetic indictment concerning such things. As Volf aptly puts it, "Churches, the presumed agents of reconciliation, are at best impotent and at worst accomplices in the strife."[9]

"Now He Had to Go through Samaria"

As Jesus prepared the Twelve for their engagement in a ministry of reconciliation that was to reach to the very ends of the earth, he often took them out of the familiar and put them in circumstances that would prove challenging. One such occasion was their journey through Samaria, recorded in John 4. One verse in this passage probably seems relatively insignificant to most readers of the New Testament: "Now he had to go through Samaria" (v. 4). Jesus, while journeying with the Twelve from Judea to Galilee, passes through the region that lay between the two, Samaria. But what is the meaning of the words "he had

---

8. Norman Anthony Peart provides significant insight into both of these areas, especially as applied to black-white issues, in *Separate No More* (Grand Rapids: Baker, 2000).
9. Volf, *Exclusion and Embrace*, 36.

to go"? Should they merely be understood as a geographical "ought?" In fact, many Jewish contemporaries found other routes for this journey. It was not uncommon for a Jewish traveler to cross the Jordan River and go north, through Perea and the Decapolis, before crossing the river again into Galilee. The trip through Samaria was both undesirable and potentially dangerous for Jewish travelers, and therefore many simply avoided this route.

It seems more likely that the "ought" in this case is missional, not geographical. Christ came to earth "to seek and to save what was lost" (Luke 19:10). This mission was given to him by his heavenly Father, to whom Jesus was utterly submitted throughout his earthly sojourn (John 5:19). As the story of John 4 unfolds, Jesus makes it clear that the Father is seeking persons who would worship him in spirit and truth (4:23) and that he, Jesus, has come to accomplish his Father's work (4:34). For all *these* reasons, he had to go through Samaria. After his ministry to the woman of Samaria, Jesus invites the Twelve to join him in doing the Father's will and work. "Open your eyes," he tells them, and you will see that the fields are "ripe for harvest" (4:35). Even as he said these things, a crowd of curious Samaritans was making its way toward Jesus and his disciples (4:30). What followed were two days of fruitful labor among these Samaritan villagers—much to the surprise, no doubt, of the apostles.

The Samaritans were, for the Jews, a people who were both very near them and very far from them. Geographically speaking, they lived right next door. But culturally, ethnically, and religiously, they were worlds apart. Each believer and every church community must consider the following: Which people may represent such a Samaria to me, to us? Do I, do we, have to pass through this Samaria, as Jesus passed through his? If so, what will this mean in practical terms? It often seems that it is easier for people in our church communities to cross an ocean for a brief "missionary" visit than to cross the street to build lasting relationships with neighbors who are near us but unlike us. It is also apparent that many learn how to navigate their entire lives without ever truly passing through the world of such neighbors. Do we "have to" pass through our "Samarias," whatever they may be? Yes, we do—*if* we are committed to doing the Father's will and fulfilling his work.

"The Word Became Flesh and Dwelt among Us"

Of all the biblical truths that should shape our thinking about loving and ministering across cultures, none is more significant than the incarnation of Jesus. Jesus is the ultimate picture of what we must become as Christians. This is true, of course, in every sense. It is certainly true in regard to learning how to love our neighbor, for the incarnation provides a glorious display of the heart of God.

The motives for the incarnation are several. The Son *exegeted* the unseen God for us (John 1:18). He glorified the Father by accomplishing his work (John 17:4). He described this work as seeking and saving the lost (Luke 19:10), as serving and giving his life as a ransom for many (Mark 10:45). Paul summarized this by use of the term *reconciliation* (2 Cor. 5:14–21; Col. 1:15–23). Jesus came to inaugurate the eternal kingdom.

To accomplish such ends, the Son emptied himself (Phil. 2:6–7), leaving the glory of heaven in order to lead many sons to glory (Heb. 2:10). He partook, in every sense, of true humanity that he might become a merciful high priest and make atonement for our sins (Heb. 2:14–18). He "dwelt among us" (John 1:14), taking on our form, our culture, our language, and ultimately our sins and our death. Even while we were sinners, God's enemies, he loved us and died for us (Rom. 5:8–10). Jesus was, in other words, exemplary for any who are determined to love God and neighbor. For those who take seriously God's heart for all the peoples of the earth, there is nothing more important than seeking to have the mind that was in Christ Jesus (Phil. 2:5).

We will return to a consideration of the implications of the incarnation for our own lives and ministry in chapter 6. For now, note that God, determined to reconcile all things to himself, did so through his incarnate Son. For reasons we may never fully understand, the reconciling work of God required that the Son be embodied, that he be truly human, that he live and die as a true man. The author of the letter to the Hebrews writes, "Therefore, when Christ came into the world, he said: 'Sacrifice and offering you did not desire, but a body you prepared for me. . . . I have come to do your will, O God'" (10:5, 7). He writes further that by that will of God, "we have been made holy through the sacrifice of the body of Jesus Christ once for all" (10:10).

"His Purpose Was to Create in Himself One New Man out of the Two, Thus Making Peace"

There is an intriguing feature to the reconciling work of God that is described in various New Testament passages. On the one hand, that work is spoken of as though it were completed. For example, 2 Corinthians 5:18 says, "God, who reconciled us to himself through Christ." But in the very next breath, Paul says, "[And he] gave us the ministry of reconciliation." At the cross, Jesus cried out in a loud voice, "It is finished!" But has the work of reconciliation truly been accomplished? The answer seems to be both yes and no. We find here one example of the already/not yet nature of God's kingdom work.

Christ's life, death, and resurrection were without question the climactic acts of God's reconciling work. Through these acts, reconciliation has truly been accomplished. This is the inescapable testimony of the key Pauline passages in which the doctrine is taught. Note the following witnesses:

> For if, when we were God's enemies, we were reconciled to him through the death of his Son, how much more, having been reconciled, shall we be saved through his life! Not only is this so, but we also rejoice in God through our Lord Jesus Christ, through whom we have now received reconciliation.
>
> Romans 5:10–11

> All this is from God, who reconciled us to himself through Christ. . . . God was reconciling the world to himself in Christ.
>
> 2 Corinthians 5:18–19

> . . . and in this one body to reconcile both of them to God through the cross.
>
> Ephesians 2:16

> For God was pleased to have all his fullness dwell in him, and through him to reconcile to himself all things . . . , by making peace through his blood, shed on the cross. Once you were alienated from God and were enemies. . . . But now he has reconciled you by Christ's physical body through death.
>
> Colossians 1:19–22

In each of the above passages, the reconciling of humankind to God is presented as having already been accomplished through the death of Jesus Christ. In what sense, then, can the task of reconciliation be seen as something that is still underway?

First, there is the "ministry of reconciliation" and the "message of reconciliation" that, says Paul, have been committed to us (2 Cor. 5:18–19). In light of this, Paul writes, "We are therefore Christ's ambassadors," imploring people to "be reconciled to God" (2 Cor. 5:20), for although God's righteous demands—which had been violated by humankind since the fall—have been fully satisfied in Christ (1 John 2:2), this fact alone does not mean that all persons are reconciled to God. God has turned to us, but it remains for each of us to turn again to him. Thus, we must preach the good news of what God has done in Christ and must plead with people to acknowledge and receive this gift. By engaging in this ministry of reconciliation, Paul incurred much suffering. But he reckoned that he was sharing in the sufferings of Christ (Phil. 3:10), even filling up in his own flesh "what is still lacking in regard to Christ's afflictions" (Col. 1:24)!

There is a second sense in which the work of reconciliation continues. Just as individuals need to experience personally that which Christ accomplished, by turning to the God who has turned toward them in Christ, so society and, indeed, all the nations and all of creation must yet experience that which Christ accomplished. For example:

- The peoples of the earth, who have been divided through mutual hostility—such as that between Jew and Gentile—must experience that God, in Christ, has "destroyed the barrier, the dividing wall of hostility . . . to create in himself one new man out of the two" (Eph. 2:14–15). God has declared that, in Christ, there is no longer "Jew nor Greek, slave nor free, male nor female" (Gal. 3:28). But this has not been worked out fully in human experience.

- The various powers and principalities that have rebelled and boasted against God have been "disarmed" and defeated "by the cross" (Col. 2:15), but they have yet to be completely "destroyed" (1 Cor. 15:24).

- Indeed, every enemy of God must be placed under the feet of Jesus, the reconciler. The last of these enemies is death. Then will the end come (1 Cor. 15:24–26).

- Only when the end has come will the sons and daughters of God be unveiled with Christ in glory and all of creation—which has been for ages subjected to bondage—be liberated and "brought into the glorious freedom of the children of God" (Rom. 8:21).

- The "great white throne" of the judge will settle the eternal fate of all creatures (Rev. 20:11–15), and the eternal kingdom will be established in all its glory (Revelation 21–22).

All of this provides clues about our place in the ongoing ministry of reconciliation. Like Paul, we are to bear the message of reconciliation as ambassadors of Christ. But it is not merely the message of God's reign we should bear; we should also bear its life, love, and power. We are called not only to *bring* good news but also to *be* good news. We must live as those who have been reconciled to God (2 Cor. 5:15). We must pray as those who are anticipating and longing for the kingdom's full expression (Matt. 6:9–13; Rev. 22:20). And we must engage in works of reconciliation, as Jesus did during his earthly life, for it was not only in death that Christ was the great reconciler. Every word and deed of love, justice, mercy, compassion, healing, and deliverance was a reconciling act. He came to do such works while it was yet day, and he called his disciples to join him in this work (John 9:4). Indeed, he said that his followers would actually do greater works than he had done, because of the outpouring of the Holy Spirit in their lives (John 14:12). Further, it was for the doing of such good works that Christ redeemed us (Titus 2:14) and made us new creations in Christ (Eph. 2:10). God has given us his very Word so that we may be thoroughly equipped for these appointed works (2 Tim. 3:16–17).

What then is the ministry of reconciliation for us today? It is every bearing of the gospel, every good work, every prayer, and every act of worship. It is every endeavor to live out on earth that which Christ accomplished so that God's will might be done in and through our lives. What a wonder is this—that we have been called and invited to engage in the very work for which Christ came into the world! Like that of Jesus himself, the purpose of our earthly sojourn is to be engaged in the ministry of reconciliation.

In entering this work, however, we do not usurp Christ's reconciling work. Nor does our reconciling work parallel his own. The work we engage in is *his* ministry of reconciliation. It is still Christ who is reconciling all things to the Father. And, as always, this work is carried on through his body.

During his earthly sojourn, as we have seen, Christ accomplished reconciliation through his physical body (Col. 1:22). His reconciling work continues now through his spiritual body, the church. It is therefore critical that the body of Christ be gifted, equipped, built up, and mature so that it can be fully functioning (Eph. 4:11–16). But there is one critical dimension of this that Christians often miss. This body that is to be busily engaged in the kingdom work of reconciliation is made up of people who have been reconciled to God *and* to one another.

The Bible does not allow for the notion that people can somehow be reconciled to God but not to one another. John plainly disallows such thinking (1 John 4:20) just as his Lord and teacher, Jesus, had done (Matt. 6:14–15). In Ephesians 2, Paul applies the same logic to the doctrine of reconciliation. Christ destroyed the hostility that had long existed between Jew and Gentile. Thus, he himself is our peace (Eph. 2:14). His purpose in this "was to create in himself one new man out of the two . . . and in this one body to reconcile both of them to God through the cross, by which he put to death their hostility" (Eph. 2:15–

16). God makes one new man from the two, one new people from the two, and one new spiritual building from the two (Eph. 2:19–22).

The beautiful prayer of Ephesians 3:14–21 is prayed in the light of this truth. Paul writes:

> For this reason I kneel before the Father, *from whom his whole family in heaven and on earth derives its name*. . . . I pray that you . . . may have power, *together with all the saints*, to grasp how wide and long and high and deep is the love of Christ . . . that you may be filled to the measure of *all the fullness of God*. . . . To him be glory *in the church* and in Christ Jesus throughout all generations, for ever and ever! Amen. (emphasis added)

This amazing prayer, which is a celebration of how God has reconciled us to himself, is also a celebration of the fact that he has reconciled us to one another. In the same context, Paul continues with a declaration both of the church's essential unity (Eph. 4:1–6) and of its diverse gifts (4:7–11). It is in this context also that Paul speaks of the fully functioning body of Christ doing its work to the glory of God (4:12–16).

In the New Testament contexts, this reconciliation reality was a constant challenge for the churches. How could those who had for centuries been alienated from one another truly live and serve together as one— Jew and Gentile, servant and free, male and female? It was not easy in the first century. It is not easy around the globe today. But the tragedy is complicated today by the fact that many churches do not struggle with this reconciliation reality at all. We simply ignore it. We envision that we are reconciled to God in a way that does not require reconciliation with "the other." We may seek to be reconciled to alienated family members and others of our neighbors, but we are largely content to worship and serve alongside only those who are very much like us. Christ may have destroyed the wall of hostility between us, but we have grown so accustomed to the wall that we live as though it were still standing.[10] Theoretically, we may affirm that there is but one body in Christ. Practically, however, most of us seem to live as though it were otherwise.

"The Body Is a Unit, Though It Is Made Up of Many Parts; and Though All Its Parts Are Many, They Form One Body. So It Is with Christ."

We consider, finally, the biblical concept of the unity of the body of Christ. While some may view diversity in the church as something

---

10. I first heard this idea articulated by Elizabeth Conde-Frazier.

that is generally good and thus should be sought or at least tolerated, the biblical vision is significantly different. Diversity in the church, according to Scripture, is not merely good; it is essential. It is not something to be sought or tolerated; it is a reality we must obey and endeavor to preserve. Indeed, neither the idea of unity without diversity nor the idea of diversity without unity is a biblically viable option. Let us briefly explore these two notions.

First, diversity without unity is unbiblical. While the New Testament consistently affirms that there is diversity in the church, believers are continually urged to be united in spirit and in purpose. They are not to allow diversity to divide the body, whether that diversity be the result of ethnicity, culture, economic status, or preferences regarding church leadership. Believers are to accept one another as Christ accepted them. To correct the tendency toward fragmentation, biblical authors remind their hearers that they are *in fact* one in Christ. "There is one body" (Eph. 4:4), "you are all one in Christ Jesus" (Gal. 3:28), and similar passages. Furthermore, for all the diversity in the church, there must be unity around the truth of God (see, for example, 1, 2, and 3 John). Any vision of or effort toward ecumenism that does not include unity around the essential teaching of the biblical, historic, and orthodox Christian faith is a sham and must be rejected.

The second truth, that unity without diversity is unbiblical, is perhaps less obvious to many. In their daily experiences, many churches seem to shun the most obvious types of diversity (though, of course, diversity is always present in any church in the form of gifts, abilities, personalities, etc.). But the biblical vision of unity actually embraces diversity. This is evident in several important ways.

First, it is evident with respect to the Triune God himself. The doctrine of the Trinity is a lesson in unity in diversity and diversity in unity:

> There is in God genuine diversity as well as true unity. The Christian God is not just a unit but a union, not just unity but community. There is in God something analogous to "society." He is not a single person, loving himself alone, not a self-contained monad or "The One." He is triunity: three equal persons, each one dwelling in the other two by virtue of an unceasing movement of mutual love.[11]

11. Kallistos Ware, *The Orthodox Way* (Crestwood, N.Y.: St. Vladimir's Seminary Press, 1996), 27.

Thus, when we affirm that God is one (as in the *shema*—"Hear, O Israel: The LORD our God, the LORD is one" [Deut. 6:4]), we are affirming a unity that involves diversity.

The Hebrew word that describes God's unity in Deuteronomy 6, *echad*, is used to describe the unity that occurs when a husband and wife are joined together: "And they will become *one* flesh" (Gen. 2:24). Thus, marriage provides a second significant example of unity in diversity. In marriage, the individual life of neither spouse is to be lost or forfeited. Each person retains unique gifts and personality, each has his or her role to fulfill, and each will live eternally as a unique son or daughter of God. But for the course of their earthly sojourn together, they are, mysteriously, one flesh.

So it is that we read of Paul's vision of the one body of Christ, the church. Paul could not assert more emphatically than he does in Ephesians 4 and 1 Corinthians 12 the essential unity of the church, but it is unity that requires the presence of diversity. The body has many parts, writes Paul, but it is one body (1 Cor. 12:12) with Christ as its one head (Eph. 4:15). Each member of this body is unique and essential. Each belongs to Christ, the head, and each belongs to every member of the body. Indeed, the body as a whole is only as strong as its weakest members allow it to be (1 Cor. 14:26). Paul hammers these truths home to the Corinthians because so much in their treatment of one another was at odds with them. The rich abused the poor at the Lord's Table (chap. 11), the gifted and the not so gifted despised one another (chaps. 12–14), and the church had splintered into personality-centered factions (chaps. 1, 3).

Elsewhere, as we have seen, Paul makes it clear that the diversity of Christ's body also includes all manner of human distinctions that had historically separated people from one another. But our flesh seems to resist this concept at every turn. Rather than embrace diversity, we eschew it. We tend to find those who look, think, act, speak, and smell as we do and congregate with them while excluding others. It is as though I, after identifying myself as a "pinky" in the body of Christ, am now instinctively drawn to other pinkies. We are so excited to find one another that we determine—prayerfully, of course—to form a church together. We will be the First Church of the Pinkies! Absurd as this analogy is, the reality is often not much different.

Of course, no church can be diverse in every respect. In some countries and in some portions of the United States, for example, ethnic and socioeconomic diversity may not be possible for a local congregation to achieve. Other churches may choose, for missional purposes, to concentrate their evangelistic efforts on a narrowly targeted population.[12] Others may be primarily mono-ethnic and mono-cultural for other, complex, sociocultural reasons. But the concern here is with churches that have willfully barred the doors—in ways subtle or not so subtle—to prevent *xenoi* from being welcomed into their communities. How can any church that is organized in such willful opposition to the good plan of God be a true reflection of the Triune God? How can it be a properly functioning body of Christ—doing his work in the world? How can it be an agent of reconciliation when it is actually resisting God's reconciling work by its very design?

The testimony of the biblical texts is clear and convincing: God loves the peoples of the world[13] and calls us to do the same. This testimony must be equally clear and emphatic in our teaching ministries, be they in the local church or in the academy. We now turn our attention to an exploration of educational theories and practices that may prove useful as we strive to align ourselves more faithfully with the Way of the Lord.

---

12. It seems to me that in light of the New Testament vision of the church, the merits of such an approach are debatable at best. Marva Dawn argues against such use of the "marketing niche" approach and the creation of a "homogeneous church." She writes, "The gospel calls us instead to welcome everyone as God has welcomed us, breaking down barriers to discover the unity of God's diversity, the revealing of God's grace that comes from people not like ourselves" (Marva Dawn, *Is It a Lost Cause?* [Grand Rapids: Eerdmans, 1999], 56). Curtis Paul DeYoung, Michael O. Emerson, George Yancy, and Karen Chai Kim also argue against the validity of building and maintaining a church based on the racial implications of the "homogeneous unit principle" in their book *United by Faith: The Multicultural Congregation as an Answer to the Problem of Race* (New York: Oxford University Press, 2003), especially in chapter 8, "Arguing the Case for Multiracial Congregations," 128–44.

13. This is not to suggest, of course, that there is no sense in which God "hates," "opposes," or "judges" individuals or nations, for the Bible plainly speaks in such terms. To say that God's heart is "for the nations" is to affirm, simply, that "God so loved the world" and calls forth people for himself "from every nation, tribe, and tongue."

4

Salient Theoretical Frameworks for Forming Kingdom Citizens

S. STEVE KANG

God's heart for people from every nation, tribe, and tongue on earth is unmistakably portrayed throughout the Bible. As shown in the previous chapter, from Genesis to Revelation, Scripture is replete with glimpses of God's sovereign execution of gathering his people to himself. Specifically, the incarnation, ministry, death, and resurrection of Jesus Christ inaugurated the eternal kingdom of God here and now.[1] Jesus, in responding to the Pharisees' wrongheaded kingdom-gazing activities in Luke 17, declares that the kingdom of God is already active, present, and operative, if only they would open their hearts to receive it.[2] To Christians who have responded to God's gracious call to be kingdom citizens, God has graciously provided the kingdom mandates, as discussed in the previous chapter, and promises to realize the kingdom of God on earth as Christians faithfully live as kingdom citizens in thankful obedience. How then should thankful obedience be shaped and practiced in the church here and now?

This chapter brings together several strands of theory and practice from the disciplines of Christian education, educational foundations, and theology in an attempt to construct an integrative approach to Christian forma-

---

1. Tibor Horvath, "Jesus Christ, the Eschatological Union of Time and Eternity," *Science et Esprit* 40, no. 2 (1988): 179, 192.
2. Joel B. Green, *The Gospel of Luke,* The New International Commentary on the New Testament (Grand Rapids: Eerdmans, 1997), 629–30.

tion[3] that increasingly realizes the *ethos* of the shalom of Christ's kingdom in the local church and beyond. The chapter begins by discussing the faith community approach to Christian formation as the context for Christians to come together and forge kingdom-building pedagogies. It then explores some contextualized theologies that challenge Christian formation to expand the scope and purpose of kingdom-building pedagogies. The chapter concludes by exploring some critical pedagogies that enhance Christians' engagement in the world as kingdom citizens.

The Faith Community Approach to Christian Formation

If the church is to be the central sociocultural institution for Christians to be (re)enculturated as kingdom citizens, then its Christian formation must be characterized by a sense of authenticity, community, safety, and hospitality. A significant way in which the church can shape the community of kingdom citizens is through the formation of a faith community.

The faith community approach employs the faith community itself as the context, content, and method for Christian education.[4] This approach presupposes that a community of believers transmits faith to its children, as well as to its adults, through socialization or acculturation processes.[5] In other words, learning the faith happens as the members of a faith community participate, intentionally and unintentionally, in the activities of that community.

Its Epistemological Framework

Many theorists in the field of Christian education have articulated the faith community approach to Christian education during the past thirty years.[6] While these theorists have made their unique contribu-

---

3. Christian formation entails inviting, creating a space for the people of God to intentionally, habitually, and holistically engage in God-given educational moments in all aspects of life, thus invoking the Holy Spirit to work in the community and the lives of the people of God through those transforming moments.
    4. Jack Seymour, *Mapping Christian Education: Approaches to Congregational Learning* (Nashville: Abingdon, 1997), 50–53.
    5. C. Ellis Nelson, *Where Faith Begins* (Atlanta: John Knox, 1971), 183–85.
    6. Charles Foster, *Educating Congregation* (Nashville: Abingdon, 1994), 12–14; Maria Harris, *Fashion Me a People: Curriculum in the Church* (Louisville: Westminster John Knox, 1989); Nelson, *Where Faith Begins;* Parker Palmer, *To Know as We Are Known: A Spirituality of Education* (San Francisco: Harper & Row, 1993); and John Westerhoff, *Will Our Children Have Faith?* rev. ed. (Toronto: Morehouse Publishing, 2000).

tions to the development of the approach, a common epistemological presupposition underlies their theoretical proposals. They begin by critiquing the positivistic notion of knowledge and the dichotomy that exists between the notions of subjectivity and objectivity. They construe knowledge as the result of dialectical interaction among people in the community and the sociocultural ethos that permeates the community.

KNOWING AND LOVING IN COMMUNITY

For instance, Parker Palmer argues for the socioculturally constructed nature of knowledge[7] as people in community shape and in turn are shaped by their life together based on the commitment to and practice of their shared knowledge. In this sense, his epistemological reflection involves the ethical dimension. He does not simply ask, "How do we know?" but also, "How do we use and apply knowledge?" He construes knowing as having passion and purpose that involve love and commitment to the community of knowers. Palmer contends that the goal of knowledge stemming from love is the "reunification and reconstruction of broken selves and worlds."[8]

The act of knowing, then, becomes an act of love. This knowing encourages people to enter and embrace the reality of the other in an intimate way. In this process, one comes to know and is known by one's own community. This kind of knowing solidifies the bonds of persons in the community as they grow together within the rules and visions of that community. It is, therefore, through radical authenticity and love that the community is created and maintained and that people shape and are shaped by their community.

In the process, Christians realize that they are inextricably bound together and that their lives are incomplete unless committed to and shared with a faith community. This is how Christians can begin to recover together one aspect of the image of God, the interpenetration or the relationality among the three persons of the Godhead. We are exhorted to know ourselves together through God's love as kingdom citizens—as we are known by God in his infinite love.

THE NARRATIVE PROMISE AS THE "FOUNDATION" OF THE FAITH COMMUNITY

While shying away from claiming to have transcended epistemic assumptions in their theologizing, nonfoundationalists argue that the modern theological enterprise has been largely *foundational* in its epistemic

7. Palmer, *To Know as We Are Known*, 54–60.
8. Ibid., 8.

assumptions. In other words, the modern theological program has adopted "foundations"—universal and undebatable principles of argumentation—for knowledge. It assumes the existence of a privileged foundation that possesses the ability to ground the framework of knowledge and that this privileged foundation is necessary for knowledge to be meaningful.

Nonfoundationalists, on the other hand, argue that the Christian faith possesses its own background beliefs or "foundations" in its rich premodern traditions (i.e., Scripture, doctrines, liturgical practices, etc.). For them, theological reflection within the faith community must determine the community's self-understanding in Jesus Christ, who is the head of the church and in whom all things hold together, for all things have been created through him and for him (Col. 1:16–18).

For instance, Ronald Thiemann asserts that modern theologians have mistakenly associated revelation with a foundationalist epistemology, that is, a set of non-inferential, self-evident beliefs.[9] He maintains that many modern theologians have resorted to foundationalist arguments to justify the doctrines as the legitimate starting points of theology by arguing that revelation is a common intuition experientially available to all. Thiemann contends that faithfulness to Christianity's basic background beliefs, or its own foundations, which are independent of theoretical justification through the use of modern philosophical frameworks, should determine the integrity of the theological program.

Thiemann believes that God's prevenience—divine initiative—must be the central focus in conceptualizing the doctrine of revelation and initiating the formation of the Christian faith community. He submits that revelation should be conceptualized as "narrative promise"—Scripture's narration of the identity of God as the one who promises, where the promise is initiated by God and must subsequently be responded to by human beings. Thiemann is more concerned about the internal validity of revelation within the Christian community than trying to articulate a doctrine of revelation and of the church that may appeal to the entire modern world.

What then is required of those within the Christian community if the notion of God's prevenience is to be taken seriously as the preeminent foundation of the community? Lesslie Newbigin responds to a question asked by an Indonesian acquaintance: "Can the West be converted?"[10]

9. Ronald Thiemann, *Revelation and Theology: The Gospel as Narrative Promise* (Notre Dame, Ind.: University of Notre Dame Press, 1985).

10. Lesslie Newbigin, *Proper Confidence: Faith, Doubt, and Certainty in Christian Discipleship* (Grand Rapids: Eerdmans, 1995), 5–44.

Newbigin is convinced that the West can be converted only by a complete transformation of its mind—away from the distinctive patterns of Enlightenment thought and toward openness to grace, faith, and revelation. He argues that the notion of certainty has been the controlling myth of modernity. Yet he shows that even the natural sciences involve something like "faith" or a set of agreed-upon propositions within the community. Newbigin contends that the "myth of certainty" must be abandoned if the West is to be converted.

Newbigin goes on to assert that the notion of faith should be the starting point of the formation of a Christian faith community, which can in turn open the postmodern Western mind to the cultural contributions of a faith-based, revelation-based, Christian perspective. In sum, Newbigin advocates a distinctly Christian framework that rejects the notion of certainty as the chief arbitrating principle and that begins with an openness to the truth of the Christian story.

Its Theological Framework

In the past two decades, theologians calling themselves post-liberals have critiqued the nature of the relationship between Christian faith and the faith community. They have attempted to articulate a postmodern vision of the Christian faith community by critiquing yet also utilizing modern epistemological discourses.

ABSORBING THE MODERN WORLD INTO THE BIBLICAL WORLD

If faith itself is the crucial foundation for the formation of a faith community, how is the faith shaped? Hans Frei, who is considered the cofounder of the post-liberal movement along with George Lindbeck, was one of the first to argue that modernity misled the church in its use of the Bible.

In great historical detail, Frei asserts that by the eighteenth century the great reversal had taken place in the lives of people in the Christian church.[11] He contends that the world of people's daily experience became the lens through which the biblical story was interpreted; no longer did they incorporate their world into the biblical story. By way of contrast, Christians before modernity did not read the Bible to get *behind* the text so much as to get at the truth *in* the text. For them, the Bible absorbed and redefined the world on biblical terms. Frei's hope was that (post)modern Christians might recover the premodern strat-

---

11. Hans Frei, *The Eclipse of Biblical Narrative* (New Haven: Yale University Press, 1974), 17–65.

egy of reading Scripture in their own day and in their own way in the context of the Christian faith community.[12]

Frei admits that the logic of connecting the mode of factual affirmation with the mode of a religious life cannot be readily understood. He affirms that the factual affirmation of the resurrection of Christ, unlike other cases of factual affirmation, shapes a new life and that this process takes place mainly within the Christian textual community.[13] This notion of Christian formation finds much congruity in its process, though not necessarily its content, with that of Horace Bushnell, who claimed that the children of a Christian family and community should grow up not knowing what it means to grow up any way other than as a Christian.[14]

THE FAITH COMMUNITY AS A REVELATIONALLY SHAPED CULTURAL-LINGUISTIC SYSTEM

Well versed in anthropology and epistemology, George Lindbeck argues that Christianity has its own sort of "culture" and "language." Moreover, human beings are thoroughly sociocultural beings who depend on these resources to make experience possible and are shaped by their historical and cultural contexts.

Drawing from Clifford Geertz, Lindbeck considers religions cultural frameworks or mediums that engender a vocabulary and precede inner experience. He likens the function of theology and doctrine to the way grammar functions for any given language. Christian theology and doctrine are rules or regulations that govern Christian speech and life, and they are changeable and highly contextual. Moreover, theology and doctrine function as grammar in that they affirm nothing either true or false about God and his relation to creatures. They are second-order activities that speak about such assertions. Although at first glance Lindbeck does not seem to be concerned with the historicity of the narrative of Scripture, he affirms the authenticity of the biblical narrative, as does Frei, who comes close to the notion of the historical presence of Jesus as a shared knowledge within the Christian community.[15] Lindbeck criticizes cognitive-propositionalism for affirming doctrines as objective descriptions of realities that are "beyond" the narrative of

12. Ibid., 1–16.

13. Ibid., 224–32.

14. Horace Bushnell, *Christian Nurture* (1861; reprint, Grand Rapids: Baker, 1979), 10.

15. George Lindbeck, "The Story-Shaped Church: Critical Exegesis and Theological Interpretation," in *Scriptural Authority and Narrative Interpretation*, ed. Garrett Green (Philadelphia: Fortress, 1987), 161–78.

Scripture. In other words, modern evangelical theology has elevated propositional statements above the words of Scripture so that they take on a life of their own rather than shaping and being shaped by the faith community as clearly witnessed in church history.

Seen in this light, the Christian faith is best understood as a cultural-linguistic system in which the canonical texts of Scripture function as the interpretive norm, and doctrine and theology function as the grammar governing communities of practice. This narratively shaped faith community or cultural-linguistic system provides an intelligible interpretation in its own terms of the varied situations and realities its adherents encounter. It also advocates a thoroughly social and communitarian vision of human life, thereby repudiating the individualism endemic to modern life and thought. The kingdom life of Christian experience is mediated through the language and practice of particular communities, and individuals have identity only within those communal contexts. The faith community approach to Christian formation thus advocates a return to Christian religious tradition and the task of interiorizing the values of particular communities. Yet these Christian faith communities are committed to conversation with participants of other Christian traditions regarding specific shared concerns, each bringing to the conversation the distinctive voice of its tradition.

Its Theory and Practice

C. Ellis Nelson and John Westerhoff are the two prominent figures who have been instrumental in advocating the faith community approach to Christian education.[16]

TRAJECTORIES OF THE FAITH COMMUNITY APPROACH

In articulating his model, Nelson criticizes a general tendency of the church, namely, the compartmentalization of Christian education into Sunday school.[17] Sunday school, as the primary educational approach of the church, was shaped by a distinct socio-historico-religious situation of a specific time and space for a specific purpose: reading and writing and conversion of the soul.[18] Thus, Sunday school by itself fails to educate people in a holistic fashion, especially in this day and age.

---

16. Charles Foster, "The Faith Community as a Guiding Image for Christian Education," in *Contemporary Approaches to Christian Education*, ed. Jack Seymour and Donald Miller (Nashville: Abingdon, 1982), 58–59.

17. Nelson, *Where Faith Begins*, 182–211.

18. C. Ellis Nelson, *How Faith Matures* (Louisville: Westminster John Knox, 1989), 186–98.

What is critical for the faith community is reappropriating Christian traditions, re-envisioning the nature and ministry of the church and its formational responsibility, and exploring ways to live out that life of faith authentically in the present.

In clarifying the faith community model within the church education movement, Nelson highlights three crucial objectives for the Christian educator.[19] The first objective is to utilize all aspects of church life as educational means and processes. Whether in an informal, formal, or nonformal educational setting, the Christian educator must maximize every opportunity for people of God to engage in mutual critical-contextual reflection on the Christian faith.

Another objective for the Christian educator is to foster theological and ethical inquiry within the community. People should be encouraged to "bring their belief to a conscious level and then to examine those beliefs in the light of [their] knowledge of the world and society."[20] This process involves dialectical interaction between the Christian faith and the current experience of the community. Nelson also maintains that the Christian educator should create a space where people can examine the ethical norms of the Christian faith and their adherence to them.

The third objective includes the community's involvement in social justice. The Christian educator should function as a coach who prepares people for corporate life and who helps them find meaning in their life situations. Nelson reminds his readers that the coach "is deeply involved but he can't play the game for the players, and the players know it."[21]

Leaders of the faith community must recognize that people are constantly engaged in the task of interpreting their life and world, and the faith community needs to provide opportunities for people to understand two crucial elements.[22] First, they need to understand what the community that produced Scripture and the communities of subsequent generations were like. Second, they need to understand how these communities interpreted their pasts and how they understood God's presence among them. In the process, the community is to live out the interpreted Christian faith here and now and to pass on that faith by socializing the next generation. This transmission of the Christian faith—through interpretation and transformation—will continue,

19. Ibid., 111–49.
20. Nelson, *Where Faith Begins*, 10.
21. Ibid., 14.
22. Ibid., 67–94.

spearheaded by subsequent generations under the guidance of the Holy Spirit.

In sum, transmission and socialization involve passing on all aspects of faith, utilizing all means available in the community of faith, to subsequent generations. In this sense, the knower and the known are bonded together in compassion and responsibility. Thus, involvement, mutuality, and accountability become the core values that the community seeks to live out.

INTERLOCKING PHASES OF THE FAITH COMMUNITY

While similar themes of Nelson's approach can be found in Westerhoff's writings, Westerhoff employs the historic word *catechesis*, which basically means Christian nurture through acts of instruction by word of mouth. Catechesis is, for Westerhoff, a holistic approach that involves three phases.[23]

The first phase is called the "affiliative-experiencing way." It involves generating intuitive knowledge in people as they participate in "subjective aesthetic experiences—through symbols, rituals and myths of the community."[24] In the midst of this "traditioning," the community is entrusted with the authority to shape its people. It therefore involves intentionality as the community seeks to create an ongoing experience for its people in their relationships with one another. In the process, the community endeavors to create in its people the community's worldview—shaping their perceptions, faith, consciousness, and character. This involves a deliberate process of constructing the selfhood of those in the community through a variety of experiences in the community, both planned and unplanned, that provide the "data" of Christian faith in a relational-experiential manner.

In the second phase, the "illuminative-reflective way," the community encourages its people to investigate alternatives to a Christian worldview. The community encourages its people to engage in critical reflection on the tradition and to verify the authority of the community. Thus, people are encouraged to individuate as persons who have explored issues that concern them, but they are strongly encouraged to stay within the community to share their learning with the community.

The third phase, the "unitive-integrating way," invites people to continue to engage in the first two phases. In the process, they reconcile the paradox of "Catholic substance" (and its conserving tradition) and "Protestant spirit" (prophetic judgment and retraditioning). Therefore,

23. Westerhoff, *Will Our Children Have Faith?* 87–103.
24. Ibid., 91–93.

the faith community approach becomes an interplay of tradition, authority, and human development in the context of community. In that context, the members of the community are invited to follow its tradition, question its authority, engage in personal development, search for options, realize paradox, and commit to life together. In the end, however, it is ultimately through the revelation of Jesus Christ and the illumination of the Holy Spirit that the faith community and its members are enabled to live out Christ's kingdom vision as aliens and strangers in the world.

An Exploration of Salient Contextualized Theologies for Kingdom-Building Christian Formation

The etymology of the word *theology* suggests that it is the study of God. Indeed, throughout the history of Christianity, theology has been seen as the enterprise in which God is the central focus of human inquiry concerning the nature of God, the world, relationships, the presence of evil, and life commitments.[25] In a more concise manner, theology is a faith inquiry into the God-human relationship in the world. Seen in this manner, it can be postulated that the God-human relationship in human history informs and reflects the nature of God as well as the nature and functioning or vocation of the Christian church.

Until recently, Western theology has dominated the discipline with its normative truth claims and universalizing applications. More specifically, in Western theology, God's relationship with the privileged Western white male has been construed as if it represented God's relationship with all humanity. In turn, this kind of triumphant theology has coersively and thus unilaterally defined the nature and vocation of the human being.

However, an increasing number of "voices from the margin," especially from ethnic minorities in the United States, has offered a critique of and corrective to this widely held notion in the discipline of theology. These theologians begin with an articulation of their experiences as the point of departure for understanding the God-human relationship in the world. These "contextualized" theologians also critically reflect on their experiences in light of their Christian traditions. In the process, they articulate in a perspectival manner the nature and functioning of

25. Jack Seymour, Margaret Ann Crain, and Joseph Crockett, *Educating Christians* (Nashville: Abingdon, 1993), 23.

the Christian church. The following subsections discuss three strands of contextualized theologies that inform the formation of the church.

Womanist Theology/Ethics and the Exercise of Corporate Human Agency

Those engaging in womanist theology/ethics approach the God-human relationship from an oppressed black female's perspective. Naming the oppression the "colonization" of the black female mind and culture, womanist theological ethicists point to two sources that largely shaped their experience: white oppression and African-American denominational churches.[26] First, African-American women were reminded by whites in every way of their place as colored people—as biologically, socially, and culturally inferior people. Thus, their vocation was defined for them: to serve white people, both male and female, young and old, at all costs. Second, African-American denominational churches, while providing emotional support and space for faith expressions by African-American women, suppressed and contributed in rendering invisible, through their patriarchally and androcentrically biased liturgy and leadership, African-American women's thought and culture.[27]

Womanist theology/ethics exposes the racism, sexism, and classism of American society and the church and reveals how the systematic oppression of African-American women throughout history has impacted the livelihood of these women.[28] Those engaged in such theology are keenly aware of the role society has played in the construction of the selfhood of African-American women and of symbolic African-American women (anyone or any group of people who have had and continue to have life experiences similar to those of African-American women, namely, the black family, the homeless, the destitute, and the young people lost in the drug and gang culture in America).

Such theologians discuss how skin-color consciousness and the value placed on color have birthed a pathological pattern in American culture. Delores Williams calls it "white racial narcissism"—a method by which the devaluation and abuse of black people have been gradually cemented into America's national consciousness. In the process, African-American women, both actual and symbolic, have been socialized as the ultimate nobodies.[29]

26. Jacquelyn Grant, *White Women's Christ and Black Women's Jesus* (Atlanta: Scholars Press, 1989), 195.
27. Ibid., 177–91.
28. Ibid., 195–222.
29. Delores Williams, *Sisters in the Wilderness* (Maryknoll, N.Y.: Orbis, 1993).

Williams asserts that black consciousness is created by a social context that differs from that of white people. As a result, black theologians and white theologians have different mental grids, and these different mental grids determine the sources and the method each theologian uses in the construction of theological statements.

For example, Williams contends that for African-American women, the story of the non-Hebrew female slave Hagar, instead of the exodus event or the story of Abraham and Sarah, is the paradigm through which the God-human relationship must be understood. Williams reminds us that God's response to Hagar's plight was not a triumphant liberation from her oppressors. Instead, God participated in her survival, which gave ultimate purpose to her life, a sense of communal fellowship, and personal worth. The wilderness experience continues, and God is there for both actual and symbolic African-American women.[30]

Williams's reading of the Bible assumes that readers often identify with those in the Bible who depict their livelihood. Moreover, she believes that readers often view their own lives through the lenses of those biblical figures with whom they identify. Seen in this light, African-American Christian women are able to identify with the plight and survival of biblical figures who were marginalized as a result of their race, class, and gender, while privileged white Christians identify with those whose lives were marked by triumph and victory.

While the Hagar story provides Williams with a theological paradigm, black women's literary tradition provides Katie Canon with a rich understanding of the God-human relationship.[31] Appropriating Zora Neale Hurston's portrayal of the integrity of black people, Canon talks about African-American women's "invisible dignity," "quiet grace," and "unshouted courage." These salient features of African-American women were responses to the negative constitutive impact (i.e., the confluence of racism, sexism, and classism) on their selfhood.[32]

Jacquelyn Grant employs a method that focuses on the concrete reality of African-American women who not only survived but also lived a bold life with dignity and audacity.[33] Her focus on the concreteness of African-American women raises the issue of Jesus Christ as the God-human who identified thoroughly with the oppressed. For Grant, Jesus is black precisely because he not only identified with Jews but also concretely became a Jew himself. Thus, African-American women can

---

30. Ibid., 15–33.
31. Katie Canon, *Black Womanist Ethics* (Atlanta: Scholars Press, 1988).
32. Katie Canon, *Katie's Canon* (New York: Continuum, 1995), 77–100.
33. Grant, *White Women's Christ and Black Women's Jesus*, 177–91.

claim Jesus' power over death in their struggle for mutual liberation in this world.

These womanists, instead of focusing on the metaphysical nature of the human being—for example, sinful nature, eternality, material-immaterial dichotomy, and so on—understand the human being in terms of moral relationships and obligations. According to womanists, African-American women have never thought of themselves as individuals whose goal is to attain their own freedom. Instead, they see themselves, in their efforts for survival and betterment, as moral agents who exist for the common good of the community. In the process, they have sought to create a rich legacy and vision, shalom, for their community, realizing the enormous power of shaping the lives of its people, young and old, male and female, in light of powerful societal oppression. They believe that faith communities exist to set one another free and to mend wronged relationships. Thus, they view Christians as interconnected kingdom agents who mutually construct one another through interactions in a context in which sexism, classism, and racism have been and continue to be the fabric of society.

Hispanic Theology and the Recovery of Peoplehood

As a contextualized theology, Hispanic theology also seeks to understand the God-human relationship in the context of sociocultural experience. If womanist theology emphasizes the moral agency of African-American women, Hispanic theology seeks to recover the selfhood or the peoplehood of Hispanic-Americans. Both Justo González and Virgilio Elizondo,[34] in their unique social locations, ground their theological formulations in the experience of Hispanic-Americans.

González, an exiled Cuban-American, criticizes the not-so-innocent history of the United States when he points out the deep-seated racial superiority and evil intentions and deeds of Anglo-Americans in regard to those who are different from them. He contends that in U.S. history as well as in church history, the traditional doctrines of Christianity have been used in oppressive ways.[35] In the end, González argues that all human beings are created in the image of God and, as God's image bearers, must continue to work together to create God's kingdom on earth by eradicating the sins of society and the church.[36]

---

34. Justo González, *Mañana: Christian Theology from a Hispanic Perspective* (Nashville: Abingdon, 1990); idem, *Out of Every Tribe and Nation* (Nashville: Abingdon, 1992); Virgilio Elizondo, *Galilean Journey: The Mexican-American Promise*, rev. ed. (Maryknoll, N.Y.: Orbis, 2002); and idem, *The Future Is Mestizo* (New York: Crossroad, 1988).

35. González, *Mañana*, 38–42.

36. Ibid., 157–67.

As a Mexican-American, Elizondo traces the history of the Americas from the perspective of oppressed Mexican-Americans. He calls Mexican-Americans *mestizaje*, the mixed people, the new race, who were created as the result of two colonization encounters, between Indios and Spanish Catholics, then later between their descendents and Protestant Americans.[37] Elizondo exposes the confluence of a multiplicity of historical factors that brought about racism, which in turn led to rationalization, legitimization, institutionalization, and perpetuation of the violence of racism. He contends that both religions, Catholicism and Protestantism, have played a major role in this immoral atrocity in the name of God.[38]

Consequently, as biologically and culturally mixed people, and as neither Mexicans nor Americans, Mexican-Americans have internalized shame and guilt as a doubly marginalized people. Moreover, struggling with their inferiority complex, they have come to believe that to be free is to become like Anglo-Americans in every way. In his theological formulation, Elizondo claims that Jesus was a *mestizo* in every way[39] and that by identifying fully with Jesus, the *mestizo*, Mexican-Americans can reconstruct their peoplehood and live out God's purpose in the world—namely, promoting inter-mixing and celebrating it, as fiesta, in every way.

Realizing the profound impact of mainstream American society on the lives of Hispanic-Americans, both Elizondo and González challenge the church to ponder how the American West was won (while Mexicans and Indians lost) and how the American church actively consented to the expansion of the American dream. Again, not unlike womanist theologians, they believe that faith communities exist to retell the history of the church for the purpose of reconciling with one another in the name of Jesus Christ and boldly living out the shalom that comes in Jesus Christ and God's kingdom.

Korean-American Theology and the Concept of Marginal Community

Reflecting on his plight as an immigrant in America, Sang Hyun Lee appropriates the story of Abraham as the story of a pilgrim through which Asian-American immigrant Christians should articulate their identity and vocation.[40] Yet Lee focuses on positive aspects of the pil-

---

37. Elizondo, *Galilean Journey*, 7–18.
38. Ibid., 20–27.
39. Ibid., 54–56.
40. Sang Hyun Lee, "Asian-American Theology: Call to Be Pilgrims," in *Korean American Ministry*, expanded English ed., ed. Sang Hyun Lee and John Moore (Louisville: General Assembly Council—Presbyterian Church [U.S.A.], 1993), 39–65.

grimage. He spiritualizes the status of pilgrim in the United States and believes that Asian-American Christians are called to be on a sacred journey and must possess visions of a symbolic "homeland," not only for themselves but for all humankind.

Lee asserts that Asian-American theology must reinterpret the Asian-American experience in light of the understanding of Christian existence as a pilgrimage. He believes that a bicultural existence for Asian-Americans has thrust them into the spiritual wilderness. They have left the security of home in pursuit of God's promise. As a reformed theologian, the most crucial foundation for his theology is the sovereignty of God. He asks, "Why did God bring us into this American wilderness of marginality?" and "To what kind of future is God leading us?" Thus, Lee believes that Christians are called to be marginalized people who seek God's will and obey it as God's instruments in the world to accomplish his will.

Although he does not explicitly articulate the concept of marginality, Andrew Park construes the victims of sin as people oppressed by those who sin against them.[41] Utilizing the Korean concept of *han*,[42] Park reinterprets traditional doctrines of sin and salvation in the broader context of interrelationships among God, human beings, and the world. Park characterizes *han*—the result of an extended period of time of external oppression and exploitation—as resigned hope, helplessness, and resentful bitterness. In discussing some of the major roots of *han* in the world—detrimental effects of a capitalist global economy, patriarchy, racial and cultural discrimination—Park maintains that collective sin generates a great deal of personal *han* as well as collective *han*.[43] In this scheme, Park argues that when victims are oppressed and not fully restored, God's heart is wounded. God is then a co-sufferer with those who are marginalized, while human beings are seen as either victims (the marginalized) or victimizers ("marginalizers"), depending on who inflicts and who receives *han*.[44]

Jung Young Lee utilizes the notion of marginality in a more abstract manner.[45] He illustrates the Asian-American notion of marginality—the possibility of "in-betweenness," "in-bothness," and "in-beyondness." For him, the ultimate purpose of liberation from the margin is not to occupy the center by toppling the power that has dominated the margin. Instead, those on the margin should form creative and dynamic

41. Andrew S. Park, *The Wounded Heart of God* (Nashville: Abingdon, 1993).
42. Ibid., 15–20.
43. Ibid., 36–41.
44. Ibid., 69–85.
45. Jung Young Lee, *Marginality: The Key to Multicultural Theology* (Minneapolis: Fortress, 1995); and idem, *The Trinity in Asian Perspective* (Nashville: Abingdon, 1996).

cores in order to overcome the effects of marginality and to harmonize the margin and the center in their coexistence.[46]

In conceptualizing the predicament of Asian-American Christians and their faith communities, these Asian-American theologians assert that the faith community should be seen as a community in process toward the image of Jesus Christ rather than merely a socially constructed institution. Thus, the notions of journey, *han*, and marginality are points in the process toward fully realizing God's kingdom in the world. In this scheme, Asian-Americans and all other marginalized Christians see themselves as God's elect who are in the process of moving from the margins of society to the center of God's kingdom. They are called to invite those Christians who have been a part of mainstream society to journey toward the center of God's kingdom instead of remaining in the privileged societal position.

These contextualized theologies have a few implications for the practice of Christian formation. First, they challenge those involved in Christian formation to promote the well-being of the entire kingdom of God—female and male, adults and children, black and white, rich and poor—through engaging in righting relationships among all people.

Second, they call for undoing the negative impact of the social construction of the oppressed and marginalized. They also call for creating a safe and hospitable place for these people to claim and appropriate together their experiences in light of their faith traditions.

Third, they challenge Christians to welcome Christocentric engagement with a variety of theological voices and with other disciplines. They support the conviction that critical yet mutual conversations among faith communities sharpen the specific vision of each faith community in God's kingdom. Therefore, contextual theologians call for a brand of kingdom-shaping Christian formation that invokes the Holy Spirit to bring about transformation among the people of God, both locally and globally, as faith communities mutually submit to forming and being formed by one another. Toward that end, we turn now to a discussion of kingdom-building critical pedagogies.

An Exploration of Salient Critical Pedagogies for Kingdom-Building Christian Formation

Many Christians from mainstream America practice a faith based on normative theology, with its normative truth claims and universalizing

46. Lee, *Marginality*, 55–76.

applications. As a result, these Christians often tolerate hyphenated theologies and churches, for example, Native-American theology, the African-American church, and so on. Some even celebrate this hyphenating phenomenon for giving a voice to the hyphenated people in the margin. However, many do not realize that mere toleration of this phenomenon, without mutual relationships and authentic dialogue across the divides, has served to perpetuate the segmentation of the church based on race, ethnicity, class, and gender.

The church of Jesus Christ can no longer go about its business as usual without understanding and working toward its ultimate goal, which is clearly depicted throughout the Bible and culminates in Revelation 21: the glorious, eternal worship of God by the redeemed from every tribe and nation. Toward that end, it is imperative that Christian formation (re)enculturate the people of God as kingdom citizens who practice Christ's shalom. The church, therefore, must live as a faith community that shapes people as kingdom citizens. Such a faith community must be characterized by a commitment to engage in critical analysis of how the people of God have been shaped by race, ethnicity, class, and gender. As local faith communities engage in such analysis by themselves in their own liminal spaces, they will soon realize that they have been myopic in their understanding of God's kingdom vision for them. Hopefully, these communities will then seek out other faith communities that have been shaped in ways different from their own and will commit to prolonged dialogue and action in order to live out the shalom that is the mark of God's kingdom. In the process, Christians from both socioculturally privileged and underprivileged faith communities of various stripes will authenticate God's shalom in the world as aliens and strangers whose citizenship is in heaven. Toward that end, we now turn to a modest proposal of the kind of pedagogical strategy in which a local faith community should consider becoming involved.

Critical Pedagogy Described

Critical pedagogy refers to a wide range of symbolic production and cultural work—i.e., textual, verbal, and visual practices of critiquing and reformulating culture—through which people engage in the process of understanding and bringing about systemic changes in themselves and others in their respective sociocultural contexts. Inherent in the pedagogical process is the existence of human relations, specifically, power dynamics as people in society construct and are constructed by one another through the practices. There is also a sense in which dominant forms of symbolic production prevail as a segment of the society attempts either to maintain or to reform the status quo while silencing others in the society. Critical pedagogy challenges and reformulates the construction, presentation, and engagement of symbolic production and cultural work to be just and equitable for all people, especially for people whose lives have been systematically marginalized by those with power who have benefited by imposing their own values as universal prescriptions.

Critical pedagogy, especially as espoused by Paulo Freire, bell hooks, and Henry Giroux, is committed to rewriting the relationship between the theory and the practice of critical pedagogy as a form of cultural praxis (i.e., a series of reflective actions in which the loop of actions and reflections brings about habitual lifestyle) rather than merely remaining an academic exercise.[47] For them, pedagogical practice is a discursive practice that takes place in the context of particular engagements and dialogues; thus, it involves open discourse and countless possibilities. Because symbolic production and cultural work have far-reaching implications for society and people, social criticism, as it relates to human dignity, liberty, and social justice, is the point of departure for critical pedagogy.

Conscientization and Dialogical Problem-Solving Pedagogy

Many educators, both Christian and non-Christian, testify that Paulo Freire made a significant contribution to the field. Both his life and work provided rich resources for their personal and systematic transformation. Freire believed that human beings possess power to perceive their social locations and to work toward transforming their situation, despite the existence of situations and contradictions that cause human beings to remain in the status quo or to passively accept their present situation as their lot in life.[48] The prerequisite for transformation, for Freire, is that human beings realize that they can indeed conscientiously realize their life's full vision, despite the limiting situations

---

47. Paulo Freire, *Education for Critical Consciousness* (New York: Continuum, 1973); idem, *Pedagogy of the Oppressed* (New York: Continuum, 1970, 1992); idem, *Pedagogy of Freedom: Ethics, Democracy, and Civic Courage* (Lanham, Md.: Rowman & Littlefield, 1998); bell hooks, *Teaching to Transgress* (New York: Routledge, 1994); idem, *Yearning: Race, Gender, and Cultural Politics* (Boston: South End Press, 1990); Henry Giroux, *Disturbing Pleasures: Learning Popular Culture* (New York: Routledge, 1994); idem, *Border Crossings: Cultural Workers and the Politics of Education* (New York: Routledge, 1992); and Stanley Aronowitz and Henry Giroux, *Postmodern Education: Politics, Culture, and Social Criticism* (Minneapolis: University of Minnesota Press, 1991).

48. Freire, *Pedagogy of the Oppressed*, 91–92.

and contradictions, through relationships with fellow human beings and the world.

Believing that human beings are historical and cultural beings, shaped by sociohistorical conditions through language and other symbolic processes, Freire argued that only through mutually respectful relationships with fellow human beings and the world can human beings be fully conscious of reality and themselves.[49] In discussing concern for humanization, he pointed out that human beings are unfinished in the sense that they are to be and to become active participants in the world who are fully cognizant of their historical and cultural contexts. "To exist," according to Freire, is to name the world and to change it.[50] Freire contended that through continuing praxis, human beings create social institutions, ideas, and concepts. In doing so, human beings give meaning to history and culture. For Freire, then, to exist is to take political action, in its full meaning, for the purpose of naming the world.

Therefore, the goal of human beings is humanization through a self-conscious communal praxis of criticizing and reforming the limiting situations and contradictions that hinder human beings from fully realizing God's intention for them. Humanization is not merely an ontological possibility; it must become a historical reality. Freire warned, however, that the oppressed must not become the oppressors when seeking to regain their humanity. Instead, they need to become restorers of the humanity of all.

Freire was most harsh in critiquing the dichotomy of the teacher-student relationship in traditional education. This dichotomy inevitably gives birth to a "banking" style of education in which the teacher is the dispenser of sterile knowledge and the student is the passive receptacle of that knowledge. Such education becomes lifeless and petrified. This approach to education becomes a tool to maintain the status quo and to exacerbate the diametrically opposing realities of the privileged and the downtrodden, as in an oppressive society. As an alternative to the traditional banking education, Freire proposed dialogical education. Such education is committed to a concept of human beings as conscious beings, and the key methodology used involves addressing problems of human beings in their relations with the world.

Freire's methodology of dialogical problem-posing pedagogy involves three phases common to preliteracy and postliteracy education: (1) investigation: an examination and discovery of human consciousness as naïve, superstitious, and uncritical; (2) thematization: an examination of the emerging themes from investigation by reduction, cod-

49. Ibid., 76–86.
50. Ibid., 76.

ing, decodification, and discovery of new generative themes suggested by the emerging themes; and (3) problematization: a discovery and interrogation of limiting situations and their corresponding acts that hinder human beings from actualizing God's full intention for them.[51]

Freire provided a crucial example of how a facilitator approaches sharing knowledge and resources with those in need.[52] Authentic help means that all who are involved help one another in the effort to understand the reality they seek to transform together. Only through such action can those involved be free from a situation in which the helper dominates the helped.

However, Freire's critical pedagogy is not without criticism. Robert Pazmiño has aptly critiqued Freire's theological method and content.[53] In Freire's model, political analysis takes priority over biblical theology, placing the human experience, especially the struggle of liberation, over Scripture. His anthropology considers the depravity of sin only on the part of oppressors. Thus, salvation comes by joining with the oppressed in the struggle for liberation, without faith and repentance through Jesus Christ. Yet Pazmiño also points out the significant contribution of Freire's critical pedagogy to Christian formation.[54] Freire's critical pedagogy challenges the faith community to understand the sociocultural dimensions of the faith that were shaped in a concrete historical situation. It calls for Christian obligation and commitment to mutual and continuing transformation of fellow Christians in a holistic manner, especially in the context of complex permutations of race, ethnicity, class, and gender. Finally, it calls for the Western church to examine the structural sins and principalities from which it has benefited over the centuries and to commit itself to bring about the shalom that characterizes the kingdom of God.

The Engaged Critical Pedagogy

The pedagogical practices of bell hooks, who has been profoundly influenced by Freire, integrate anticolonial, critical, and feminist pedagogies. This blending of multiple perspectives has enabled hooks to formulate pedagogical practices that powerfully confront systems of domination.

---

51. Freire, *Education for Critical Consciousness*, 61–84.
52. Freire, *Pedagogy of the Oppressed*, 28.
53. Robert Pazmiño, *Foundational Issues in Christian Education*, 2d ed. (Grand Rapids: Baker, 1997), 77–78.
54. Ibid., 79–80.

Hooks contends that the pursuit of ending anticolonial patriarchal domination must be the primary concern of the engaged critical pedagogy in order to eradicate exploitation and oppression of various groups and in intimate relationships.[55] Furthermore, she aims at the complete eradication of the ideological foundation that not only legitimizes the unethical practices of patriarchy but also powerfully shapes the identity of the oppressed and exploited. Toward that end, hooks maintains that feminists must work together to confront differences among themselves.[56] In critiquing the white feminist movement, hooks urges all feminists to expand their awareness of sexism, racism, and classism as confluential or interlocking systems of domination that reinforce and perpetuate social structures.

This blending of multiple perspectives also provides perhaps the most comprehensive foundation to create (trans)formational opportunities for students to encounter and eradicate exploitation and oppression (of various groups and in intimate relationships). She describes her pedagogy as a multilayered practice of mutual freedom in which the exploited do not forcibly take away freedom from those who have exploited them but struggle to work together for authentic freedom for all, including the exploited, those who have actively exploited others, and those who have enjoyed the privilege of that exploitation simply because of their identification and/or association.[57] The most foundational basis of critical pedagogy is its reliance on a relationship between teacher and student based on mutual recognition and commitment. The relationship is characterized by respect and care for the souls of students. Moreover, conceptualizing the teacher as a healer, hooks goes beyond the conscientization of the mind. Her pedagogy is concerned with well-being and wholeness, a union of mind, body, and spirit. For hooks, pedagogy must promote students' well-being as a way of empowering students to be critical agents of human emancipation and social transformation.

This engaged[58] pedagogy values student reflection and expression. Hooks, being mindful of the power dynamics between student and teacher, does not expect students to take any risks she would not take,

55. hooks, *Yearning*, 1–13.
56. Ibid., 89–102.
57. Among her many published works, *Teaching to Transgress* is a collection of essays that reads like a testimony of a teacher who has approached education as the practice of freedom.
58. The pedagogy is called "engaged" because it does not call for eradication of exploitation and oppression merely "out there" in society. It must involve people at a personal and relational level who work to eradicate exploitation and oppression at a more global or societal level.

to share in any way she would not share. She contends that empower-ment cannot take place unless teachers are fully committed to being vulnerable and taking risks. Teachers are to create a safe place where students feel free to engage in critical learning and feel a mutual re-sponsibility to contribute to the authentic growth of all the students in the learning community. Teachers must strive to build a "community" characterized by openness and intellectual rigor. This kind of mutually engaged and holistic approach to education, hooks asserts, can bring about authentic transformation of the people involved, including the teacher.

In speaking of the critical importance of one's voice,[59] hooks con-tends that a student must be given ample opportunities and support from the learning community to discover, reflect on, test, and revise his or her own voice.[60] However, hooks asserts that the personal en-gagement in developing one's voice must be critically evaluated in re-lation to the complexity of the structures of domination. Such a con-textual evaluation is necessary in order for the person to be fully conscious of his or her life's situation and vocation in the learning community. In sum, the *telos* of the engaged pedagogy is to promote critical consciousness among human beings, especially the silenced in society, and to elucidate and eradicate the factors (i.e., sexism, racism, classism, etc.) that determined the social construction of the self and the community.

Hooks's engaged pedagogy invites a faith community to acknowl-edge the complexity that each person, shaped by various voices, au-thorities, and values in unique sociocultural contexts, brings to that community. Even the Christian faith that each person possesses and practices has been profoundly shaped by his or her sociocultural sit-uation. Moreover, the faith community itself has been systemati-cally shaped by the same factors that shaped each person, as well as by the people themselves. Therefore, Christian formation must be approached with deliberateness and intentionality. The formation process is a journey in which the faith community commits itself to engage mutually in teaching-learning, healing, and other formation processes in the name of Jesus Christ and through the power of the Holy Spirit.

59. A voice is "a speaking personality, the speaking consciousness. A voice always has a will or desire behind it, its own timbre and overtones" (S. Steve Kang, *Unveiling the So-cioculturally Constructed Multivoiced Self: Themes of Self Construction and Self Integra-tion in the Narratives of Second-Generation Korean American Young Adults* [Lanham, Md.: University Press of America, 2002], 5.

60. hooks, *Yearning*, 41–49.

Border Pedagogy

For Henry Giroux, if pedagogy is to be authentically practiced as a form of political, moral, and social production in which education is not construed as transferring codified knowledge of the privileged to maintain the status quo but as a world-transforming endeavor through which society becomes more just and liberating for all people, pedagogy and educational reform must be approached as a sociocultural project. Giroux confesses that, until recently, he grossly underestimated both the structural and the ideological constraints operative in educational institutions in the United States.[61] As a result of the prevailing conservatism within school systems, many leading journals in education and even radical and critical educators have resorted to maintaining the status quo in regard to educational policies and practices.

In his methodology, Giroux seeks to combine the modern notions of critical reason, agency, and the power of human beings with the postmodern notions of contingent and reflexive discourse. Such discourse is a socioculturally situated dialogical discourse in which one's assumptions, social construction, and culturally mediated practices are interrogated, reformulated, and practiced in community.

Giroux is concerned with developing a democratic public philosophy that focuses on enhancing the quality of public life. Rejecting a form of cultural uniformity, Giroux envisions an authentic democratic society in which individuals, as active social agents with various differences, together create society for the purpose of greater and mutual social transformation and justice. Giroux charges neoconservatives such as Allen Bloom with conceptualizing culture as a warehouse of goods that can be contained as a canon of knowledge or information.[62] Education for them involves passing on the canon in order to maintain social order and control while consigning difference to the margins of history. Seen in this manner, pedagogy becomes secondary, merely a transmission process of the canon.

Instead, Giroux conceptualizes his pedagogy as border pedagogy. This concept presupposes the existence of epistemological, cultural, social, and political borders that construct the discourse of history, power, and difference, which in turn constructs the self and society. For Giroux, who is influenced by Jacques Derrida, focusing on the issue of difference is of critical importance.[63] Giroux calls for a pedagogy that examines how differences between groups develop and are maintained

61. Giroux, *Border Crossings*, 149–60.
62. Ibid., 92–95.
63. Giroux, *Disturbing Pleasures*, 113–18.

as empowering and disempowering sets of relations. His pedagogy allows people to analyze how their identities and subjectivities, both as individuals and as groups, are constructed in multiple and contradictory ways. Thus, differences are to be not only affirmed but also transformed for the purpose of emancipation of society—through democracy, citizenship, and public spheres.

Border pedagogy provides spaces for teachers and students to reconceptualize, in community, their experiences and their roles in society. Thus, border pedagogy helps people to become "border crossers" as they commit themselves to understand otherness in its own terms. The ultimate goal of Giroux's project is to envision and realize borderlands in which the constitutive resources from diverse cultures sanction the construction of new identities within existing configurations of power.

Border pedagogy challenges those in the faith community to acknowledge their God-given responsibility to be border crossers in order to work toward the mutual transformation of faith communities and the world. Mutual transformation must begin, however, with people understanding otherness in its own terms. True shalom rules over God's kingdom on earth as those in adjoining borderlands humbly come together, repent of their sins against God and one another, and see God's face.

Conclusion

In modern Christian higher education in America, we hear much about the integration of faith and learning as an important process and *telos* of educational institutions. Upon graduation, students from these Christian universities and colleges are exhorted to continue this integration process throughout their lives. While this noble call merits lifelong pursuit, such an integration inadvertently places too much emphasis on the ability of individual Christians to rationally and systematically pursue the heart of God. In fact, much of the time, the faith and learning integration model has tended to equate the fruit from the intellectual pursuit of natural revelation—through natural and human sciences, humanities, and the arts—with that of special revelation gained through worship, proclamation, and theology. Moreover, the task of Christian theology has largely shifted its audience base from the church, to whom it owes its beginning and allegiance, to mainstream academia. Particularly, conservative Christian theology (theology espoused by Christians who have a high view of Scripture) has been content to correlate the gospel to the sociocultural trappings of mainstream America. As a result, conservative Christians have been largely content to maintain the status quo of American society (in education, politics, economy, etc.), desiring to fit into mainstream America and enjoy the benefits of allegiance. This cycle continues where many conservative Christians seek to maintain the social status that comes as a result of keeping in step with American values and ways of life. In the process, many well-meaning American Christians have lost what it means to be the people of God's eternal kingdom, living as aliens and strangers in the world.

This chapter sought to introduce three theoretical frameworks that potentially engender Christians to become and continue to be formed as kingdom citizens in this world. It began by discussing the Christian faith community's foundational role in the formation of kingdom citizens. Christians, God's elect in Jesus Christ, are called by God's grace to be the community in which the foundation is none other than God's historical revelation in Jesus Christ and its enduring legacy in the church through the witness of the Holy Spirit. The faith community is thus exhorted to enter into and dwell in the biblical reality, re-socializing itself as the earthly manifestation of God's eternal kingdom. This re-socialization of the community involves the ongoing process of cultivating the Christocentric virtues and practices that are informed by the biblical narrative, which functions as the grand narrative of God's eternal kingdom.

This re-socialization or formation process must take its cues from the vastness of God's kingdom, namely, the communion of saints, which inextricably brings together the saints throughout history and all places. Compellingly, contextual theologians remind us that theology as a second-order reflection is very much shaped by the sociocultural context in which theology is done. They criticize Western theology for seeking to articulate a theology of the privileged European and American triumphalistic church, which has attempted to promote its brand of theology as universal or normative to all. Womanist theologians contend that the notion of power relations among people on the basis of gender, race, and class must be reflexively and mutually engaged. Hispanic theologians remind us that the church of Jesus Christ is responsible to reflect critically and humbly on its own history and to offer reconciling peace to those graciously gathered together as kingdom citizens. Korean-American theologians, with experience as displaced and disposed people, challenge the church to live as aliens and strangers in the world. Rather than seeking to fit into society, the church, the gathering of kingdom citizens, is to see itself as a societal fringe from which it is called to engage the world creatively and boldly as God's peculiar people with a unique worldview and lifestyle.

Lastly, we discussed how critical pedagogies strive for nothing less than social reconstruction. Their scintillating criticism of a brand of education that seeks to maintain the status quo of the privileged is a direct challenge to the shared sociocultural values of many conservative Christians in America. For these ideologues, authentic freedom is none other than freedom for *all* human beings, through the reconstruction of society, to be what they desire to be. Toward that end, they propose and tirelessly work to bring transformation to the consciousness as well as to the concrete life situations of both the oppressed and the oppressors. As gathered kingdom citizens in the world, the church's various faith communities, God's instruments of genuine freedom and peace, must come together locally and globally to deliver one another from the encumbrances and bondages that have historically hindered the church from becoming the earthly witness of God's eternal kingdom. In the end, the road to societal reconstruction is possible only when kingdom citizens gather together and authentically live out the kingdom life in the world. In that we pray, "Your kingdom come, your will be done on earth as it is in heaven" (Matt. 6:10).

5

Prejudice and Conversion

ELIZABETH CONDE-FRAZIER

Christian education in a context that is diverse in terms of gender, class, culture, and ethnicity requires a multicultural sensitive pedagogy, or a pedagogy of reconciliation. Such a pedagogy is part of creating a borderland or a space for the discovery of mutuality and common ground amid our differences. The goal of a reconciliation pedagogy is to facilitate a journey whereby we are sensitized to our assumptions about our culture in order to understand another culture's content and context from within, even while we are without. It allows us to see the structural sin in each culture and how difference has been maintained for empowerment or disempowerment so that we might envision the healing and transformation of the world. Doing this is a process of border crossing that moves us from our ethnocentricities and prejudices to an appreciation of differences. This makes it possible for us to respect and learn from other cultures. It also enhances our ability to understand and interact with biblical texts, themselves a variation of cultures, and to relate them to our present changing realities.

The task of the teacher, among others mentioned below, is that of a broker between power and powerlessness in the classroom. In the classroom, worth, dignity, language, articulation, and appropriately expressed anger are empowering. On the other hand, discrimination, putdowns, silencing, fear, lack of confidence, depression, and hopelessness are the signs of disempowerment among us. Compassion, acquaintance with the suffering of students, the form of syllabi, criteria for grading, cooperative learning, and rituals can be catalysts for empowerment in the teaching/learning setting. A ritual that is empowering is that of remembering. The Evangelical Covenant Church of Southern California, for example, remembers its journey as immigrants. This made it possible for members to tap into their resource of compassion and to partner with their Latino/a brothers and sisters in ways relevant to the context of the Latina community. Remembering facilitated their envisioning and creating together for the kingdom of God.

As kingdom citizens, we seek to be light. In today's world, in which globalization enhances the ills of consumerism, helping to bring about social justice is an integral part of acting as kingdom citizens. To act in this manner, we need to create coalitions of Christians working together. Deeper relationships are needed among us to achieve this. Paul reminds us that we are "to equip the saints for the work of ministry, for building up the body of Christ, until all of us come to the unity of the faith and of the knowledge of the Son of God, to maturity, to the measure of the full stature of Christ" (Eph. 4:12–13 NRSV).

For us to become kingdom citizens, we need to transform our prejudices, which disconnect us from one another and create unjust relationships among us, making us unrighteous people. Becoming righteous entails a spiritual journey that brings us to reconciliation with one another. This journey may begin with hospitality or the welcoming of one who is different from us. The next step is to encounter the other person by engaging in dialogue and the rituals of sharing our lives, such as table fellowship, playing together, praying, or disagreeing. Sharing brings us to a place where we begin to see the world through one another's eyes. When we are away from one another, experiences in the world remind us of our neighbor and how he or she might be affected by or contribute to our experiences. Compassion then makes way for a shared passion, for a place of woundedness in the world and a sense of calling to bring shalom or well-being to this woundedness. On this journey we are transformed. For this transformation to take place, we need to explore the barriers to it. Prejudices are some of the strongest barriers. To understand more clearly what we are working to transform as we move from hospitality to shalom, we need to explore how prejudices are constructed and how conversion transforms them at personal and communal levels.

Prejudice

Multicultural education is concerned with the sensitivity, skills, and spirituality necessary to teach all students more completely. It involves an awareness of their value as human beings that comes from understanding that God created each one in his image. It is teaching people to recognize the image of God reflected in each culture. Clearly, not everything in culture reflects God's image. Multicultural Christian education focuses first on the treasures of God manifested in each culture and person. When worthiness is ascribed to all persons, positive interaction can take place. This creates community, and it is within community that we earn the right and may develop the practice of helping one another transform the elements that are not life producing and therefore are not reflective of God's values.

Christian educator Kathleen Talvacchia speaks about a multicultural sensitive pedagogy as a "conviction and an ethical orientation that a teacher brings to a teaching context that grounds pedagogical action."[1] The teacher also strives for the empowerment of all students in the learning process. This entails understanding learning styles and how they may be connected to culture and making content relevant. It also has implications that go beyond pedagogy and that have to do with justice and equity in the educational system. Talvacchia names this empowerment of students a "moral necessity of a good society."[2]

In his book *Latin American Journey: Insights for Christian Education in North America*, Robert Pazmiño uses the work of Ricardo García to discuss a multicultural model of education.[3] He suggests that such an education involves not only the study of ethnic cultures and experiences but also a commitment "to creating educational environments in which students from all cultural groups will experience educational equity."[4] Pazmiño posits that a multicultural model has two educational movements. The first movement focuses on one's ethnic identity formation. The second seeks a common ground for community in a global city and deals with the realities of ethnic and cultural plurality. These two movements help us come to a dialogue with those from different backgrounds in the fullness of our own ethnic identity.

This model leaves room for exploring the ethnic heritage of others in order to appreciate and learn from them.[5] Pazmiño's theological under-

---

1. Kathleen T. Talvacchia, *Critical Minds and Discerning Hearts: A Spirituality of Multicultural Teaching* (St. Louis: Chalice Press, 2003), 10.
     2. Ibid.
     3. Robert W. Pazmiño, *Latin American Journey: Insights for Christian Education in North America* (Cleveland: United Church Press, 1994). See also Ricardo García, *Teaching in a Pluralistic Society: Concepts, Models, and Strategies* (New York: Harper & Row, 1982).
     4. Pazmiño, *Latin American Journey*, 117.
     5. Ibid.

pinnings include the claim of unity in Jesus Christ based on the experience of Pentecost.[6] In this experience, the Spirit pointed to Jesus as the source of human understanding and unity. In Christ, our differences are transcended not because they are made uniform but because we can share the gifts of our culture with others while receiving the gifts of their heritage as well.

This transcendence embodies the spirit of the incarnation and allows us to think of ourselves and others with sober judgment (Rom. 12:3). Cultural differences are no longer used to exalt one and dominate another. Ethnocentrism, on the other hand, is an inequity in power dynamics that creates hegemonies and metanarratives. A metanarrative is a grand story that offers an interpretation of the history and values of a people. Such grand stories may be imposed over the stories of people considered minorities or marginal to secure the interests, values, and history of the dominant people over those of others. In education, this may be done under the guise of academic excellence or core content. These metanarratives oppress and fragment peoples by setting up relationships based on inferiority and superiority. Appreciation for one another begins a process whereby we can see one another with new eyes and eventually learn to participate with one another in the world in ways that model equal partnership.

To reach this point, multicultural education must in some way address prejudices and discrimination. Education may at times foster prejudices, especially when they have not been named as such. Teachers must be aware of this as they make decisions about what to include in a curriculum. Whose reality is not included and why? How will students learn to live in a world with persons who may not be represented in the classroom but whom they will encounter and serve by way of their vocations? Has an exclusion or inclusion of material helped to prepare them for a changing world and church?[7]

6. Ibid., 118.

7. Philip Jenkins writes about the changing trends in Christianity today and how they are changing the form of the church. A great factor to be considered is the changing demographic of the church from a Western church to a predominantly Latin American, African, and Asian church. The political forces of non-Western countries influence the form the church is taking in them. Church leaders will need to be prepared for cross-cultural communication and interaction. Seeing things from the political and sociohistorical perspective of others is not something we are used to doing in the United States, where we assume that the world revolves around us. Our citizens, therefore, are not educated for world leadership, while the strength of nation states wanes and the definition of citizenship becomes more cosmopolitan. For further discussion of these issues and how they affect the church in this millennium, see Philip Jenkins, "The Next Christianity," *Atlantic Monthly*, October 2002, 53–68.

Prejudice is defined as a special type of prejudgment. Gordon Allport's work in the mid fifties made a classic contribution to the understanding of prejudice.[8] He concludes that "prejudgments become prejudices only if they are not reversible when exposed to new knowledge."[9]
Professor of psychology Harold D. Fishbein examined various definitions of prejudice and looked at what they have in common to come to
his own definition. He states, "Prejudice is an unfavorable and unreasonable negative attitude directed towards others because of their
membership in a particular group."[10]

Attitude is defined by psychologist Howard Ehrlich as follows: "an interrelated set of propositions about an object or class of objects which
are organized around cognitive, behavioral, and affective dimensions."[11]
Cognitive dimensions have to do with the degree to which a belief is assumed (All Puerto Ricans carry knives, or some Puerto Ricans carry
knives), the intensity with which a belief is accepted (I sort of agree, or
I strongly disagree), the extent to which a belief is positive or negative
(All Asians are very intelligent, or all Asians tend to do well academi-
cally), and whether a belief forms the core or essential aspect of an attitude or is peripheral and can be changed without having much effect on
the attitude.

The behavioral dimension of attitudes reflects the linkage between
one's beliefs and one's intentions to behave in particular ways. The affective dimensions of attitudes have to do with the emotions or feelings
evoked in relationship to the object of one's attitudes. One may have a
strong attraction to something or may feel repulsed by it.

Ehrlich's framework reveals the complexity of attitudes. In regard to
Christian education, this framework allows one to reflect on the different areas that need to be addressed if one's teaching is to influence prejudices, attitudes, and behaviors in positive directions.

An unreasonable negative attitude cannot be easily modified even
when a person is exposed to new data that conflicts with the information on which he or she based the attitude. This poses a challenge for
an educator who seeks a change in attitude through the presentation of
new information. In this case, the teacher would need to look into the
experiences an individual has had with the target group and reflect on
these experiences. Perhaps the individual has never had significant ex-

8. Gordon W. Allport, *The Nature of Prejudice* (Cambridge, Mass.: Addison-Wesley,
1954).
9. Ibid., as quoted in Harold D. Fishbein, *Peer Prejudice and Discrimination: Evolu-
tionary, Cultural, and Developmental Dynamics* (Boulder, Colo.: Westview Press, 1996), 9.
10. Fishbein, *Peer Prejudice*, 5.
11. Howard Ehrlich, *The Social Psychology of Prejudice* (New York: Wiley, 1973), 4.

periences with persons from the other group, or perhaps there has been limited experience, but it has been negative. Creating opportunities for experiential learning may be one way to approach the situation.

Family, friends, books, schools, and the media influence cognitive, social, and emotional understandings. Over time, these may change. For example, individuals may mature, making them capable of changing their beliefs, attitudes, and behaviors. Structuring the classroom as a temporary community of inquiry in which various experiences and means of conveying information are part of the learning environment could provide a positive point of intervention in the life of a prejudice.

Discrimination and acting negatively toward people because of the group to which they belong are not always based on prejudice. When acting on behalf of an institution, one may carry out a discriminatory policy without having feelings of prejudice. However, when a person is acting on his or her own, prejudice and discrimination may exist in tandem. At this point, they feed each other in a vicious cycle. Discrimination becomes the action of a prejudicial belief or attitude. But we do not always act in discriminatory ways. Other factors determine actions, such as socially accepted behavior or sympathy in a crisis situation. For this reason, in a church setting, it may not be socially acceptable to carry out discriminatory actions, but it may still be possible for persons to hold prejudices about others.

At one of the Promise Keepers rallies, one of the leaders confessed his sin of prejudice.[12] He explained how, whenever he shook hands with an African-American person, in his mind he wiped off his hand. He had not noticed this until the Holy Spirit made it evident to him. Notice how there was no explicit behavior but an internalized one instead.

Two theories are frequently cited to explain changes in prejudice: contact theory and Lewinian theory. Allport is responsible for contact theory. He suggests that three conditions must be present for contact to work in reducing prejudiced attitudes: (1) equal status among the parties involved, (2) pursuit of common objectives by the groups (cooperation), and (3) deep and genuine association (intimacy) among those involved. This is achieved through working, studying, and sharing leisure time together consistently over a period of time.[13]

Lewinian theory, developed by Kurt Lewin, postulates that there are driving and restraining forces and that their equilibrium or alteration can cause an attitude to remain in place or change. A simplified example would be as follows: I work out at the gym three times a week. The factors that

---

12. Promise Keepers, *Stand in the Gap: A Sacred Assembly of Men: Highlights* (Washington, D.C.: Promise Keepers, 1997).

13. Fishbein, *Peer Prejudice*, 215–16.

drive me to do this are the need to lose twenty pounds to avoid knee replacement surgery and enjoyment of my friend's company. Other factors restrain my going to the gym. These are the early morning hour at which I must get up, the cold temperature in the gym, and the lack of time to refresh my energies before the work day begins. Taken together, these driving and restraining forces determine how often I work out at the gym. Eliminating the restraining forces would increase the frequency of workouts.

Lewin determined that group belongingness and interdependence of fate serve as restraining forces. The first is similar to group identity, and the latter is based on cultural/historical factors such as collective memory of history, language, religion, and morality.[14] Other scientists later used field theory to discuss additional restraining forces such as social interactions. Some of these are discomfort caused by the expectation of inappropriate social behavior by out groups, inhibition, or uncertainty.[15]

Fishbein's work in determining what elements contribute to the elimination of prejudices suggests that efforts should be made to eliminate discrimination first; then one can move toward a modification of prejudices. He reports that the most successful experiences for accomplishing prejudice modification are cooperative interactions between persons of different groups.[16]

His experiments revealed that empathy brought about by cooperative ventures reduces prejudice. If there is reinforcement of such experiences, then a reduction in prejudiced attitudes may also be observed. This holds important implications for teachers. The experiments were done with groups of students, each group containing different ethnic groups, genders, and so on. Cooperative interaction was carried out through cooperative learning in the classroom and was consistently found to have positive effects in reducing discrimination and prejudice. Cooperative interaction involves positive goal interdependence. Groups working and communicating with one another will share rewards or resources and will perform complementary roles. This suggests that teachers should look at how they facilitate interactions among diverse people in the classroom as part of the curriculum.

Role playing has also proven to be an effective way to change attitudes. Persons in the dominant group may be asked to play the role of a person

14. See K. Lewin, *Resolving Social Conflicts* (New York: Harper & Row, 1948).
15. See J. Donaldson, "Changing Attitudes toward Handicapped Persons: A Review and Analysis Research," *Exceptional Children* 46 (1980): 504–14; and C. L. Evans, *The Immediate Effects of Classroom Integration on the Academic Progress, Self-Concept, and Racial Attitudes of Negro Elementary Children* (Ph.D. diss., North Texas State University, 1969).
16. Fishbein, *Peer Prejudice,* 268.

from a minority group. It has been found that after playing a role and reflecting on what took place and what their feelings were, college students
became less prejudiced.[17] The development of empathy for persons of a minority culture or race during the simulation experience was a driving force
for the development of more positive attitudes toward these persons.[18]

Conversion

The above understandings were garnered from the social sciences.
Theologically and pedagogically, transformation demands that we speak
of conversion. Some paradigms of conversion focus on conversion as an
event, while others see it as a process. The Pauline paradigm as described
in the Book of Acts (9:1–19; 22:1–21; 26:1–23) focuses on the radical aspects of the event of Paul's conversion. The Petrine or Markan paradigm
of conversion focuses on Peter's conversion as a process of transformation until there is a conversion of his inner self. As Christian educators,
we are to prepare people not only for an initial encounter with Jesus as
Savior but also for an ongoing process of turning from sin to God. Conversion in this discussion, therefore, is an ongoing journey into the mystery of the reign of God.

In the Old Testament, the Hebrew word *shub* means to return to
Yahweh, turn from sin, and renew the vows with Yahweh. In the New
Testament, various terms focus on this phenomenon. *Epistrephō* refers
to the turning of unbelievers to God (Acts 3:19; 26:20). Another New
Testament term is *metanoeō*, which means to change one's mind or to
adopt another view. This term is connected to both the previous one
and to *pisteuō*, which means to believe or adhere to, trust or rely on.

These terms imply that the life we appropriate in conversion involves
turning to God and God's world and work, changing our minds, and
adopting a new worldview so that we ally ourselves with the values and
life of commitment associated with the realm of God. In this work, we
are enabled by the power of the Holy Spirit. In this ongoing journey of
many turnings, the church is renewed. The goal of this renewal is to enable members to follow Christ into new paths that cross new frontiers.[19]

17. See J. L. Clore and K. M. Jeffrey, "Emotional Role Playing, Attitude Change and
Attraction toward a Disabled Person," *Journal of Personality and Social Psychology* 23
(1972): 105–11.

18. Fishbein, *Peer Prejudice*, 249.

19. For further discussion, see Orlando E. Costas, "Conversion as a Complex Experience: A Personal Case Study," in *Gospel and Culture*, ed. John Stott and Robert T. Coote
(Pasadena, Calif.: Carney Library, 1979).

Richard Peace suggests a sequence of phases or movements for this process that include insight, turning, and transformation.[20] Transformation entails coming to a new way of perception so that there is a radical reinterpretation of the past. The past is then reconstructed as part of a new understanding of God and the world.

Prejudices are hard to change because they resist even new information that conflicts with the views held. This is why the spiritual journey suggested in this chapter includes various steps. Each step includes cognitive and affective dimensions. The epistemology that guides them is relational and entails interaction with contextual, practical, and theological assumptions. Hospitality and encounter are seen as a period of awareness. Compassion is seen as an empowering grace that allows transformation to take place. Passion and shalom are the decision making and action that follow awareness and thus complete the transformation. Pazmiño defines transformation as a process that takes one beyond the "existing or dominant forms to a new or emergent perspective and reality."[21] It is also "creating alternatives that present new and better possibilities for all of human life."[22]

Transformation takes place in a context of people, events, ideologies, expectations, and orientations. Factors for fostering change need to be multiple, interactive, and cumulative. The classroom experience must be seen as only one factor within the educational ecology of persons. Realizing that there is no one process or simple consequence of a process that will bring about transformation, teachers must approach the educational task with great humility.

Lewis R. Rambo, professor of psychology and religion, posits that four components within the journey of conversion interact with one another. These components are cultural, social, personal, and religious.[23] The cultural and social elements involve social institutions and mechanisms. The personal component involves the intrapersonal dynamics of the person. The religious dimension relates to the influence of God. As they interact, these components may have varying weight in a person's life. It is helpful to look more closely at each component, for each informs a selection of teaching materials and techniques.

20. Richard Peace, "The Conversion of the Twelve: A Study of the Process of Conversion in the New Testament" (Ph.D. diss., University of Natal, South Africa, 1990), cited in Robert W. Pazmiño, *Principles and Practices of Christian Education: An Evangelical Perspective* (Grand Rapids: Baker, 1992), 41.

21. Pazmiño, *Latin American Journey*, 55.

22. Ibid.

23. Lewis R. Rambo, *Understanding Religious Conversion* (New Haven: Yale University Press, 1993), 7.

Culture is mediated through stories, rituals, and symbols that are often adopted unconsciously. Language is an element of culture, and a person's sense of reality is rooted in language. Language transmits cultural perceptions and values. Rambo points out that culture constructs the intellectual, moral, and spiritual atmosphere of life.[24] It is within symbols and stories that the methods of religious change lie. Although the traditional mode of teaching tends to be conceptual and theoretical, cognitive perception alone will not bring change. Narrative, which includes the affective and the cognitive, is needed to help people find the symbols and experiences on which they can build new paradigms. Different languages have a variety of words that encapsulate powerful concepts and symbols that can move thinking in new directions.

I have the privilege of teaching in a multicultural context in which many of my students speak languages other than English as their first language. As dialogue becomes intense, a student may contribute a word in his or her language that enriches the understanding of a concept or experience we may be grappling with. We note the word without translating it, for many times there is no translation. We adopt the word as part of our meaning making and use it in future discussions and essays.

The social context includes the relationships between persons and the expectations and ideologies of the groups they belong to. The experiences of a person act as forces that impede or move that person toward transformation. These may be crises, rewards, or punishments of the immediate social environment, self-realization, or intellectual influences.

The religious component explores the encounter with the "holy," looking at how persons come into a relationship with God and how this encounter provides a new sense of meaning and purpose. This relationship is essential and at the core of the whole process of transformation. After teachers have facilitated experiences and reflection on them, provided information, created community among students, and evoked memories and stories, they have reached their pedagogical limits. It is the Holy Spirit who convicts people and leads them to truth about God, themselves, and others. In Luke's account of many conversion stories of individuals (Acts 8:26–38; 9:1–19) as well as large groups (Acts 2:14–41), conversion is a gift that comes from God. God initiates the conversions. God directs events in the conversion stories and creates the occasions that lead to the change of the masses.[25] Teachers, as they partner

---

24. Ibid., 8.
25. See Beverly Roberts Gaventa, "Conversion in the Bible," in *Handbook of Religious Conversion*, ed. H. Newton Malony and Samuel Southland (Birmingham, Ala.: Religious Education Press, 1992), 49.

with God, provide opportunities to usher in the Spirit. These opportunities may include a variety of class activities and experiences, such as the devotions at the beginning of class, times of silence when students can hear God speaking to the class by way of the discussion of the subject matter, the discussion itself, or an interactive drama exercise and its debriefing. Without fail, breakthrough moments come by way of such opportunities.

Ultimately, conversion is a progressive interactive process that impacts not only an individual but a community. Therefore, a breakthrough is only one point in the progression. Affirmation and support are needed if this breakthrough is to be long lasting so that it might serve as the ground on which other changes can be constructed. The breakthrough entails reflection on the revelation received. We can see this in Paul when he comments on his own conversion and the revelation he received. He explains how it brought him to a point of reinterpreting his past and future (Gal. 1:1–24).

Theological images of conversion are helpful to the Christian educator for determining the stages of learning. For example, the theology of Karl Barth focuses on an awakening.[26] Conversion is a waking and rising from sleep and moving counter to one's previous direction. In a classroom, awakening may come as new information is introduced. There are several questions I ask my students to think about when I introduce new information and different perspectives: (1) What has happened to me because I have this new information? (2) How does this information assist me to make connections between God and the world, between myself and God, or between myself and others? (3) What kind of person am I as a result of this added information? (4) How is the Holy Spirit working in my life so that this information is appropriated in my life to help me respond to a changing world around me?

This set of questions helps students reflect at the cognitive level. However, because this is an awakening in the totality of one's being, feelings are also part of it. Following are the questions students are asked to reflect on: (1) Why do I open or close my mind to this new information? (2) Am I reacting to a person or to preconceived prejudices rather than to the new idea or information? (3) Would the same information given by someone else or in a different way make a difference in how I accept it? (4) Am I allowing the Holy Spirit to work in me to help me in my attitudes toward others so that I may be more patient in my understandings?

26. See Karl Barth, *Church Dogmatics*, trans. G. F. Bromiley (Edinburgh: T & T Clark, 1958).

In the classroom, dialogue is for clarification and reflection. Reflection may lead us to ask more questions as well as to challenge the new information. We may also express new ideas and discuss the implications and implementation of the new information. This helps us make connections with what is new. These connections may be with information as well as with persons and/or communities that had previously been unimportant to us. Such relational connections bring us to commitments that change our relationships with others and bring us into partnerships with others in the work of God in the world. Connections between information and action were important to Jesus, who emphasized the doing and not only the hearing of the Word (Luke 6:46–49). Action was always a sign of one's conversion. John the Baptist challenged persons not only to repentance and baptism but also to a change of life. Peter and Paul did the same. It is the new action that redefines a person's sense of meaning and purpose in Jesus. It is a reorientation.

Liberation theologies place much emphasis on this dimension. For example, feminist Rosemary Radford Ruether writes about the grace of conversion from patriarchal domination as an opening up to "a new vision of humanity for women and men that invites us to recast and recreate all our relationships."[27] Liberation theologians challenge us to understand the radical action that conversion invites us to. This action is related to the kingdom of God. Conversion is the process that gives us entry into the kingdom. It is made concrete in Jesus' actions and is by grace offered to us through Jesus. For liberationists, to place oneself in the perspective of the kingdom means to participate in the struggle for the liberation of those who are oppressed by others or the struggle of those who suffer and die for want of human dignity.[28] Conversion is both an announcement as well as a transforming action whose focus is the fulfillment of the kingdom.

Common to each of these theological images of conversion is the sense of a truth that breaks in on one in a continuous way, awakening the need to express oneself by way of new actions. These actions give proof of the transforming power of the gospel as they are initiated and carried out by God's grace. Grace takes place through the teaching of the church in its multiple forms. In the evangelical understanding of conversion, salvation is depicted as a growing discovery of the unsearchable riches of Christ. It is "constant rediscovery of the gospel of grace, and an openness to the reforms which the Spirit will prompt in

27. Rosemary Radford Ruether, *Sexism and God-Talk: Toward a Feminist Theology* (Boston: Beacon, 1983), 186.

28. See Gustavo Gutierrez, *A Theology of Liberation* (Maryknoll, N.Y.: Orbis, 1973); and James H. Cone, *A Black Theology of Liberation*, 2d ed. (Maryknoll, N.Y.: Orbis, 1986).

those who keep turning again to become as little children."[29] Gary Parrett's story confirms that the sins of prejudice are the last to go. How does Scripture address this?

Jesus incarnated God's wisdom in his teaching and living so that he modeled what he taught. The purpose of his teaching centered on the values of God's kingdom. This took the form of the two great commandments: to love God with all our heart, soul, mind, and strength and to love our neighbors as ourselves (Luke 10:27).[30] In his theology of education, Peter C. Hodgson describes the central image of Jesus' teaching as an open community of freedom where God's wisdom, rather than human wisdom, prevails. He explains that "divine wisdom overthrows the dominant logic of the world (hierarchical, authoritarian, juridical, dualistic) in favor of a new logic, that of grace, love, and freedom of noncoerced and fully reciprocal communicative practices."[31] In multicultural Christian education, this is the goal. Jesus brought this type of wisdom to his teaching when he used parables. He utilized them to bring his hearers to a discovery of a deeper meaning of a tradition. At times this discovery also led to the reformation or modification of the tradition.

A parable central to moving from prejudices to embracing those who are different is the parable of the good Samaritan (Luke 10:25–37). The parable comes forth as Jesus is challenged to interpret what one must do to inherit eternal life. In the Luke account, Jesus is asked a question, which he answers with a question of his own: "How do you read it [the law]?" (Luke 10:26). The two great commandments are the reply from the lawyer, and Jesus then reassures him, "Do this and you will live" (Luke 10:28). The two great commandments placed together love for God and love for one's neighbor, showing that there is no dichotomy between them. However, in Jesus' time, the Pharisees had elevated the importance of the study of the Torah. The pronouncement of Akiba was "study of the law is of higher rank than practicing it." Jesus' response to the lawyer reflects a contrasting view. Eternal life is found not only in knowing the commandments but in living them. In his commentary on Luke, R. Alan Culpepper suggests that Jesus' response gains him the

29. David H. C. Read, "The Evangelical Protestant Understanding of Conversion," in *Handbook of Religious Conversion*, 143.

30. For further discussion of how the two great commandments form the foundations of teaching, see Robert W. Pazmiño, *Basics of Teaching for Christians: Preparation, Instruction, and Evaluation* (Grand Rapids: Baker, 1998).

31. Peter C. Hodgson, *God's Wisdom: Toward a Theology of Education* (Louisville: Westminster John Knox, 1999), 140.

upper hand so that the lawyer attempts to rally by posing a controversial question: "And who is my neighbor?"[32]

The question is controversial because it is a question about boundaries. How we order our boundaries in society is a subject that generates controversy at any time. The Lukan passage reflects the boundaries of Judaism; there were specific rules regarding how Jews should treat Gentiles or Samaritans, how priests should relate to Israelites, and how men should treat one another. Today, we too have boundaries. I live in California, one of the border states with Mexico. At least once a week there is an article in the newspaper about border issues with our Mexican neighbors. The incidents of September 11, 2001, have drawn our attention to what used to be a quiet border, the Canadian border with the United States. In all times, boundaries are about different groups establishing their positions, power, and privilege. Maintaining boundaries is vital to maintaining social order. In Jesus' time, it was also a religious duty. This is why, in the conversation with Jesus, the lawyer asks the question as one who brings a definition of the limits of required neighborliness.

There are two main characters in the story. The first is the victim. He is noticeably undefined. We are not given much detail about his personal life, race, religion, or trade. The phrase "a certain man" is the only descriptor. The priest and the Levite come in and out of the story fairly quickly, but their behavior reflects an attitude about the practice of the commandments and the limits of neighbor. Their actions shatter the expectations and hope of the unfortunate traveler on his way to Jericho as well as those of the hearers who identify with him.

The Samaritan is the third man who comes by the victim. In picking him to be the helper, Jesus challenges the prejudices of his hearers and invalidates all stereotypes about Samaritans. "Community can no longer be defined or limited by such terms."[33] Culpepper's analysis of the passage shows that there are many verbs or types of actions assigned to the Samaritan. When the Samaritan sees the man on the road, he has compassion for him. He is moved to deep pity and shows mercy. He bandages his wounds, he pours oil and wine on them, and so on.

At the end of the parable Jesus asks, "Which of these three do you think was a neighbor to the man who fell into the hands of robbers?" (Luke 10:36). The lawyer answers, "The one who had mercy on him" (Luke 10:37). Culpepper claims that Jesus turned the issue from the

---

32. R. Alan Culpepper, *Luke: The New Interpreter's Bible*, vol. 9 (Nashville: Abingdon, 1995), 229. The following insights are drawn from Culpepper's comments.
33. Ibid., 230.

boundaries of required neighborliness to the essential nature of neighborliness so that neighbors are defined actively and not passively.[34]

In the parable, Jesus integrates the knowledge of the law with the practice of it. The duty of being a neighbor becomes an expression of love of God. It is by showing mercy that we demonstrate that we are among the heirs of the kingdom. The reign of God is characterized by showing compassion to those in need regardless of race, religion, class, reign, or culture. The parable implies that the boundaries of neighbor have been expanded so that the "other" is now within the parameters of neighbor. It closes the distance of difference and does away with the notion of otherness. Jesus' parable shatters the stereotypes of social boundaries, cultural difference, and class divisions. The activities of the kingdom expose the injustice of social barriers that categorize, restrict, and oppress various groups in any society.[35] To love God and neighbor will often challenge us to reject society's accepted prejudices and discriminatory practices in favor of the codes of the reign of God, who ushers in a society without distinctions and boundaries between members of the one race, the human race.[36]

Conclusion

Prejudice is the bifurcation of a professed commitment to Christ and acts of commitment. Conversion is the process whereby the grace of God integrates our knowledge of God's will with our practice of it. A Christian education that seeks to bring people from prejudice to conversion is in partnership with the Holy Spirit. Such an educational task utilizes a pedagogy that combines the cognitive and the experiential. It must create opportunities of collaborative learning between groups that have a history of prejudice between them. Reflection is important for naming the insights and convictions of the Holy Spirit in this process. The collaborative learning and the reflection must be done over a consistent period of time in order to bring an awareness of sin as well as alternative actions of faithfulness.

Conversion is a turning to new patterns and habits that are aligned with the commandment to love one's neighbor as well as the alien in one's land. It demands a process of constant reinforcement of the way of the Spirit by the community committed to faithfulness. The Chris-

34. Ibid.
35. Ibid., 232.
36. Biologists challenge us by reminding us that "race" as we have defined it is a sociocultural construction. Biologically, there is only one race, the human race.

tian educator's task needs to go beyond the traditional setting of the classroom. Communal and relational forms of teaching and settings that facilitate these forms are necessary.

Preparing to teach in this way involves confession of prejudices on the part of the educator in the midst of a community of teacher and learners who together covenant to form a community of truth telling, accountability, and critical thinking for faithful and radical living. The stories of struggles with prejudice, confession, and conversion, along with the biblical story, are the components of the narrative that can be used as the text for teaching. Ritual and symbol can be significant for marking and celebrating the moments of turning toward God.

6

Becoming a Culturally
Sensitive Minister

GARY A. PARRETT

Each perfect gift from heaven's heights
Descends from God, the Lord of lights,
Who knows full well our ev'ry need,
And ev'ry prayer of faith will heed.

When we were held by sin's fierce chain,
Heaven's great loss was our great gain.
For grasping not his throne above,
Christ came to us—Redeeming Love!

You know the grace of Christ our Lord:
Though he was rich, he became poor,
That we, through his true poverty,
Would be made rich eternally.

To such a wondrous, Servant-King
Our tribute we will gladly bring,
In sacrifice henceforth to live:
As we've received, we freely give.

To God the Father, God the Son
And God the Spirit—Three in One,
Be all the glory, pow'r and praise,
From ev'ry heart through endless days. Amen.[1]

1. Gary A. Parrett, "Doxology" (2003). To be sung to the hymn tune OLD ONE HUNDREDTH.

As discussed in the previous chapter, the harsh reality of prejudice is a formidable obstacle in both our own spiritual progress and in the lives of those we seek to serve and teach. To address this arena of sin, true conversion is required—not merely an initial conversion to faith in Jesus Christ but also ongoing conversion to the way of Jesus by the power of the Holy Spirit.

This chapter considers such issues by examining the person of the teacher or minister. Rather than looking at *how* to teach in ways that are culturally sensitive, this chapter focuses on a vision of *who* the culturally sensitive minister—servant, friend, teacher—can be. The word *becoming* in the chapter's title suggests that cultural sensitivity requires ongoing growth and development. The model pursued here is that of an incarnational ministry, an approach patterned after the greatest cross-cultural minister who ever lived—the Lord Jesus Christ. The vision of an incarnational ministry is surely not original, but hopefully the particular approach to this vision taken in this chapter will offer some fresh insights.

To bring many sons and daughters to glory, the eternal Son of God became the Son of Man. He came to earth as a first-century Palestinian Jew who was raised in the small Galilean village of Nazareth. His incarnation was motivated by love both for humans, whom he came to save, and for his Father, whom he longed to obey and honor. The apostle Paul plainly imitated this pattern, as his words in 1 Corinthians 9:19–23 testify:

> Though I am free and belong to no man, I make myself a slave to everyone, to win as many as possible. To the Jews I became like a Jew, to win the Jews. To those under the law I became like one under the law (though I myself am not under the law), so as to win those under the law. To those not having the law I became like one not having the law (though I am not free from God's law but am under Christ's law), so as to win those not having the law. To the weak I became weak, to win the weak. I have become all things to all men so that by all possible means I might save some. I do all this for the sake of the gospel, that I may share in its blessings.

Paul, in becoming all things to all people, never ceased being Paul. Nothing was removed from his essential character. It is probably true, however, that some things were *added* to his character because of incarnational experiences. But he never compromised his faith or resorted to sin to reach others. The same things could be said, of course, about Jesus. In becoming man, he did not cease to be God. Nothing was removed from his essential character. Something was added to him, however: a truly human nature and experience. Yet such loving identification with humans never led him to disobey his Father in heaven.

Before moving to meditations on and implications of the incarnation of Christ for ministry, let me first offer an important caveat. While the incarnation is an essential model for cross-cultural ministry, it can be misunderstood and misapplied. The greatest danger is, perhaps, that the one seeking to become culturally incarnate to serve others might take upon himself or herself an unhealthy "messiah complex." Although we must imitate Christ in sacrificial love and service toward others, we cannot do so in several key respects. We do not enter a culture from "above," as Christ did. We approach others as equals, not as superiors. Nor are we sent directly from the bosom of the Father, as the Son was. We come to another culture from the bosoms of our own cultures, which are not pure or divine. Further, as Sherwood Lingenfelter and Marvin Mayers point out, we can never be truly incarnate in another culture, as Jesus was. Jesus was, in their terms, "a 200 percent person"—100 percent God and 100 percent man. Eternally God, he became an authentic human being.[2] For us, this is an unrealistic goal, since we cannot be born into another culture and raised within that culture during the span of our lives while still retaining our own original culture. "As finite human beings we are constrained by the limitations of our minds, our life histories, and our personal abilities. Few of us have the emotional strength to endure the changes that full incarnation in another culture would require." Yet "the goal of becoming at least partially incarnate in the culture of those to whom we minister is, by God's grace, within our grasp."[3] In other words, "The challenge is to become what Malcolm McFee . . . calls 150 percent persons."[4] With these cautionary notes now sounded, let us continue.

Two Visions of Christ's Incarnational Ministry

Many years ago, I heard someone say that if we could reduce the entire earthly ministry of Jesus to a single scene, or a snapshot, we might focus in on the scene described in John 13. There we find the Lord of glory, stripped of his outer garments, stooping to wash the feet of his disciples. Another intriguing suggestion is that there is an amazing par-

2. Sherwood G. Lingenfelter and Marvin K. Mayers, *Ministering Cross-Culturally: An Incarnational Model for Personal Relationships* (Grand Rapids: Baker, 1986), 15.

3. Ibid., 121.

4. Ibid., 15.

allel between that scene in the upper room and Paul's hymn-like[5] description of Christ's incarnation in Philippians 2.[6] (See the two accounts placed side by side.)

Two Visions of Christ's Incarnational Ministry

John 13:3–17	Philippians 2:5–11
Jesus knew that the Father had put all things under his power, and that he had come from God and was returning to God;	Who, being in very nature God,
so he got up from the meal, took off his outer clothing,	did not consider equality with God something to be grasped, but made himself nothing,
and wrapped a towel around his waist.	taking the very nature of a servant, being made in human likeness.
After that, he poured water into a basin and began to wash his disciples' feet, drying them with the towel that was wrapped around him. . . .	And being found in appearance as a man, he humbled himself and became obedient to death—even death on a cross!
When he had finished washing their feet, he put on his clothes and returned to his place. "Do you understand what I have done for you?" he asked them. "You call me 'Teacher' and 'Lord,' and rightly so, for that is what I am.	Therefore God exalted him to the highest place and gave him the name that is above every name, that at the name of Jesus every knee should bow . . . and every tongue confess that Jesus Christ is Lord, to the glory of God the Father.
Now that I, your Lord and Teacher, have washed your feet, you also should wash one another's feet."	Your attitude should be the same as that of Christ Jesus.

With these two amazing portraits in view, let us consider some implications of Christ's incarnational ministry for our own ministries. The following should be viewed as meditations on, rather than expositions of, John 13 and Philippians 2. In particular, the following discussion focuses on the implications of these two passages and of Christ's incarnation for ministry across cultures.

5. We will not here join the debate concerning whether this famous passage was truly a hymn that Paul took up for his purposes or perhaps composed himself or merely has a hymn-like structure and feel.

6. Many expositors have noted the parallel thoughts between the two passages. See, for example, R. C. H. Lenski, *The Interpretation of St. John's Gospel* (Minneapolis: Augsburg, 1943), 913; and F. F. Bruce, *The Gospel of John* (Grand Rapids: Eerdmans, 1983), 280. An explicit comparison between the two texts in their totality is made by Philip W. Comfort and Wendell C. Hawley, *Opening the Gospel of John* (Wheaton: Tyndale, 1994), 209–10.

Being Secure in the Love of God

All those who seek to step out of their own cultural comfort zones in obedience to God and in sacrificial love for others must have a foundational security in God. Jesus was "in very nature God." But "grasping not his throne above, Christ came to us—Redeeming Love!" Secure in his divine identity, the Son willingly "let go," in some sense, for our sakes. The John 13 passage actually begins with the declaration that Jesus was about to show his disciples "the full extent of his love" (v. 1). Whether this is a reference specifically to the foot washing or to the entire drama of his passion that was about to unfold, this much is clear: Jesus moved forward in love from a place of incredible security in his Father's love. He knew that the Father had put all things under his power, that he had come from God and was about to return to God (v. 3). In the full light of such security, "he got up from the meal, took off his outer clothing," and began to wash his disciples' feet.

This was an incredible, jaw-dropping act of love. The full impact of the story is largely lost on contemporary readers, removed as we are from the cultural context in which the story took place. But we know that this was an act of amazing humility and vulnerability. Loving others in such a way is incredibly risky business. This is especially so when that love involves moving out of our own cultural comfort zones into the great unknown territory of someone else's world. To risk such love, we must be secure in a prior love. The old Gaither song surely had it right:

> I am loved, I am loved, I can risk loving you.
> For the one who knows me best, loves me most.
> I am loved; you are loved. Won't you please take my hand?
> We are free to love each other. We are loved.[7]

When my wife and I accepted God's call to move to New York City in 1985, it was a significant move for us in every respect. We were moving from one coast to another, from a small city to one of the world's largest, from an adult ministry to a youth ministry, and from a white American ministry setting to a Korean-American setting. For me, an incredibly shy and introverted person, becoming a pastor to several hundred youth in such a context represented a huge risk. Even now, all these years later, I marvel that I said yes to the invitation. But there were several things that freed me to do so. First, I knew that even if I were an absolute failure in the eyes of these youth and in that church, my wife

7. William J. Gaither and Gloria J. Gaither, "I Am Loved" (1978).

would still love me. Second, I knew that the family and friends I was leaving behind would lovingly receive me back again—even if I returned in humiliation. And most significantly, I believed God had called me to go. My going was, I truly believed, an act of obedience. The key verses that most encouraged me in those days were Psalm 37:23–24: "If the LORD delights in a man's way, he makes his steps firm; though he stumble, he will not fall, for the LORD upholds him with his hand." I truly believed that even if I had mistaken God's direction or had been right about the move but simply proved to be incompetent for the task, God would still love me. If I fell, he would pick me up, brush me off, and send me off on another journey of faith. The same sense of security has enabled every ministry move and adventure I have taken since.

If we are to love others, we must be secure in God's love for us. As Scripture says, "We love because he first loved us" (1 John 4:19). This should not be seen as an excuse *not* to love others, as though we can ignore God's commands until all our doubts and insecurities have been answered by God. The fact is we will always have a measure of doubt and insecurity until we see Christ face-to-face. Until then, we walk by faith, not by sight. But we will find it difficult to give away what we have not ourselves received. Before doing business with others, ostensibly for their good, we must do business with God, who has acted for our good. Before engaging in the good works God has prepared for us, we must experience his gracious salvation, which involved no work of our own (Eph. 2:8–10). Listen to the wisdom of St. Augustine on this point:

> Christ came chiefly for this reason, that man might learn how much God loves him, and might learn this to the end that he might begin to glow with love of Him by whom he was first loved, and so might love his neighbor at the bidding and after the example of Him who made Himself man's neighbor by loving him, when instead of being His neighbor he was wandering far from Him.[8]

Removing Outer Garments

Secure in the Father's love for us, we are now free to begin loving others who may be, in certain respects, very different from us. To love within a cultural context other than our own, we will likely need to let go of some things that have always been precious to us. For Christ to become incarnate as a human, he had to "empty himself," Paul tells us.

8. St. Augustine, *The First Catechetical Instruction* (Westminster, Md.: Newman Bookshop, 1946), 23.

The exact nature of the famous *kenōsis,* or "emptying," of Philippians 2:7 has been debated for many centuries. In what sense did the eternal Son of God empty himself when he became man? While we may be unable, this side of glory, to answer that question completely, we can say the following with relative confidence. The Son let go of the glory and splendor he had enjoyed with the Father and the Spirit from all eternity. He laid aside certain rights and prerogatives that were rightly his. As Paul states elsewhere, "For you know the grace of our Lord Jesus Christ, that though he was rich, yet for your sakes he became poor, so that you through his poverty might become rich" (2 Cor. 8:9). On the eve of his death, Jesus prayed, "And now, Father, glorify me in your presence with the glory I had with you before the world began" (John 17:5). It also seems clear that the Son let go of the private exercise of his divine attributes. That is, though he retained these attributes—such as omnipotence and omniscience—he used them only as directed by his Father. As Jesus explains, "I tell you the truth, the Son can do nothing by himself; he can do only what he sees his Father doing, because whatever the Father does the Son also does" (John 5:19).

In these and perhaps other ways, the Son emptied himself when he came to us and for us, but by no means did he cease to be divine when he became human.[9] Even though he left behind the glory of heaven, even in his humanity his followers beheld "his glory, the glory of the One and Only . . . full of grace and truth" (John 1:14). It is not that something was removed from his essence or from his character. Rather, something was added—full and true humanity. Nor did his self-emptying spell compromise. Though he was tempted in all ways, even as we are, he never succumbed to sin (Heb. 4:15).

The image from John 13 furthers reflection on this point. There we read that Jesus "got up from the meal" and "took off his outer clothing" before proceeding to wash the feet of the Twelve. When we serve and love others in a cultural context unlike our own, are there some "outer garments" we must remove? If so, what might these be?

Surely, none of us needs to empty himself or herself of the glory of heaven or the free exercise of omnipotence. But there are indeed some

9. See, for example, the following remarks from R. C. H. Lenski, *The Interpretation of St. Paul's Epistles to the Galatians, to the Ephesians, and to the Philippians* (Columbus, Ohio: Wartburg Press, 1937), 780: "Paul does not say that Christ emptied himself of his equality with God. . . . He does not say that Christ 'exchanged' his equality with God for equality with a slave. . . . God's form and existence in God's form and the consequent condition of equality with God are immutable." F. F. Bruce comments, "The form of God was not *exchanged for* the form of a servant; it was *revealed in* the form of a servant." He notes that in this act, Jesus "manifested the form of God on earth more perfectly than would otherwise have been possible" (*Gospel of John,* 280).

trappings of our own homelands and cultures that we must let go of to serve others. Such things in and of themselves may be either good or bad. Or perhaps they are morally neutral. But each of us must consider what aspects of our own cultural heritage and experience may hinder the cause of becoming incarnate in another culture.

To consider such things aright, we must be at least somewhat culturally self-aware. Indeed, the teacher who seeks to apply the gospel to any cultural context must be committed to cultural self-understanding. Without this commitment, the teacher will often be seen as trying to remove splinters from the eyes of others while remaining ignorant of the large amounts of lumber hampering his or her own vision.

Such a self-understanding is important regardless of the context in which one ministers. Whether I, as a teacher, am seeking to apply the gospel to my own culture or to that of others, it is necessary that I first consider how my culture has affected my understanding and practice of the faith. How is my reading of the Bible affected by my cultural lenses? Which passages, doctrines, stories, or themes may I have overlooked? Which have I tended to overemphasize? At which points have the values of my culture clashed with those of the gospel? If I identify no such points, perhaps I have adopted what H. Richard Niebuhr called a "Christ of culture" perspective and have been basically uncritical of my culture.[10] If I can identify such points of tension, how have I responded to them? Have I submitted to the claims of the gospel? Or have I instead capitulated to the cultural gods and found ways to rationalize my choice?

Admittedly, honest self-reflection in these areas is difficult to achieve. Lesslie Newbigin, reflecting on his preparation for missionary service in India many years ago, wrote, "Obviously, I studied Indian religion and culture with the intellectual tools of a twentieth-century European. But with what tools could I study my own culture? There is a Chinese proverb that says, 'If you want a definition of water, don't ask a fish.'"[11]

If I belong to a given culture and am ministering to people who, for the most part, share the same culture, we may together be essentially blind to how that culture is affecting our perspective. This type of problem is even more vexing if the group in question represents the majority culture within a larger context. For example, in the United States, whites may come to view themselves as the "cultural norm," or worse,

10. H. Richard Niebuhr, *Christ and Culture* (San Francisco: HarperSanFrancisco, 2001).

11. Lesslie Newbigin, *Foolishness to the Greeks: The Gospel and Western Culture* (Grand Rapids: Eerdmans, 1986), 21.

they may view themselves as being somehow *a-cultural* or unaffected by cultural issues. It is highly unlikely, of course, that someone would so explicitly confess such a thing, but the perspective may display itself nonetheless. Consider some of the books that are written to address multicultural education. Whether the setting in view is the public school, the university, or the local church, one tendency is clear: The authors and editors of these books often fail to deal with white Americans in the same way that they deal with other Americans.

Two fairly recent titles in Christian education—Barbara Wilkerson's edited work, *Multicultural Religious Education*,[12] and *What Color Is Your God?*[13] by James and Lillian Breckenridge—illustrate this point. Both of these works offer readers significant help in wrestling with issues of culture and multicultural education in Christian contexts. Wilkerson's book, in particular, is a weighty resource of valuable and provocative material. Yet as rich as the content of these books often is, the *structure* of each can leave readers with the impression that white Americans are culturally neutral, or that ministry among whites does not require the same level of cultural awareness that is required in other settings. Each book has chapters devoted to religious education in particular ethnic settings: among African-Americans, Hispanics, Native Americans, and Pacific-Asian-Americans. (Actually, in certain respects, these chapters are problematic in and of themselves.)[14] But there are no chapters, in either book, about ministry among white Americans.

Several passages in Wilkerson's book actually point out the problem white Americans may have with such cultural myopia. Quoting David Ng in the book's opening chapter, Wilkerson writes that "cultural majority churches" need to "learn cultural awareness, including awareness of what Ng identifies as their own 'invisible, weightless, knapsacks of cultural imperialism' that must be unpacked."[15] In the book's final chapter, Virgilio Elizondo sounds a similar warning: "Western tradi-

---

12. Barbara Wilkerson, ed., *Multicultural Religious Education* (Birmingham, Ala.: Religious Education Press, 1997).

13. James and Lillian Breckenridge, *What Color Is Your God? Multicultural Education in the Church* (Wheaton: Bridgepoint, 1995).

14. While such chapters can, in a very broad sense, provide helpful clues for ministries among people of these cultural backgrounds, they also have the potential danger of flattening out differences among groups and of unwittingly misleading readers into stereotypes and oversimplified understandings concerning the persons in question. Work such as this, then, is both potentially helpful and potentially harmful. Thus, a good deal of space (not merely a passing remark) in any such writing should be devoted to providing disclaimers and guidance to the reader.

15. Barbara Wilkerson, "Goals of Multicultural Religious Education," in *Multicultural Religious Education*, 22.

tion is regarded as 'Tradition,' while everything else is regarded as local tradition. Western theologies are regarded simply as theology, while the theologies and methodologies of other cultures are regarded as ethnic or particular theologies."[16] Other passages in the book could easily be cited in this regard as well. My concern with the book, then, is not with its "explicit curriculum" but with its "implicit curriculum." Ironically, the structure of the book may serve to undermine some of its most emphatic content.

A similar problem is evident in *Preaching to Every Pew: Cross-Cultural Strategies* by James R. Nieman and Thomas G. Rogers.[17] The book offers much wise counsel for preaching in diverse settings, but preaching among white Americans does not seem to be within the authors' scope. For the book, the authors interviewed ministers who serve in congregations "with a significant presence of Native American, Latino, or Asian participants, or where the participants lived in economic hardship." Admitting that their omission of similar attention to African-Americans may seem strange to readers, they suggest that "there are already many rich resources in that area" and that "the presence of African-Americans (and others not targeted) was amply reflected through those we did interview and the places they served, even when such groups were not our primary focus."[18] The authors do not seem to believe that people would think it "strange" that white Americans are not specifically attended to in the book. Are we to understand whites as among the "others not targeted"? Does the fact that some of the ministers they interviewed were white mean that this population was "amply represented" in their work? Have the authors assumed that their readers will be mostly white and therefore will have to "cross cultures"? Or have they concluded that those who minister among whites do not have to wrestle with issues of culture in quite the same ways as those who minister among other groups of people?

In each of these books, such questions are left unanswered. Readers are left to wonder about the omission of due attention to the challenges of ministering in white American cultural contexts. Is it because each of these books is targeted toward white readers? None of these books says so or gives such an impression. But what if there were an assumption in place that most readers are white or are at least sufficiently exposed to the dominant culture? Surely, the critical problem is under-

16. Virgilio Elizondo, "Benevolent Tolerance or Humble Reverence," in *Multicultural Religious Education*, 397.

17. James R. Nieman and Thomas G. Rogers, *Preaching to Every Pew: Cross-Cultural Strategies* (Minneapolis: Augsburg, 2001).

18. Ibid., 18.

exposure to minority cultures, is it not? Indeed, such underexposure *is* a problem. Yet it is surely no more a problem than the fact that many white evangelicals have under-examined their own cultures. While the authors of the books in question are, in fact, culturally literate and sensitive people, many of their readers may not be so. A white reader could well be lulled into thinking that working through issues of culture is simply not as important when working with white Americans as when working with others.

It must be noted again that each of the above-mentioned books offers significant insight into issues of ministry within and across cultures. Further, each of these authors is clearly committed to promoting understanding among persons and groups of diverse backgrounds. Is it not significant then that we find what may be evidence of cultural myopia even among those who are so personally invested in combating that phenomenon? Discerning readers will surely find evidence of the same sort of limitation in the writings of the three authors of this present work. Rather than being alarmed by such things, we should allow them to challenge and instruct us. Our task is not an easy one. We will never be free from a certain amount of cultural bias in our perspectives. Yet while pure objectivity is beyond our grasp, this does not mean we cannot or should not strive for it. At the very least, we must pursue a conscious and responsible subjectivity.

How can we who teach and serve others gain understanding in this area? The most important thing we can do when dealing with intercultural issues is develop and deepen *relationships* with people from backgrounds that are significantly different from our own. In the context of such relationships, we are challenged by the different perspectives of our new friends. Newbigin, still reflecting on his own missionary experience, remarks:

> As a young missionary, I was confident that the critical evaluations I made about Hindu beliefs and practices were securely founded on God's revelation in Christ. As I grew older, I learned to see that they were shaped more than I realized by my own culture. And I could not have come to this critical stance in relation to my own culture without the experience of living in another, an Indian culture.[19]

Newbigin's comments remind me immediately of how my own understanding of white American culture has been affected by my immersion in Korean-American culture. I suppose I must agree with his conclusion that, short of such an immersion experience in another culture,

19. Newbigin, *Foolishness to the Greeks*, 21.

true cultural self-knowledge is difficult to come by. However, I do believe it is possible to grow in these areas if we intentionally build and
nurture significant relationships with people from other cultures and
listen to both their words and their lives.

Even limited exposure of this type can cause enough cognitive dissonance to stimulate significant learning. Recent political events helped
to encourage such a learning process for some of the students on my
own campus. The historically unprecedented presidential election of
2000 featured a hotly contested battle between George W. Bush and Al
Gore. The outcome was not decided until weeks after the November
election when the United States Supreme Court finally intervened, rul-
ing 5 to 4 in favor of Mr. Bush's cause. Throughout the campaign, the
election, and the weeks that followed, a deep fissure that exists between
Americans was brutally exposed for all to see.[20] The country divided
nearly evenly between the two candidates. Two of the more striking
points of divide were between black and white Americans and between
urban and rural residents. An overwhelming majority of blacks and ur-
banites supported Mr. Gore, while most whites and rural Americans
supported Mr. Bush.

As all of this unfolded on the national level, the seminary where I
teach became something of a microcosm of these things. At the school's
largest campus, located in a rural area and with a largely white student
body, faculty, and staff, sentiments seemed to favor Bush and his Republican Party. Thirty miles away, at our urban campus, many among
the mainly Hispanic and African-American community were in the Gore
camp of supporters. One of my students, a young white man, was among
a number of students from the larger, suburban campus taking courses
at the urban campus as the election and its aftermath unfolded. He re-
ported to me afterward how stark the contrast was between mealtime
conversations at the two campuses. Questions about who was trying to
"steal the election" were answered, for the most part, in precisely opposite ways on the two campuses of this one seminary. This experience was
perhaps more educative and formative for the student in question than
were any of his formal courses that fall semester. No doubt, the experience was challenging for the students of both campuses who were in relationship (albeit of a limited nature) during that turbulent season.

In incidents such as these, being removed from one's own context
and becoming engaged at deep levels of conversation about significant

20. Lawrence E. Adams has addressed aspects of this fissure and the issue of Christian responsibility in such an age in *Going Public: Christian Responsibility in a Divided
America* (Grand Rapids: Brazos Press, 2002). Surprisingly, Adams pays only scant attention to the role of race or ethnicity in this national divide.

matters seem to expand one's perspective. Sadly, such experiences are not common for most American evangelicals. When we do rub shoulders with Christians of other ethnicities and cultures, often at large-scale events that are held only occasionally, they are often brief encounters, and the conversations do not probe beneath the surface of pleasant exchanges.

We may come to understand our cultural selves better through assuming the roles of active learners, the ones being served by others. As one who is regularly in the position of leader, teacher, minister, servant of others, I have become aware of a tendency to have feelings of condescension toward others. Certainly, this is at least unconsciously strengthened by the fact that I am white, male, and American. To address this—an attitude that I believe to be not only arrogant but plainly sinful—I have sought to be the learner, the one receiving service, instruction, or other forms of grace from another, especially from someone who is unlike me in terms of ethnicity, nationality, gender, life experience, educational background, theological perspective, or in other significant ways. I may take such a posture by reading and studying books, by enjoying art—music, film, paintings, sculpture—by sitting under preaching and teaching, or simply by being in conversation with others and consciously being a listener and learner.

In my recent travels to Sri Lanka, I was asked to teach young pastors about various aspects of pastoral theology and ministry. I accepted these invitations with gladness and rejoice that I was, apparently, able to contribute to the understanding of the brothers and sisters there. A major reason for accepting the invitations, however, is that I am eager to learn. I am painfully aware of how limited my understanding of Christ and his church is. When I first traveled to this island nation, I anticipated that I would learn as much as I would teach. I was wrong. Without doubt, I learned far more than I taught. Being with these pastors and their parishioners was sobering, humbling, challenging, and powerfully formative. As I witnessed these kingdom people and kingdom workers who toil daily in a land that has been divided by civil war for twenty years and devastated by poverty, my vision of the world, the church, the ministry, and the Lord himself was vastly enlarged. Yet I realize that even with these opportunities, my global exposure is miniscule at best.

When we begin to acknowledge how little we truly know, we are in a position to begin to acquire wisdom. But we must be intentional about learning from those we have previously barely even known. I recently heard the lead pastor of my church describe his ongoing conversations with a homeless man who had been attending our church. The pastor had been meeting fairly regularly with the man and spoke of how much he was learning in those conversations. He had begun to envision occasions in which this newcomer could share his insights with the rest of the generally affluent congregation. Finally, the pastor spoke of his desire for the church to somehow be a blessing to his homeless friend. Being a benefactor was not, however, his first or chief concern in the relationship. He was not approaching this as a relationship between himself as the greater party and his friend as the lesser. They were equals. Each had something significant to bring to the life of the other. As we minister to persons with cultural backgrounds unlike our own, we too will be wise to approach the relationship as one of mutual blessing, instruction, and edification. In fulfillment of the pastor's hopes, this man has began sharing his story in a series of small group meetings in the church. Those of us who have attended one or more of these sessions have come under this man's instruction, even as he has sat under the instruction of many of us who have preached and taught in the church.

Through these types of experiences and relationships, we can grow in our understanding of our cultural selves. We can become increasingly aware of what our cultural trappings, our "outer garments," may be. For some, perhaps these will include an obsession with the clock, a desire to protect one's privacy and safeguard individualism, a commitment to democratic forms of leadership, a carefree spirit in worship, an egalitarian attitude toward elders. Westeners can profit from reading the experiences of others who have preceded them in moving outside Western contexts.[21] For others, there will be entirely different sets of garments that need to be dealt with. In any case, these things—not necessarily either good or bad in and of themselves—may need to be removed in love and humility if we seek to serve in another cultural context. Removing them may be painful, but it need not injure or compromise our essential identities. On the contrary, far from having something precious taken away, we will likely discover that something precious has been added. In losing our lives for the sake of the gospel, we will find deeper, truer lives.

Putting on New Garments

As we have seen, none of us can be truly incarnate in another culture as Christ was for our sakes. Nevertheless, we can and should seek to

21. Lingenfelter's and Newbigin's experiences, for example, are helpful in this regard. Similarly, helpful insights about walking in humility and respect when relating to persons of other cultural and religious backgrounds can be found in the recent work of Sri Lankan evangelical leader Ajith Fernando: *Sharing the Truth in Love: How to Relate to People of Other Faiths* (Grand Rapids: Discovery House, 2001).

identify with any culture in which we are called to serve, following the examples of both Jesus and the apostle Paul. Paul was determined to "become all things to all people" for the sake of the gospel. For the sake of "bringing many sons to glory" (Heb. 2:10), the eternal Son of God "shared in their humanity" (Heb. 2:14), was "made like his brothers in every way" (Heb. 2:17), and was "tempted in every way, just as we are— yet was without sin" (Heb. 4:15). In Philippians 2, Paul writes that Jesus took on "the very nature of a servant" and was "made in human likeness." To wash the disciples' feet, Jesus, having taken off his outer garments, put on a new garment—a towel, wrapping it around his waist in readiness to serve (John 13).

When we are called to minister in a cultural context other than our own, we must seek to identify with that culture for the sake of the gospel. Such action is motivated by servant love and, as is the case whenever we strive to be servants of others, requires deep humility. But as we do so, we must wrestle with the issue of how much of that culture we can take upon ourselves while retaining our integrity. Put otherwise, what ought to happen when the gospel is introduced into a particular culture and the call to discipleship is sounded in that context? This sort of "Christ and culture" question has challenged and perplexed Christians throughout the ages. Space does not allow us to probe this fully here but only to offer a few suggestions.

To begin with, when the gospel truly penetrates a culture, it becomes enculturated in that setting. It cannot remain detached from or unaffected by the culture. As Newbigin says, "There can never be a culture-free gospel."[22] In gospel ministry today, the role that culture plays is complex on all sides. The gospel is carried into a given culture by messengers who have a culture of their own. The messengers' understanding of the gospel has been deeply influenced by that culture. The new recipients of the gospel, even in their initial hearing of the gospel and certainly in any subsequent adoption of it, are deeply influenced by *their distinct* culture. We may be disturbed by such thoughts, but we should not be. Consider the incarnation of Christ. God's coming to us was not culture free. Jesus Christ was not a generic human being. He was a particular human. God came to us in the person of Jesus Christ "within a particular human culture, conducting his ministry in the language and culture of those among whom he lived."[23] He was a first-century, Middle Eastern, Jewish man. He was raised in Nazareth, a particular town in Galilee, a particular region of Israel. He was raised by a

---

22. Newbigin, *Foolishness to the Greeks*, 4.
23. Charles Kraft, "Gospel and Culture," in *Christianity in Today's World*, ed. R. Keely (Grand Rapids: Eerdmans, 1985), 274.

particular family and participated in a particular form of Jewish religious life. This uniqueness did not, however, limit him in any way from being the Savior of the world. Neither does the gospel lose its power when it takes root in a given culture.

Charles Kraft writes, "Human beings cannot live outside of culture or think except in cultural categories. So if God is to reach us at all, it has to be within the cultural 'water' in which we live."[24] This has obvious implications for those who minister in the name of the Lord. As my friend Adrian DeVisser, a Sri Lankan pastor, has written, "The minister of the Gospel cannot communicate without concerning himself with the culture, because communication is inextricable from culture. Just as Christ became flesh and dwelt among men, so propositional truth must have cultural incarnations to be meaningful."[25]

The gospel enters a culture and finds particular expression in that culture. But this expression is not mere acceptance of the culture. Jesus truly became a part of his culture, but his response to that culture was one of critical engagement. At times, he seemed to affirm cultural practices. Consider, for example, his participation in the wedding celebration at Cana in Galilee. Not only did Jesus bless the gathering with his presence, but he also provided wine so that the celebration could continue. Likewise, Jesus faithfully participated in the religious festivals of Israel. He regularly attended the synagogue in his hometown of Nazareth (Luke 4:16). On the other hand, Jesus challenged and even condemned many of the practices of his countrymen and fellow Jews. He was relentless in his attacks on the hypocritical practices of many religious leaders (Matthew 23). He did not campaign for the overthrow of the political powers in place during his lifetime, but he was unafraid to speak candidly about them and to them (see, for example, Luke 13:32, in which he refers to Herod as "that fox").

Niebuhr suggests that there are various responses to the Christ and culture dilemma. He calls these "Christ against culture," "Christ of culture," "Christ above culture," "Christ and culture in paradox," and "Christ the transformer of culture." The enduring usefulness of Niebuhr's insights is evidenced by the fact that the book was recently reintroduced in an expanded edition in honor of the fiftieth anniversary of its original publication. A further tribute to the work's significance is the sheer volume of those who have interacted with his paradigm—both favorably and critically—throughout the years.

24. Ibid.
25. Adrian DeVisser, "Gospel and Culture," in *Navodaya Compendium: Faithful to Our Call* (Katunayake, Sri Lanka: New Life Literature, 1995), 57.

One of Niebuhr's most important contributions to the issue is pointing out that there is no simple answer or single answer to this dilemma. Although one may adopt a particular stance as a basic position, that person may well find it necessary—under certain circumstances—to advocate a different response. Thinking along these lines, I would like to suggest that in every Christ and culture encounter, there are a number of responses that may be appropriate. These can be plotted on a continuum (see fig. 2).

Celebrate   Connect   Challenge   Condemn

Fig. 2. A Range of Responses as the Gospel Encounters a Culture

When we enter a new and unfamiliar culture, we can expect to find a spectrum of cultural values, symbols, and other phenomena. As shown, in any given culture, we can expect to see reflections of the image of God, for all have been created in that image. We can just as surely expect, on the other hand, to find clear evidence of our fallenness, for we all bear the image of fallen Adam as well. Since the culture is complex, so too is the range of responses to that culture.

The gospel always becomes incarnate in a given culture, but it never does so uncritically. Immediately after stating that there can be no "culture-free gospel," Newbigin hastens to add the following: "Yet the gospel, which is from the beginning to the end embodied in culturally conditioned forms, calls into question all cultures, including the one in which it was originally embodied."[26] Along these same lines, Bishop Stephen C. Neill wrote that "the Gospel can serve as the destroyer, the preserver, and the creator of cultures."[27] As the gospel went forth into the world, Neill points out, "Christians found it necessary to distinguish between those things which must immediately and totally be forbidden, those things which were undesirable and—it was hoped—would gradually die out, and those which were merely cultural, representing no more than differences of habit and tradition."[28]

As we enter a culture with the gospel, our aim fixed on making disciples, we come with the conviction that God has already been at work in this context. The doctrines of divine omnipresence, general revelation,

26. Newbigin, *Foolishness to the Greeks*, 4.

27. Stephen C. Neill, "Religion and Culture: A Historical Introduction," in *Down to Earth: Studies in Christianity and Culture*, ed. John R. W. Stott and Robert Coote (Grand Rapids: Eerdmans, 1980), 6.

28. Ibid., 8.

and the *imago Dei* assure us of this. Thus, we can expect that among any people group there will be things beautiful and praiseworthy. It is wise to look first for these and to celebrate them. There will be other things that seem to be, to use Neill's terms, "no more than differences of habit and tradition." Such things are neither celebrated by the gospel nor condemned by it. We can begin to consider how to make use of such things as points of connection for the sake of the gospel. As we spend more time in a given culture and gain a proper understanding of it, it will become evident that the gospel directly challenges certain values and practices of the culture. Indeed, further investigation may make it clear that a practice is plainly condemned by the gospel.

Those things that are praiseworthy and worthy of celebration and those things that may provide viable means of connecting with the culture without compromising the faith can become "new garments" that we take upon ourselves for the sake of the gospel. Again, as we have seen, Jesus' blessing of the wedding at Cana is an example of celebrating a particular cultural practice. Paul's use of the imagery of athletic games in his correspondence with the Corinthians (1 Cor. 9:24–27) and in his letters to Timothy (2 Tim. 4:7–8) provides us with an example of connecting for the sake of the gospel.

On the other hand, Jesus and Paul both condemn other cultural practices. In the same chapter in which we read of the wedding at Cana, we read of Jesus' impassioned rejection of certain cultural practices that had defiled the temple (John 2:12–17). A chapter after we read of Paul's connecting with the Corinthians through athletic imagery, we find him uncompromisingly condemning the cultural practice of participating in pagan festivals that honored false gods (1 Cor. 10:14–22). Jesus had become truly incarnate in his Jewish world. Paul was obliged to "become all things to all people." But neither merely embraced their cultural contexts in an uncritical fashion. Their approaches to culture were thoughtful indeed. Christ was not merely "against culture," nor was he interested in becoming "the Christ of culture" in his first-century context.

If the incarnate Son of God and the inspired apostle needed to think and act carefully in regard to culture, surely we must be even more cautious in our approaches. Before celebrating or connecting with a value or practice, we had best understand it as well as possible. This may be even more important in terms of challenging or ultimately condemning a cultural practice. Personally, I have learned to be very cautious in this area because of the fear that I may be too eager to condemn a practice that I simply do not adequately understand. A wiser course to take would be to encourage those disciples who are indigenous to the culture to investigate their own practices in light of the gospel, to allow them to see for themselves how the gospel challenges or indeed condemns certain practices or values. Whenever possible, such work should be done by those native to the culture. Of course, there may well be cases in which such tasks fall to the newcomer. But these should be exceptions, not the norm.

Finally, unless we have examined our own cultures in the same way we examine another, it is hypocritical of us to presume to pass judgment on the cultural lives of others. Only when the plank has been removed from our own eyes will we be in a position to help our brothers and sisters deal with the specks in their eyes. There will certainly be areas in which we can serve others and spur them on to greater obedience to Christ, but we are unqualified to do so until after we have taken such an approach with ourselves.

It may be helpful at this point to show how this approach to culture has been working itself out in my ministry among Korean-Americans. I hesitate to do so because I freely confess that, in spite of nearly thirty years of interaction with Korean culture in various forms and settings, I still have only limited knowledge of that culture. This is not feigned humility; it is simple fact. The examples I now put forth, then, are offered with apologies to my Korean and Korean-American friends.

Thankfully, long gone are the days when I was tempted to publish a tract outlining the shortcomings of the Korean Christian movement. Throughout the years, as I have come to understand the Korean culture and the Korean church better, my appreciation for both has deepened. In speaking like this, I have no pretense that I am responding to "pure Korean culture." For one thing, cultures are not static but dynamic and, as such, continually evolving. This helps explain why many Korean-American youth have complained to me throughout the years that their parents—first-generation Korean-American immigrants—are often more "Korean" than Koreans who still live in Korea. Second, my perception of "Korean values" are, like all perceptions, limited in various ways. What I am responding to are the cultural values and experiences I have come to understand as and associate with Korean culture. I will summarize my responses in terms of three broad categories. First, some of the values and practices I have discovered through my interaction with Korean and Korean-American people have become as new garments to me. Others I can only appreciate from afar—I could not wear them even if I wanted to do so, for I can never become a truly "200 percent person" in another culture. Finally, there are other Korean values and practices that I would not take upon myself even if I could. Let me briefly illustrate each of these responses.

The cultural forms I have tried to take upon myself include things I consider to be critical points of connection and things I regard as worthy of celebration. It is likely true that language and food are critical ports of entry into any new culture. This certainly seems to be true in Korean culture. Saying even a few simple greetings in the Korean language nearly always produces warm smiles when I meet first-generation Koreans, as does saying yes to a serving of kimchee as part of my dinner. Recognizing these things, I have endeavored to learn the Korean language (it has been no easy task) and to enjoy Korean food (thankfully, a much easier and more delightful task for me). I do not consider Korean language or food to be more praiseworthy than those I grew up with (although a diet of Korean food is probably far healthier than the tasty fare I was raised on). But I do consider it worthwhile to have invested time in coming to use and enjoy both. In terms of language, I devoted eight months to rigorous formal study in Korea and countless years of unofficial tutoring at home and elsewhere. In terms of food, I have had to be willing to try new things (and keep trying them) and to have my tastes expanded.

There are other values or practices in the Korean culture that I have taken not merely as points of connection. They are truly praiseworthy "garments." For example, I have found the Korean attitudes toward elders to be far closer to the biblical model than those in my own cultural upbringing. When I first started dating my wife, I learned to rise when her parents entered the room. At first, I regarded this as simply cultural sensitivity. Only later did I discover that Scripture commands such behavior (Lev. 19:32). The Korean tradition of being generous to aging parents—providing for their needs and caring for them even at great expense to oneself—seemed very strange to me at first. But I have come to understand that this is very much in keeping with the spirit of biblical mandates (1 Tim. 5:4–8). The strong communal emphasis in Korean culture strikes me as more biblical (Acts 2:44–45; Phil. 2:1–5) than the preservation of privacy and individualism that my own culture prizes. When, after enjoying a lunch with Korean-American friends, I find myself fighting over the right to pay the entire bill rather than reaching for a calculator to make sure I do not pay more than my fair share, I somehow feel more like Jesus for the effort.

There are other Korean cultural practices and traits that, praiseworthy though they seem to be, I find myself unable to fully lay claim to. In particular, two Korean words capture qualities that will never be fully mine in the way they belong to others. The first is *han*.[29] This word is

---

29. For further discussion of *han*, see chapter 4.

often used to describe the deep pathos of the Korean people, cultivated through centuries of national endurance of great difficulties—especially those inflicted by foreign powers that invaded the Korean peninsula and oppressed the Korean people for extended historical periods. Even in recent history, Koreans have endured great hardship. Koreans of my in-laws' generation, for example, lived through two devastating wars—World War II and the Korean Conflict—were raised under Japanese occupation, during which time they were forced to abandon much that was fundamental to their Korean identities, and watched their nation be divided by superpowers. My father-in-law has no knowledge of what became of his father and countless other relatives who lived only a few miles north of his own home, in Seoul, because they lived north of the thirty-eighth parallel. Older members of Korean churches remember well what it was like to live through severe persecution and extreme poverty. *Han* sometimes manifests itself; sometimes it does not. But it *is* there, within the very soul of many Koreans. I can hear it when I listen to traditional Korean singing and when I join a contemporary Korean gathering of prayer. It seems to me that *han* is, in certain respects, akin to the heart of him who was "a man of sorrows, and acquainted with grief." I admire the quality, but, although I can experience it as an observer and perhaps assimilate it in limited ways, I can never fully possess it myself.

The second word is *yulshim*. This might be translated as "zeal" or "fervor." I have come to see that *yulshim* marks much of what is done in Korean culture. From the demonstrations at university campuses in Korea, to the passion of striking employees in a Korean company, to the daily dawn prayer meetings that draw multitudes of Korean Christians, *yulshim* seems to be ever on display. I have longed to imitate the Korean Christians in their zeal to pray and evangelize, but I continually prove to be no match for them. There are some garments we may admire in a shop window, and yet they remain, for one reason or another, beyond our ability to own. *Han* and *yulshim* seem to be such garments for me.

Finally, there are some Korean cultural values and practices—as I understand them—that I do not desire to take upon myself. As is often the case, the things I have in mind are in some ways the reverse side of the coin of those traits I most admire. Respect for elders, for example, can be overdone. Some Korean Christians insist that their children continue to obey them even when they are married adults. The practice of asking the bride to leave her parents and, with her new husband, live with and be subservient to her new in-laws seems to be at odds with the clear biblical teaching of Genesis 2:24. Similarly, the quality of *yulshim*, which can lead to great and heroic acts of faith, can also lend itself to competition and pride. I have known Korean Christian leaders who seemed to measure spirituality by how few hours of sleep they were getting each night because of all the work they were doing "for God."

Of particular concern to me is that the strong communal emphasis—eminently worthy of praise in many respects—sometimes leads to an unhealthy and oppressive conforming tendency in the culture. The community sets standards of what is good and beautiful, and those who do not appear to meet those standards are often belittled or worse. In our ministry among Korean-Americans, my wife and I have witnessed the devastation wrought among young people when they are perpetually compared with those who *do* satisfy community standards. Such soul-crushing teaching must be confronted by the gospel of him who ministered chiefly at the margins and calls his followers to do the same and by the message of the great love that God has lavished on us all (1 John 3:1).

There is another potential negative outworking of this communal ethos. The Korean word for "our" or "ours" is *uri* (pronounced *oo-ree*). My Korean language professor once explained to the class that the root of this word is the same as that used for the large stone walls that are traditionally built around Korean homes. These walls are imposing structures of protection, often topped with broken glass or barbed wire to ward off would-be intruders. As I was learning the language, I was struck by how often the word *uri* was used in Korean television news broadcasts—especially in combination with *nara*, the word for nation. "*Uri nara . . .*" I would continually hear as I watched the news report. The strong national identity can prove to be powerfully unifying, of course, but it can also be very divisive. When *uri* creates an unhealthy "us against them" mentality, it must be challenged by the wall-destroying gospel (Eph. 2:14).

The examples I have cited are limited, of course, but I hope they serve to illustrate the varied responses that may be appropriate as we seek to become incarnate in a given culture. As we have seen, the gospel challenges every culture, but it does so in love. While there are "garments" of a given culture that we cannot or should not seek to wear, there are many others that we can and must try to put on. What, then, can we take upon ourselves from a new culture? What new garments, what form, can we assume in this context? We can and must, without compromising the gospel or our identity as children of God, take upon ourselves the elements of a culture that will enable us to serve that culture faithfully. This includes whatever is praiseworthy in that culture as well as whatever language, forms, customs, and practices may be useful for connecting with that culture at deep and significant levels.

Washing Feet

To what end do we seek to enter the cultural world of another? We become "incarnate"—to whatever degree this is possible—for the purpose of loving and serving others. The only other appropriate motivations are to glorify God and to obey his will. But these, too, are realized only as we sacrificially serve others. Such things alone constrained the Son of God to become one of us (see, for example, Mark 10:45; Luke 19:10; 1 Tim. 1:15; Heb. 2:10–18). We do not enter a culture, as Christians in too many ages and in too many places have done, to impose our cultural standards on it. We dare not enter to oppress or terrorize or exert our own authority. It is unthinkable to assume seats of honor or to claim the highest places as our own.

> Forgive us, Lord, the harm we do
> When we refuse to follow you.
> Forsaking love, we grasp at pow'r;
> Come, heal our sickness in this hour.[30]

Over the last few years, as I have ministered in Sri Lanka, this point has been driven home to me. The greatest obstacle to the spread of the gospel in that land, I have been told by Sri Lankan church leaders, is the history of the church there. The Christianizing-civilizing-colonizing history of the church in Sri Lanka has had a negative effect on the views of Christianity among contemporary citizens of the island. Portuguese Catholics, Dutch Reformed, and British Anglicans have all had their "incarnations" in Sri Lanka. Without question, each colonial episode featured a mixture of good and bad intentions and experiences. But what remains in the consciousness of many Sri Lankans today is a skewed understanding of the gospel, owing in large part to abuses done in the name of Christ by Christians who came to that land from other cultures. As discouraging as this history is, I have been greatly encouraged and instructed by the vigorous efforts of contemporary Sri Lankan pastors and workers to incarnate more faithfully the gospel in that culture today.

In every sense, we must enter a culture to love and serve in that context for the sake of the gospel. This is true even when we find that the gospel must challenge or condemn a cultural practice. In fact, the best means of challenging a prevailing cultural practice may well be one that seems counterintuitive to us. Taking up one practice or attitude within the culture may prove to be the best challenge to another practice or attitude in

---

30. Gary A. Parrett, "The Wondrous Cross Brought Down the Wall" (2003).

that culture. For example, Jesus' act of taking up the servant's towel in utter humility was the most powerful means possible of condemning the disciples' attitude of pride and their ambition for places of honor and recognition (see Mark 10:35–45). So, too, the cross—in all its apparent weakness— proved to be the ultimate display of God's power in condemning and defeating sin and its consequences (1 Cor. 1:18ff.). This is part of the fundamental mystery of the incarnational mind-set: God's way of sacrificial love boasts unparalleled power in touching and transforming hearts.

There is another noteworthy feature of the foot washing: Jesus washed the feet of his disciples *one pair at a time*. Each of the Twelve were individually cared for by the Lord in the upper room. One by one, the disciples experienced this wonder of wonders as God himself stooped to wash each one's dirty feet. It seems likely that this was an awkward, time-consuming experience for the apostles. Perhaps time seemed suspended, as each one awaited his turn. We know that Peter protested aloud; we can guess that the others joined his protest in their hearts. Judas was there as well. What was going through his mind as Jesus made his way—slowly, foot by foot—toward him? Jesus washed all the feet that night, even those of his betrayer. Another pair of feet belonged to him who would call down curses on himself while denying any knowledge of the foot washer. And most of the other pairs of feet, if not all of them, would soon be scurrying for cover as the moments of darkness fell. Jesus washed them all that night, and he did so one pair at a time. Each of the Twelve was a unique individual. He had loved them not only as a group but also as unique persons. The same was true on this his final evening with them. So it must be with us.

When all is said and done, the command that confronts us is not "Love another culture as your own" but "Love your neighbor as yourself." Each neighbor—whoever he or she may be—must be loved in all his or her divinely crafted uniqueness. This means that if we are called of God to "go" from our place and minister among "all the nations," we must do more than study about that target culture. If I am called to minister, for example, to the Haitian immigrant community in the urban center near me, it will prove helpful to learn all I can, before I go, about that cultural context. This may involve reading books or talking with people who know that context, especially those who are a part of that context. But none of this excuses me from my far more fundamental obligation: When I have joined myself to that context, I must come to know and love individuals.

In fact, too much pre-study *of* a given cultural context can have unintended detrimental effects on ministry *in* that context. Like the man who has heard God's Word but has not put it into practice, I may be self-deceived, thinking that I know all I need to know. I can never faithfully and fully portray an individual by using only the broad brushstrokes of a limited understanding of his or her culture. In the first place, culture is simply too complex for that. Even more significantly, each individual is far more than a mere product of his or her culture.

Those who seek to minister with cultural sensitivity face a confusing task and will doubtless find that they continually have much to learn, unlearn, and learn all over again. James Nieman and Thomas Rogers's pursuit of cross-cultural strategies for preaching is helpful on this point. The authors note:

> Culture is *plural.* Anthropologists no longer speak in the singular about *"the* native," as if each group has a single, monaural culture. Instead, even seemingly homogeneous groups are composed of multiple cultures that are not sealed but porous, influencing one another through cultural borrowing that now spans the globe.[31]

In their book, Nieman and Rogers look at culture through a variety of lenses, those of ethnicity, class, displacement, and belief. Their argument, based largely on interviews with a number of ministers serving in a wide variety of ethnic settings, is that each of these lenses offers a necessary perspective for seeking to preach with cultural sensitivity.

Certainly, the complexity of culture involves far more than the four layers these authors probe. To illustrate, let us consider the case of a young woman who was part of a church project that I and several others worked on years ago. I will call her Sandy. Suppose I was a new pastor in Sandy's church and desired to minister to her in a culturally sensitive way. How could I equip myself for the task? As a shepherd, I would be committed to knowing my sheep, each one, individually, seeking the same spirit in which our Lord Jesus, the Good Shepherd, ministers to his own (see John 10:10–30). I might ask the question, "Who is Sandy anyway?" How might I answer this query? Sandy is a Korean-American, teen-aged girl. These few descriptive words, by themselves, evince the complexity of the challenge. I must understand something about the meaning of "American" and of "Korean" and of the hybrid form, "Korean-American." But there is also the matter of being a teenager in America. Thus, I must also know something about so-called youth culture and the various potential influences it can have on Sandy. She is a young woman, not a young man, and this too is a critical piece of who Sandy is. But the case is more complex still.

Sandy lives in a particular geographical region of the United States. She is part of an evangelical church youth group. It is a Korean-American

---

31. Nieman and Rogers, *Preaching to Every Pew,* 15.

youth group. She reports to me that it is very different from the other Ko-rean-American youth groups in her area. She thinks the "climate" is more spiritual in her church than it is in others she has visited. Sandy has a warm and supportive two-parent, two-sibling family. She attends a par-ticular high school and, at that school, "hangs" with a particular group of friends. We could, of course, continue the exercise, but the point should be clear. A person's culture is multilayered and exceedingly complex.

It would be grossly inadequate to describe Sandy, culturally, as being simply Korean-American. It would be positively tragic to think, further, that knowing that Sandy is Korean-American is to know Sandy. If we return to the command "Love your neighbor as yourself," we under-stand that it is not simply tragic but actually sinful to reduce Sandy in this manner. How do *I* want to be loved by others? I want people to take the time to know me as a whole person, not as simply one member of one particular category. On the other hand, neither do I want another person to ignore a part of me—my ethnicity, for example—or dismiss it as being unimportant in the scheme of things, for that *is* part of who I am. It is not *all* that I am, but it is a significant *part* of my identity.

Reflecting on the example of Sandy, we may speak of two errors we should strive to avoid. First, we should not be overly obsessed with ra-cial, ethnic, or cultural difference, for then we fail to do justice to the complexity of individuals and may end up stereotyping. The critics of multiculturalism often score valid points here.

At the other end of the spectrum, however, lies an equally (or perhaps more) dangerous error, that of so-called color blindness. Well-inten-tioned people often view themselves as color-blind when it comes to mat-ters of race or ethnicity. My wife has heard this from friends who say they do not see her as Korean but simply as Holly. I have heard similar things from Korean-American friends who tell me that they do not see me as white or American. In most of these instances, there is a loving intention at work. We can even hear in this perspective the longing of Martin Luther King Jr. for the day in which a man would be judged not by the color of his skin but by the content of his character. But there are at least two fundamental problems with so-called color blindness of this sort.

First, it simply is not true that any of us is or ever could be color-blind. We *do* see the color of those we meet; it is usually one of the first and most striking things we notice about a person. And when we do no-tice a neighbor's color, we have some response or reaction to that fact alone. There is simply no use denying these things. But a second and even more significant problem is that it is, in fact, an unworthy aspira-tion. Even if we could be color-blind, we should choose not to be, for a person's color is part of who he or she was designed to be by the good and all-sovereign God. Further, it bespeaks something of importance about that person's realities—past, present, and future. There is no evidence that this part of a person's reality will vanish when we are all in glory (see Rev. 5:9–10; 7:9–10). Again, we may ask, How would I want my neighbor to love me? My own response to this is that I want to be loved for *all* of who I am. I do not want parts of my being dismissed as though they were insignificant.

When we too quickly dismiss a person's ethnicity and physical appearance as unimportant, we may, in the process, also be dismissing the painful experiences caused by those who have taken offense at his or her appearance. The weight of such experiences can often be a heavy burden borne daily by mind and spirit. Consider this passage from a young Chinese-American man who has lived and worked in the epicenter of American power:

> Do I seem scary to you? Probably not. I am a friendly looking guy, not menacing in the least.
>
> Do I seem foreign to you? Now, that is a more interesting question. What makes a person look foreign? There is, of course, the face. My skin is yellowish. My hair is black and straight. My eyes are brown, almond-shaped. But that is not all there is to it. Context matters, too, at least as much as content. In one memorable photograph from a trip to Beijing, I'm standing in front of the Gate of Heavenly Peace at the Forbidden City. Next to me, oblivious to the camera, is a Chinese passerby, my age roughly, my height, with something like my facial structure. There is reason to think we might be related. Yet somehow it is patently obvious who is the American in that picture. My clothes (college T-shirt, shorts, Birkenstocks), my bearing (arms akimbo), my smile (easy; straight teeth), and something else, ineffable, all give it away. My wife calls this the "Eric, but for an accident of history" picture.
>
> Context matters. Now put my image, so obviously American, under a headline about a plot by the Chinese government to sway our elections. How do I look now? Make it a black-and-white head shot, grainy. Are you starting to wonder? Add a caption about my having "no comment." Does it occur to you suddenly that English might not be the first thing out of my mouth?[32]

This story describes the pain of one whose appearance has made him the object of particular forms of thought, attitude, and action. Hearing the story illustrates an important "love your neighbor" principle: One of the most meaningful ways to love is to listen authentically. If I could encourage readers of this present work to begin honing one

32. Eric Liu, *The Accidental Asian: Notes of a Native Speaker* (New York: Random House, 1998), 117–18.

skill in order to respond to the issues raised in this book, I would urge them to sharpen their capacity to hear. This is surely the most basic of all spiritual disciplines, is thoroughly biblical and God honoring, and has helped the church find its way over some of its most difficult terrain during its many centuries of existence.[33]

The reality of cultural complexity we have been considering is part of the reason why I have long cringed at the use of terms such as Generation X, or postmoderns,[34] or the youth culture. These terms—which are frankly created and used chiefly by white, Western academicians—may serve some useful purposes in thinking about broad categories of people. But I fear they may, in the end, do more harm than good. A student of *the* youth culture—as if there really were such a thing—may think that she knows how to minister to teenagers because she understands youth culture, but she will be in for some surprises. In countless contexts, she will discover that there are other identifying marks of the kids—issues of national origin, race, ethnicity, socioeconomics, and so on—that are as powerful or more powerful in their lives. And as we have seen, an individual cannot be adequately understood by a single or simple broad brushstroke. It is not particularly helpful to say that such complexity can be expressed by reducing these youth to various subcultures. By what wisdom would we subsume a child's ethnicity—a nonnegotiable part of his reality—under an artificially constructed "youth culture" imposed on him by observers who live neither in his skin nor in his neighborhood?

Therefore, as we move across cultures to meet others—going boldly in the security of divine acceptance—we must strip ourselves of our outer garments, take up the servant's towel, and begin the work of washing feet, one pair at a time.

Affirming Christ's Lordship

Jesus, having loved his own to the full, "put on his clothes and returned to his place." Having laid down his life for his sheep, Jesus was

33. A full volume could easily be written on the biblical doctrine of listening. Some highlights would include consideration of the *shema* of Deuteronomy 6:4; the prophetic refrain "hear the word of the LORD"; careful study of the foundling church, especially in passages such as Acts 6, 13, 15, 17, and 18; and the command of Jesus in both the Gospels and Revelation: "Let the one who has an ear, hear."

34. Some will note that I have mentored a doctor of ministry track called "Ministry to Postmodern Generations." But in this track—which I was asked to lead—I work overtime to complicate the cultural understanding of my students.

exalted to the highest place and given the name above every name. Of him shall all creation confess, "Jesus is Lord!" Let us draw out three final thoughts from these things.

First, a question: When we have loved others, must we return to our own places? In fact, some will choose to stay put, adopting the new culture as their own and hoping that the new culture will, in turn, adopt them as its own. Others will stay even though they are fully aware that they will always be as a *xenos* (stranger) in this new land. Many, perhaps most, however, will return to the places from whence they came. But if they have truly loved, they will return as changed people. They may take up the familiar "garments" they once laid aside, but they will have new garments as well. Jesus did not cease being God when he became incarnate. Neither did he cease being truly man after resuming his place of glory. His incarnation changed him forever. The same will be true of us—if we have truly loved.

Second, a reminder: The point of all incarnations of divine love is that the lordship of Jesus Christ be affirmed to the glory of God the Father. By loving and serving incarnationally, we affirm that Jesus is Lord of all creation, not merely of our own spheres. Further, we affirm that the ultimate goal of loving another person is not that we might feel better about ourselves, nor even that the other person might be somehow aided by our "sacrifice." Instead, the ultimate goal is that the lordship of Jesus is declared and God is glorified.

Third, and finally, it is one thing to profess that Jesus is Lord of our lives; it is another to manifest the truth of that affirmation through obedience. Jesus told the Twelve that they were indeed *orthodox*—for they rightly called him "Teacher" and "Lord." But they now had to *do* the things they had learned. *Orthopraxis* must accompany orthodoxy. A servant is not above his master; if Jesus washed feet, so must we. A third *ortho-* is implicit in the John 13 and Philippians 2 passages: *orthopathy*.[35] In both passages, the *pathos* of Jesus is on full display. His heart is inclined to love his own sacrificially, to suffer loss on their behalf,

---

35. Perhaps the best articulation of the idea of biblically appropriate *pathos* is found in the writings of the great twentieth-century Jewish scholar Abraham Heschel. Heschel argues, for example, that the very evident *pathos* of the prophets is a reflection of the heart of God. He consistently affirms that "to the biblical mind the conception of God as detached and unemotional is totally alien" and is, instead, a view that emerges from the influence of the Greek philosophers. See Abraham J. Heschel, *The Prophets*, vol. 2 (Peabody, Mass.: Prince Press, 1962), 37ff. While some Christian thinkers may reject the idea of a divine *pathos* and argue instead for belief in the impassability of God (from the Latin *passio*, which is the term that corresponds to the Greek *pathos*, both terms literally referring to "suffering"), it is impossible to argue that Jesus, whose *passion* the church ever celebrates, was void of *pathos* or that Christians should be.

and, mysteriously, on behalf of the whole world (1 John 2:2). Is our *pathos* aligned with his?

The above meditations are intended as just that—meditations on the incarnational love of Jesus and its implications for us. We have focused attention on how this might look in a rather long-term relationship across cultures, but the same principles would apply to short-term relationships as well. Even in a first encounter with one who is a *xenos*, we can follow these principles. In fact, we can do the same with any neighbor, regardless of his or her ethnicity. When we desire to love, serve, and teach others, much depends on the inclinations of our own hearts. Having considered this in some depth, we now turn to congregational and educational strategies for forming such hearts in ourselves and in those we are called to serve.

7

The Formation Process
in a Learning Community

S. STEVE KANG

Theologian Karl Barth wrote, "To say atonement is to say Jesus Christ."[1] In Jesus Christ, God condescended, lived, and offered his life in true obedience. The obedience of the Son of God was purposive and effective.[2] His obedience was also revelatory. Jesus not only disclosed to us the eternal reality of the Triune God but also unveiled to us what it means to live as God's redeemed and thus how to live as kingdom citizens in the world. Christ exhorts those who are called to build up kingdom citizens through the teaching ministry of the church to partake in his incarnational ministry, as discussed in the previous chapter. A crucial dimension of participation in Christ's incarnational ministry is growth as a socioculturally sensitive teacher. As such, teachers are called to teach students, as kingdom citizens in this world, to engage various cultures and to transform society in the name of Jesus Christ. However, as seen in the previous chapter, a socioculturally sensitive teacher is not simply "credentialed" by securing a formal education or ordination or by involvement in a certain number of cross-cultural ministry projects. Instead, those who are called to participate in Christ's incarnational

1. Karl Barth, *Church Dogmatics IV/1* (Edinburgh: T & T Clark, 1956–75), 158.
2. John Webster, *Barth* (London: Continuum, 2000), 120–21.

ministry must seek to cultivate a *habitus Christi* throughout their lifetime, for we know that most often transformation takes place at the intersections—through mutual formation processes in which kingdom citizens together engage the dizzying array of this world's cultural permutations. In the process, we are called to invite, to create a space for the people of God to intentionally, habitually, and holistically engage in God-given formational moments throughout all aspects of life, thereby invoking the Holy Spirit to work in the community and lives of the people of God through those transforming moments. Indeed, teaching "requires devoted people, called by God, to make a difference in the lives of individuals, communities, and societies."[3]

For this purpose, true learning involves a holistic, formational process as an opportunity for the Holy Spirit's transformational work, which often takes place in and through the faith community. It consists of encouragement, empowerment, and guidance as people mature in the image of Christ and commune with the Triune God. The formation process simply becomes an invitation for students to enter, evaluate, and engage the various aspects of God's kingdom reality, which the teacher, subject matter, and learning activities seek to depict. Toward that end, teachers must constantly evaluate epistemological issues, sociocultural assumptions, and responsible scholarship as they explore theological trajectories, biblical narrative, and teaching-learning processes that provide the most compelling opportunities for students to encounter the Holy Spirit's transforming work.

Taking full advantage of what the learning community entails and offers is vital in forging a formation process. In general, the role of the learning community in conceptualizing formation has been routinely assumed rather than adequately understood and intentionally incorporated into the formational endeavor. Beginning with birth and ending with the last rite at the tomb, human beings function in varying degrees in communities such as families, circles of friends, neighborhoods, classrooms, workplaces, congregations, cultural enclaves, nations, and so on. In these intertwining spheres of life, informal and formal education constantly takes place.

God's elect in Jesus Christ, who are now gathered as the church in this world, are to be in communion with God's saints in time and space. This means that God's elect are, as Christ's community, to commune with the saints of the past and the present and for the saints of the future. Moreover, this communion should not be limited to the elect's geographical, homogenous, and preference-based surroundings. In

3. Robert Pazmiño, *The Basics of Teaching for Christians* (Grand Rapids: Baker, 1998), 7.

God's sovereignty, the global village of the world has become the *neighborhood* in which Christ's love must be practiced, shared, and extended. For many of us who have been socialized within individualistic cultures and privatized forms of Western Christianity, such a notion of communion is seen not only as an optional task but also as a theologically and culturally untenable one. Nevertheless, kingdom citizens are called to live as local faith communities, constantly seeking to benefit other, dissimilar parts of Christ's global church and growing in communion with saints, near and far, in an ever more interlocking manner. Through such God-honoring relationships and mutually building interactions, we shape and are shaped by the various parts of Christ's global church as kingdom citizens in this world.

At a more local level, as we teachers fully commit to encountering and being shaped through the communion of saints in God's time and space, we model authentic kingdom citizenship to our students. Such commitment signals that we are ready to hear and follow God's voice, through Jesus Christ and Scripture, in the context of historical church traditions and the rich experiences of the global church. Wherever holistic Christian formation takes place, we open ourselves up to appreciate, consider, and appropriate together the kingdom norms—values, patterns, and products—that are unfamiliar and unnatural to us. As we realize how much we have been shaped by and have lived by the sociocultural values, patterns, and products of *this* world, we begin to examine our present lives through kingdom norms; we wait upon the Triune God to shape us as the body of Christ so we can live out the kingdom norms here and now. In the process, we invite students to embark with us on this holistic, spiritual pilgrimage as kingdom citizens in this world. We must acknowledge that it is the Holy Spirit who has been working and continues to work in students' lives and that the Holy Spirit is the sovereign Lord of their individual lives and the transforming teacher within the learning community and the entire formation process.

For that reason, in the formation process, in which the Holy Spirit is the Lord and transforming teacher, we enter and embrace the reality of others and allow others to enter and embrace our own. When we commit to share our beliefs, experiences, knowledge, and feelings and, in turn, embrace the unique contributions of others, we know and are known as the citizens of God's eternal kingdom community. The more self-disclosure and embracing of one another there is—in terms of sharing the values, assumptions, and life views that are being sanctified through the work of the Triune God—the more potential there is for formation to take place among citizens of the kingdom community.

Transformation, again, takes place as a learning community and its individuals avail themselves of the Holy Spirit, who gently confronts with formational moments that "can foster a sense of wonder and awe about God and the amazing variety of God's creation"[4] *and culture.* As previously discussed, culture should not be seen as antithetical to the goodness of creation but as the result of God's intention for human beings to fill the earth through the processes, patterns, and products of human formation, which still unmistakably imbues and witnesses to God's splendor—despite the fact that it is "presently perverted and distorted by human disobedience to his will."[5]

To this end, the socioculturally sensitive teacher is to work hard to create a learning community in which the love of God is learned and practiced among already and not-yet kingdom neighbors near and far. Such a learning community should be characterized by a genuine posture of honesty and openness and, most importantly, receptivity to the Triune God's works of transformation. In this sense, learning communities are bonded together in compassion and responsibility; involvement, mutuality, and accountability are the core values that the learning community seeks to embody. The remainder of this chapter discusses some components of the formation process within such a learning community.

The Synergy of the Learning Community

Members of a learning community who desire to learn and grow together as kingdom citizens should enter into a mutual socialization process with one another. In short, the learning community, small or large, acting as the one body of Christ, is responsible for its collective formation. The modern word *synergy* gets its meaning from the Greek *synergos,* meaning "working together," through which the formation process will achieve a greater result. Recently, the students in one of my graduate courses, as a course assignment, were invited to investigate a country from Martin Gannon's *Understanding Global Cultures*[6] and present their findings to the class. In addition to preparing a handout describing the unique features of the nation, each student was to share one of Gannon's images or metaphors of the country through

4. Ibid., 50.

5. Richard Mouw, *When the Kings Come Marching In,* rev. ed. (Grand Rapids: Eerdmans, 2002), 11.

6. Martin J. Gannon, *Understanding Global Cultures: Metaphorical Journeys through Twenty-three Nations,* 2d ed. (Thousand Oaks, Calif.: Sage, 2001).

which fellow classmates could enter into the reality of that nation. For example, a student who was responsible for showcasing the nation of Turkey re-created the atmosphere of a Turkish coffee shop. Another student brought in a statue of the dancing Shiva, wore an Indian sari, and discussed her findings about the various cultures of India. Another student played Italian opera music in order to provide a "metaphor" for the nation of Italy while discussing the rich descriptions of that country. No doubt these images are indelibly imprinted on each class member's mind.

In the process, each student realized the importance of depicting his or her assigned nation adequately. He or she was the sole person responsible for a particular nation and for accurately displaying that nation's culture(s) and God's love for that nation. Students' individuality and uniqueness were disclosed as they sensed fellow students' openness and encouragement. More importantly, they sensed the connectedness between the Lord of their lives, their small learning community, and the nations they were presenting. In the process, the members of the learning community understood their vital roles in the community and became intentional in forging deeper relationships with one another, in class as well as with the global cultures, whose king is none other than the Triune God.

The Teacher and Students as Fellow Learners

Christian spiritual formation is a mutual pilgrimage among teacher and students. They are fellow pilgrims in a journey of discovery and intentional practice of God's kingdom in this world. All too frequently, people perceive formation as a damaging hierarchy in which the teacher is "the one who knows" and the students are seen as empty receptacles. Indeed, if this hierarchy is the primary mode of relationship between the teacher and students, the task of creating a formational atmosphere can easily become thwarted, and the richness of true formation will not be experienced. The teacher must utilize her authority appropriately to make it clear from the beginning that she is on the pilgrimage along with her students and is open and expecting to learn from them just as the students are expected to learn both from one another and the teacher. To achieve this, the teacher must consistently convey humility and openness in her interactions with students.

In a sense, to want to learn is to humble oneself. For a teacher to break away from the social norm of what is typically meant by "teacher" takes courage and commitment to the mutual formation process. Students remember not only *what* they learned in a class but also *how* they experienced the subject matter and *how* the teacher approached the subject matter and the students, especially in light of her allegiance to the sociocultural patterns, processes, and products of God's kingdom here and now. Students need to realize for themselves that formation never really comes to an end. In setting an example, teachers are to exhibit three important attitudes. First, the teacher is to model a love and desire for growth in witnessing to God's splendor, which is manifested in cultures near to and far from her own sociocultural location. Second, the teacher is to model a deep respect for all people and an understanding that one, especially a Christian, can learn from every person regardless of race, ethnicity, class, gender, or age. Specifically, this may involve inviting guest speakers who are *not* typically considered "authorities."

For some time, I have brought undergraduate students with unique cultural experiences and vocational trajectories into graduate-level courses. My aim is that graduate students be exposed to a particular topic from perspectives different from the perspectives of those traditionally seen as "experts." Recently, Lauren, an undergraduate senior, shared about her six-month internship working with disenfranchised women in black townships around Pietermaritzburg, South Africa, and how that internship, among other experiences in her life, led her to commit her life to serve disenfranchised women in the inner city of Chicago. I also invited Jennifer to share about her simple obedience to God's leading, which resulted in three years of ministry among male prostitutes in the Chicago area. Beforehand, I encouraged the graduate students to be fully present, with respect and receptive hearts, for the session. The class with Lauren and Jennifer was one of the most transformational times I have experienced in my teaching career.

Third, the teacher should allow herself to acknowledge humbly and freely that she does not know everything about her own sociocultural location and her areas of expertise. In the session with Lauren and Jennifer, I spoke truthfully about the strong impact the two undergraduate students had had on my life as I had witnessed their simple obedience to Christ and their quest to do God's work in various cultural settings. I shared a few stories of my experiences with the undergraduates, including my cross-cultural blunders when visiting Lauren in South Africa as her faculty mentor. As students witnessed my attitudes toward the two undergraduate students, I sincerely hope they were able to approach the learning experience as humble co-learners and will continue to seek both to learn and to create a formational process in their future ministries.

At the same time, however, it is necessary to recognize that the teacher's "co-learning" with her students must be paired with appropriate teaching authority. The socioculturally sensitive teacher must always make clear that, although she is learning alongside her students, she is nevertheless a guide and facilitator, and she has full authority and responsibility in the classroom. If this is not consistently clear, the classroom will become chaotic or relativistic, and there will ultimately be less freedom in which to learn, express, and grow. Classroom discussions have the potential for both freedom and limitations; passions can rise, and the teacher must be keenly sensitive as to when to intervene and exercise authority in facilitating the discussion. When students feel that their sociocultural assumptions and identities are being challenged or interrogated, it is only natural for them to become defensive and argumentative. They are then more likely to close themselves off from possible opportunities for transformation.

In two of my classes, we had a series of sessions surrounding Michael Emerson and Christian Smith's *Divided by Faith*.[7] While most majority students are in principle committed to racial reconciliation, many of them become defensive when they learn that one part of the book traces the Christian roots of racism and that in another part of the book the authors document the inadequate understandings and sociocultural tool kits that conservative Christians possess in terms of racial reconciliation. I take such a "crisis" in my learning community as a wonderful opportunity for formation to occur. When students' viewpoints differ from those of other students and even those of the teacher, it is an opportunity for the teacher to model respect. The conceptual leap to respecting those of other cultures should be welcomed as an opportunity for transformation. Therefore, as socioculturally sensitive teachers, we have the privilege to create a formation opportunity. We are responsible for negotiating a graceful balance between authority and humility, thus strengthening the delicate fabric of God's kingdom norms in such a way that the learning community as a whole is able to function fruitfully and effectively for Christ and his kingdom in this world.

The Teacher as Model and Friend

Not only is modeling important in conveying the teacher's attitude toward learning, as mentioned above, but it is also an essential and per-

7. Michael Emerson and Christian Smith, *Divided by Faith: Evangelical Religion and the Problem of Race in America* (New York: Oxford, 2000).

haps the primary way in which students learn from the teacher. Formation that is "kingdom-normed" is preoccupied with the living of an authentic kingdom life. True knowing or transformation in Christ involves not only our thoughts or assent to a set of beliefs but also our attitudes, actions, and lifestyles. In the learning community, small and large, we must constantly ask, "How can we facilitate the formation process in such a way that students can genuinely enter into the kingdom reality?" The teacher is an integral part of this process as she shares how she struggles to envision that reality and live in that reality in the world and as she avails herself as a model, literally, a miniature representation of something, to students in their pilgrimage as kingdom citizens.

As an imperfect model of a kingdom citizen, I look for areas of my life that might serve as connecting points or openings through which students can witness aspects of the kingdom reality. Rather than merely using certain aspects of my life as an illustration for a thought I want to communicate, I try to paint a picture of how I struggle to let the kingdom reality engulf all aspects of my life in this world. One major goal in my teaching, then, is to model how we are to live in this world as aliens and strangers, continually being transformed so that our commitments and life trajectories are based on our eternal communion with saints in God's kingdom. As an example of the formation process, I invite students to observe how I receive, analyze, and appropriate the kingdom reality from the many contexts of my life. I ask them to be conversation partners with me in such endeavors. In the process, I hope they will learn to receive, analyze, and appropriate the kingdom reality from their own life contexts within the context of the learning community.

In this sense, the learning community functions as a sociocultural context in which its participants can reveal their assumptions, commitments, interests, gifts, and life trajectories in such a way that their fellow participants can witness and thus encourage the Holy Spirit's work in their lives. Such an openness also provides the opportunity for fellow participants in the learning community to offer criticisms and challenges from their perspectives, which are shaped by the work of the Holy Spirit in them. Thus, the learning community is nothing less than a sacred space in which the Holy Spirit guides the mutual transformation process. Toward that end, the teacher serves as a priest who embodies God's redemption of all creation and all culture and reminds fellow pilgrims of this redemption. The teacher also takes on a prophetic role in that she challenges fellow pilgrims to continue to envision and dwell in God's kingdom reality. When fellow pilgrims witness the teacher consistently and resolutely struggling to live out the kingdom reality in this world, they will want to consider and emulate her attitudes and actions.

When the teacher does not take the sociocultural dimension of Christian formation seriously and does not authentically live out kingdom norms in and outside the learning community, students will probably not take her seriously *inside* the learning community. The learning community then fails to be the generative kingdom life that the participants desperately need. When teachers do not avail themselves to students outside the learning community, specifically to allow students to witness the ways in which they live out the kingdom reality, formation becomes contrived and stops being transformative. Demanding as it may be for teachers, Christian formation must exceed the boundaries of the learning community. The teacher must take the time to know—and to be known by—her students.

In my own experience, when I invest myself in friendships with students outside the limited confines of the learning community, often becoming a kind of pastor-mentor-friend to them, we develop a mutual respect for one another as "real persons" who struggle to live out God's kingdom vision for the world here and now. Time and again, such efforts enhance the quality of the experience in the learning community, and we learn to dwell in the kingdom reality in an increasingly more tangible and mutual manner. This happens as I freely admit my limitations and students see that we have the same struggles. Thus, we are able to relate to one another on a deeper level of transparency, and students are more willing to be intentional about engaging in the formation process.

The Teacher as Enabler

In stressing the importance of outside interactions, we must not downplay what happens within the learning community. The ways in which a teacher interacts with her students in the confines of the learning community are particularly important because within the learning community formation is intensified as both the teacher and students choose to enter the formation process and seek the Holy Spirit to transform them. Therefore, the classroom must be a safe and hospitable place. The teacher ought to be intentional about fostering a sense of mutual love and respect within the community. The teacher must also encourage a commitment within the community to enter into one another's lives. In doing so, the teacher helps the students experience themselves as an integral part of the learning community.

One way in which I try to foster such an atmosphere is by discovering the God-given strengths, gifts, and experiences unique to each student and then by calling on each student to share those strengths and gifts with the community throughout the learning process. I encourage students to share their learning in substantial *and* creative ways, utilizing various assignments that are designed to maximize students' holistic encounters with the subject matter. Similarly, whenever possible, I permit wide latitude in learning experiences so that each student can respond to the course content in a way consonant with his or her unique personhood and vocational goal. While this can initially frustrate those who are accustomed to boundaries and tightly defined requirements, the ensuing freedom permits a richness and depth of understanding as well as products that are not only substantial but also enjoyable and transformational for all. I also try to create a safe and hospitable environment by encouraging students to take on the perspectives of those they might consider "others"—a person or group with different life experiences and circumstances. In that way, students are persuaded to think outside their own experiences and assumptions about a given issue. They often feel enabled to broaden their limited horizons and also develop many significant relationships with those they once considered to be others.

As an example, Daniel, a student of mine, learned much about how the blue-collar workers at our college's physical plant perceive their tenuous and troublesome relationship with the institution's white-collar workers. Such a class analysis enabled Daniel to learn a great deal about how God's kingdom can be so easily divided along the socioeconomic line. A personal benefit for him was that he developed some lasting relationships with several physical plant workers. Kristi is another example. She was interested in learning about the experience of African-American female students at a predominantly Caucasian residential college. She spent an entire semester as a participant observer. In the end, Kristi not only became a strong advocate for the female minority students on campus but was also invited to enter the subcultures of these students.

Another way I try to enable students is in the area of sociocultural analysis. For instance, after reading Jonathan Kozol's *Amazing Grace*,[8] chronicling the horrific realities of living in the South Bronx, I invite students to divide into groups of two or three and have them present a biblical or theological exposition on God's heart for the downtrodden and for the cities. In the process, students encounter God's heart for the

8. Jonathan Kozol, *Amazing Grace: The Lives of Children and the Conscience of a Nation* (New York: HarperPerennial, 1995).

downtrodden in passages of Scripture or juxtapose a city in the Bible with the South Bronx. Such a project allows students to interact more deeply with God's heart for the poor as well as their plight. Students often muse about their response, as kingdom citizens who are called to embody Jesus Christ, to such vexing world problems. The learning community, when perceived as a community that also yearns to realize God's kingdom, has much potential to function as the body of Christ, in which each member is different yet uniquely necessary to complete the whole.

Teachers must also believe in their students and continually urge them to exceed what they see as their limitations. Encouragement and appreciation are crucial components in a learning community, but if these are not combined with stretching and challenging holistic encounters, formation will cease to take place and the community will become stagnant. Feeling safe does not necessarily mean always feeling comfortable. The teacher must have the courage to push students out of their individual as well as collective comfort zones. To be able to pinpoint where a student is complacent or limited in her assumptions, abilities, experiences, and vocational trajectories, the teacher must know each student well and have his or her trust. Whatever the areas of complacency and limitation may be, it is imperative for the teacher to gently challenge her, in specific ways, to move beyond those limiting situations. In turn, the teacher should invite students to voice their questions and reflections to the teacher as well as to fellow members of the learning community. The teacher might consider instituting a policy in which a student cannot speak a second time until a majority of fellow students has spoken. This can foster a sense of equality and mutual respect, and it can ensure that the conversation is balanced rather than dominated by a few more vocal students or by a single point of view. This is one of the greatest challenges the teacher faces in the classroom, but with intentionality and foresight, a space for all to contribute can be created. This is particularly important in order to hear what the shyer, less vocal students have to say. A simple, "Let's hear what a few others have to say, maybe someone who hasn't said anything yet" can be enough to elicit sharing from quieter students. Moreover, since students who represent non-majority cultures of the community often feel silenced and marginalized, it is imperative for the teacher to observe and converse with such students and try to draw forth the gifts that they bring to the learning community. In the process, the learning community will be strengthened and God, the giver of every good gift, will be glorified.

The Teacher as Innovator

To promote a holistic learning experience that consistently encounters the kingdom reality, the teacher should develop creative ways to present ideas, challenges, and growth opportunities. Creative teaching methods might include the use of sociocultural narratives, generative themes and images, music, case studies, media analysis, simulation, group work, research projects, field trips, and more. These various methods provide opportunities for students to enter into the formation process in a holistic and realistic manner. They are invited to use not only their reason but also the holy imagination, intuition, and senses that have been entrusted to all human beings by God the Creator and are being continually sanctified by the Holy Spirit.

For instance, in one course, I ask students to enter into a reality by choosing two varying perspectives that are shaped by different epistemological positions (i.e., critical realism, naïve idealism, instrumentalism, etc.). After reading and reviewing the epistemological positions, students write two short essays, in first-person narrative form, describing an issue or topic from these two varying perspectives. Students then discuss an issue using one of their perspectives. After the discussion, students try to guess which position each student was taking during the discussion.

Sometimes I prepare a devotional from a particularly moving book about a wretched story of an inner-city family. Other times I invite students to write in free form, stream of consciousness about a sociocultural narrative we read together. Sometimes I assign readings on a theological topic written not only from the perspective of the Western church but also from non-Western and minority perspectives, in which cases the issues of race, ethnicity, class, gender, and generation are intertwined. Or I invite students to present a chapter from a book on the immigration history of both majority and minority ethnic groups in a city such as Chicago. Then the students showcase ethnic groups in an oral presentation complete with props to help fellow learners engage in the reality of that culture. The options are endless. These and other methods should be used, where appropriate, to encourage formation that is kingdom advancing. Creative teaching methods should not be used merely for the sake of variety.

I am particularly fond of field trips, planning at least one horizon-expanding trip for almost every class I teach. Such trips usher students into the reality of the topic or people in focus. These trips also deepen the sense of a learning community as students encounter new experiences together in a different environment. Living near a major city provides a phenomenal opportunity for this type of field trip. On a recent field trip to Chicago, students divided themselves into groups according to the areas they wanted to visit. Multicultural enclaves such as Chinatown or areas where Germans, Swedes, Latinos, Koreans, or East Indians congregated were an option, as were religious centers such as a Ba'hai temple in a wealthy suburb and a Hindu temple. Based on the itineraries I provided, each group of students spent several hours exploring parts of the city. At the beginning of their multicultural and religious quest, each group was provided with a sheet with tips on transportation and food, background information, and what they might encounter in the neighborhoods they were visiting. After several hours of exploration, the groups met in a central location and enthusiastically shared not only stories but also ethnic samplings of food and other artifacts.

In another course, I take students who have not had much exposure to church history to a Benedictine monastery that has preserved much of its tradition from the sixth century. For another course, I require students to visit churches or other Christian organizations that work with population groups different from the majority population of those organizations. This allows students to observe and analyze how members of these organizations attempt to live out the kingdom life in this world. Finally, over the years my family has considered it a ministry to invite my classes to our home for a full course Korean meal and wide-ranging guest speakers. Among other benefits, this experience has aided in deepening relationships between myself and the students in a more holistic manner.

Ethnographic research is a particularly transformative practice to which socioculturally sensitive teachers can expose students. The crux of ethnographic research is to understand the behaviors of people and the meanings they make of their experiences within a specific sociocultural context. It is an excellent bridge from one culture to another, as students with teachable hearts engage another culture. This is a painstaking, involved process that requires intentionality on the part of students as well as the teacher. The teacher's role is to provide a thorough examination of the various paradigms of epistemological perspectives, such as critical realism and social constructionism. Clearly, this examination is necessary if one is to accept another culture as valid and equal in worth to one's own. It is crucial to understand that no one culture or subculture is inherently wrong or right. For example, it was a new realization for one student that the abundant littering she found in South America is due more to a lack of formation (no "Give a hoot, don't pollute" or "Help keep America lookin' good" slogan from the media) than to an inherent lack of cleanliness of the culture. Therefore, from many observations, interviews, artifact collecting, literature review, data coding, data analysis, and so on, students are enlightened and able to take in a new subculture without judgment.

Ethnographic research, when done with a spirit of humility and openness, provides the researcher with access to another's world—an opportunity to touch, think, and feel within that world—in order to better understand that world and its occupants. Ethnography leads to greater understanding, hospitality, and ultimately shalom—peace—among the researcher and those from whom she is learning. This, when coupled with intentional cultural and multicultural exposure, fosters a unique generosity of spirit. No doubt, our Lord Jesus Christ exuded this same spirit. There is no limit to innovation in creating learning communities that provide opportunities for the formation of kingdom citizens.

The Teacher as Questioner

In terms of what is being learned, a realistic look at difficult issues is vital to the formation of kingdom citizens. Making space in a learning community means allowing students to raise questions that may not have easy answers. When a teacher makes space for formation to take place, she listens more than she speaks. She guides the questioning process rather than giving answers that close the discussion, thus discouraging further questioning. Often, the learning community's process of questioning and learning is much more valuable than the final conclusion. One such example occurred with a discussion of Randall Balmer's *Mine Eyes Have Seen the Glory*,[9] which explores a wide variety of evangelical groups, ranging from a Christian film company to a Christian rock group to a Billy Graham Crusade to a small, fundamentalist Bible college. As students explored the forces and influences that shaped these groups, they engaged in the deep work of soul-searching and introspection. Again, allowing students to struggle with a difficult issue is important in the formation process. As difficult as it may be, teachers should resist the temptation to bring instant closure. Instead, they should leave difficult questions unanswered—and perhaps even raise relevant counterpoints—if the nature of the question is complex, as the most important questions usually are.

9. Randall Balmer, *Mine Eyes Have Seen the Glory: A Journey into the Evangelical Subculture in America*, 3d ed. (New York: Oxford, 2000).

Difficult questions should, of course, never be ignored because often the most difficult questions are of the greatest value in formation. Teachers should raise the real issues in class, the issues of greatest importance, with a spirit of honesty and inquiry. Questions about theodicy, remedies for structural sins, the silence of God, racism, classism, sexism, the modern captivity of the church, ethnic cleansing, generations of hatred among certain groups, injustice, and the mysterious nature of faith are some of the critical issues that I encourage students to tackle. For example, when studying the issue of racism in the church, I provide the students with a copy of a letter from the president of a conservative Christian college defending the school's policy of limited African-American enrollment. I also provide articles published by a so-called white Christian supremacy group about the biological superiority of those with a white European background. This is a sad, even tragic reality that exists and is a part of modern American church history. As a Christian teacher, I have a duty to remind students that issues such as racism are not a problem of those who overtly champion the cause but a complex issue that is endemic in the church of Jesus Christ, which often and unfortunately mirrors the patterns and attitudes of society at large.

The teacher should encourage students, as kingdom citizens, to invest thought and energy into considering these important issues. The teacher should take every opportunity to expose students to the rich variety of persons, experiences, and "othernesses" that exist in the communion of saints who represent God's kingdom in the world. These exposures might happen during field trips to new places, by watching videos of people whose backgrounds or cultures are different from those of the students, or simply by encouraging open dialogue among all students within the learning community.

As a follow-up to reading Balmer's book, I showed a short clip of the PBS documentary of the same title. Students were fascinated by the contrast between a backwater African-American Pentecostal congregation in Mississippi and Willow Creek Community Church in the comfortable Chicago suburb of Barrington, Illinois. In the rich discussion that ensued, a student contemplated his own tendency to relegate "emotional experiences" to the lower-class minority races. Another student admitted stereotyping African-American males as the source of all social problems in America.

When the learning community experiences these encounters, they become God-ordained opportunities for spiritual formation. Through these experiences, more often than not, the Holy Spirit brings about transformation in members of the learning community as well as in those whom the members have and will have contact with. In a safe and hospitable learning community, members have the freedom to challenge one another's stereotypes and worldviews. Change, growth, and strengthening of kingdom citizens are propelled by critical reflection on one's beliefs. Although discussing challenging issues can be temporarily uncomfortable and threatening to some, when it is done within a safe community of mutually respectful, patient, and understanding members who welcome the opportunity to learn from one another and to grow, these discussions—however passionate they may become— can be incredibly powerful and transformative.

A Learning Community That Is a Holistic, Loving, God-Glorifying Community

In a learning community, we come to know ourselves as we are known by God. True learning is a holistic process of formation and transformation, occurring best in and through a safe and hospitable learning community in which members yearn for God's kingdom to be realized in their lives as well as in the world. The teacher and the students are traveling together on a pilgrimage toward the ever intensifying vision of God's kingdom. Together, they encourage one another to enter the formation process so they can experience eternal communion with the Triune God as they have communion with fellow saints of God's historical and multicultural kingdom.

As we learn to engage fully with the world as kingdom citizens, we must strive to forge effective methods of teaching that help Christians to understand and live wholly within that kingdom. This chapter introduced some methods that have helped students to critique their faith journeys. It explored the ways in which a committed community is a loving and thus life-transforming community. This chapter also revealed some possible ways to integrate various Christian practices and church life in order to fulfill the constitutive/constructive role of the faith community. In our individually wrapped, highly segregated world, it is imperative for Christians to become border crossers, to live as kingdom citizens with robust kingdom theologies, to be fully present in two worlds simultaneously, and, ultimately, to draw the lost world to Jesus Christ himself, who is our only peace.

8

From Hospitality to Shalom

ELIZABETH CONDE-FRAZIER

This chapter provides a spiritual journey as the framework within which the biblical and theological principles and the educational theories proposed in the preceding chapters can be carried out. Additional critical pedagogies and methods accompany each segment of the framework.

Culture has been defined as the total pattern of a people's behavior that is learned and transmitted by the symbols (language, rights, artifacts) of a particular group. These symbols focus on certain ideas or assumptions that become a worldview.[1] Culture expresses the values and purposes of each community as well as its sensitivities and spirituality.

Evangelicals historically have been concerned that cultural influences not challenge or dilute the authority of Christ and his Word. We cannot, however, ensure this by avoiding culture. We cannot isolate ourselves from our culture. Our very understanding of Christ and his Word is mediated to some degree by our culture. We are products of our culture, and we therefore read Scripture and formulate theological understandings through cultural lenses. A cultural perception of Christian truth and Scripture can be used to enhance our understanding of the

---

1. W. A. Dyrness, "Christianity and Culture," in *Evangelical Dictionary of Theology*, ed. Walter A. Elwell (Grand Rapids: Baker, 2001), 212.

gospel "until we all reach unity in the faith and in the knowledge of the Son of God" (Eph. 4:13).[2]

Throughout history, the church has taken different positions on the relationship between faith and culture. What stands in the midst of these diverse views is the acceptance that faith is transmitted in cultural forms. Faith also calls us to be in relationship with one another regardless of our cultures. How one relates cross-culturally and how these issues play out in an educational environment are the topics at hand.

James Whitehead and Evelyn Eaton Whitehead consider the role of culture in their method of theological reflection.[3] They suggest three outcomes of the interplay between the tradition or the beliefs and practices of faith and culture. In the first, tradition, displaying Christianity in its prophetic role, challenges the culture. In the second, tradition is challenged by the culture. This can be seen in movements such as the civil rights movement, itself influenced by religious convictions, that have challenged Christianity to self-examination and reformation. In the last, tradition uses the resources of the culture to carry out its own mission. One such resource can be the social sciences. I often make use of the social sciences as a resource for multicultural Christian education. I use them as a tool that informs educational practices and also facilitates a dialogue to clarify and challenge educational practices.

Many have understood multicultural Christian education to be about the how-to's of teaching. According to this view, such education involves teaching in ways that go beyond linear thinking and relating to students who are not of the dominant culture. The references in this work will include some of that information. But multicultural teaching and ministry involve more. They involve a heart or a spirit for a journey that will transform us. For me, multicultural teaching has entailed developing an understanding of my own prejudices and how the work of the Holy Spirit in me modifies and slowly eliminates them. It is the spiritual journey that makes this type of teaching challenging and life producing. The how-to's will help us produce results, but such results are often superficial and temporary. Multicultural Christian education is not a program or a set of results. It is a ministry and, as such, must bear fruit. Fruit is seed producing, which means that it contains the seeds for continuous life to come forth. This type of teaching must involve the entire teaching/learning environment, the students, the administration, the congregation, the chapel services, the connections the school has with the community and the board of trustees, and their vision for the

---

2. Ibid., 214.

3. James D. Whitehead and Evelyn Eaton Whitehead, *Method in Ministry: Theological Reflection and Christian Ministry* (San Francisco: Harper, 1980).

entire teaching ministry of the school. It is for this reason that multicultural teaching is a spiritual journey that touches the heart of the barriers that have been present in our society and that have hindered us from creating relationships that bear witness to the kingdom of God.

Several spiritual practices are involved in this spiritual journey. They are hospitality, encounter, compassion, passion, and shalom. These insights are not unique. When I have presented them in different settings, people have resonated with them because the Spirit who leads us to all truth (John 16:13) had already been leading them on this spiritual journey. This chapter explores a spirituality for multicultural living, teaching, and ministry by presenting the theological and biblical foundations of each discipline and by exploring the implications that each has for teaching. Epistemological and pedagogical considerations are also a part of this discourse.

The Biblical Roots for a Christian Spirituality of Multicultural Living

A Christian way of life is composed of various activities that provide concrete ways for us to flourish. A spiritual practice is carried out, therefore, not because it works but because it is good. It is a way of connecting with God, our neighbors, and our environment. The outcome of the practice is beyond us, but it is something we do together consistently. In this way, we help one another grow. We learn the practices in small increments of daily faithfulness. A Christian practice of spirituality is one that is part of our daily lives and is "all tangled up with the things God is doing in the world."[4] To become so entangled makes us partners in God's reconciling love for the world. Becoming multicultural people or congregations involves yearning to be partners with God in the ministry of reconciliation.

As we saw above, the New Testament and early church communities developed in a multicultural context. Early on, they had to cross cultural boundaries. The incarnation and Pentecost informed the New Testament legacy on these matters. The Holy Spirit reveals Jesus Christ, God incarnate, to us. The Spirit reveals the Word that became flesh and lived among us and summons us to continue to incarnate God in the world. What does it mean to incarnate God today? Hispanic theologian Samuel Solivan explains the meaning of incarnation by pointing first to

4. Craig Dykstra and Dorothy Bass, "Times of Yearning, Practices of Faith," in *Practicing Our Faith*, ed. Dorothy C. Bass (San Francisco: Jossey-Bass, 1997), 8.

the Gospel of John: "The Word became flesh and lived among us, and we have seen his glory, the glory as of a father's only son, full of grace and truth" (John 1:14 NRSV). This begins to inform our attitudes toward diversity. Solivan posits that the incarnation requires "that divinity take on a foreign identity as flesh . . . our human existence."[5] We are called to venture into the world of our neighbor, which may be different or even strange to us at times yet also very much like our own. The incarnation calls us to dislocate ourselves from that which is familiar and to relocate ourselves in fellowship with those who are different from us. It is in the incarnation that we behold the glory of God. As we move to the Pentecost event, the account of the outpouring of the Spirit of God, we find that it discloses to us what God wills in the world: unity amid diversity. "Not a suspension of difference but the free and liberating inclusion of difference mediated by the Holy Spirit in hope, love, and peace."[6]

Pentecost points us toward some of our goals for becoming a multicultural community. It reveals that the church is a multiethnic, multilingual, and multiracial body. It shows that diversity is enriching and enabling of Christian unity rather than threatening. The Spirit enables us to value and affirm our own culture while engaging in effective ways with another culture. Pentecost also invites us to appreciate the many ways that faith is expressed in the practices of Christians from various cultures.[7]

These goals challenge both the cultural minority church as well as the cultural majority church. First, cultural minority churches need to assist their members to identify themselves as full human beings, people with experiences, histories, and aspirations. Second, cultural majority congregations need to become aware of their own cultural imperialism. They need to affirm the cultural heritage of each person and teach attitudes of respect and appreciation for other cultures. Respect is not demonstrated by becoming blind to cultural differences. This simply renders them invisible. Instead, we must acknowledge the differences and participate in them. In the Book of Acts (16:15), when Lydia met Paul, she challenged him by saying, "If you have judged me to be faithful to the Lord, come and stay at my home" (NRSV). Jesus also

5. Samuel Solivan, "The Holy Spirit-Personalization and the Affirmation of Diversity: A Pentecostal Hispanic Perspective," in *Teología en Conjunto: A Collaborative Hispanic Protestant Theology*, ed. José David Rodríguez and Loida I. Martell Otero (Louisville: Westminster John Knox, 1997), 59.

6. Ibid., 60.

7. Adapted from the original goals in Barbara Wilkerson, "Goals of Multicultural Religious Education," in *Multicultural Religious Education*, ed. Barbara Wilkerson (Birmingham, Ala.: Religious Education Press, 1997), 26–27.

placed himself in the position of encountering Gentile peoples (Matt. 15:21–28; John 4:4–26). This is where we need to position ourselves.

Ultimately, exposure to another culture at the relational level helps us to realize that politics, education, and history are culturally influenced. This awareness or consciousness raising will help us to develop strong analysis and relational skills. It will help us to develop a more balanced approach to cultural diversity that involves a healthy curiosity about other cultures and appreciation, true valuation, and respect of other cultures and people from those cultures.[8]

Hospitality

The first step in multicultural living is hospitality. It is a practice that brings us into closer alignment with the basic values of the kingdom. It is a part of worshiping Jesus. In Matthew 25, to offer food, shelter, and protection to one of the little ones is to offer it to Jesus. Luke 14 and the parable of inviting those who cannot repay us to the banqueting table is another image of hospitality. During the fourth and fifth centuries, the church founded various institutions for the care of pilgrims and the poor. The monastic communities held the demands of hospitality in tension with the ideal of separation from the world as they carried the Christian tradition of hospitality through the Middle Ages.[9]

Hospitality creates a place where we are connected to one another. It is a space that is safe, personal, and comfortable. It is a place of respect, acceptance, and friendship. A pastor going through a traumatic divorce sought hospitality. His friend invited people who had also gone through the experience of divorce to meet the pastor at his home. As they shared their journeys with him, they offered him empathy and hope. He was included in an environment that was life giving. His friend offered him a life-sustaining network of relations.

Notice that the place of hospitality offers attentive listening and a mutual sharing of lives and life stories. When I pastored in New England, people often wished to get to know Hispanics, and our congregation was invited to countless potluck dinners. It was difficult to make these experiences meaningful because there were many barriers between us. On one occasion, I arranged an evening when we could share our lives with one another. Both communities chose four people to share, and we had a passionate, humorous, and dramatic time of story-

8. See Kathy Black, *Culturally Conscious Worship* (St. Louis: Chalice Press, 2000).
9. Christine D. Pohl, *Making Room: Recovering Hospitality as a Christian Tradition* (Grand Rapids: Eerdmans, 1999), 6.

telling. This required of us an openness of our hearts and a willingness to make our lives visible and available to one another. Hospitality calls us to enlarge our hearts by offering our time and personal resources.

Christine Pohl writes about the recovery of hospitality as a Christian tradition. She notes that because acts of hospitality participate in and reflect God's greater hospitality, they connect us to the divine, to holy ground. It is a practice of worship as well as a life-giving practice.[10]

Hospitality is related to human dignity and respect for persons. The theological basis for this respect is that the image of God is found in every person. Also, we were made for others, and we depend on others. We can sympathize with the needs and suffering of others because we have a common nature.

Hospitality as recognition involves respecting the image of God in others and seeing their potential contributions as being of equal value to ours. Valuing is of the utmost, for when persons are not valued, they become socially invisible and their needs and concerns are not acknowledged. Therein lies the root of social injustice and suffering. Pohl rightfully points out that hospitality begins a journey toward visibility.[11] It is a spiritual journey that brings us from practicing hospitality on a one-on-one basis to practicing hospitality that defies the social arrangements of class, ethnicity, or race. In this way, the practice of hospitality rearranges our relationships.

When we practice the rearrangement of relationships through even the smallest act of respect and welcome rather than disregard and dishonor, we point to a different system of values and to an alternate model of relationships. Through this act of resisting the devaluing of people, we witness to the importance of transcending social differences and breaking sociocultural boundaries that are exclusive. This practice also helps us to resist the temptation of working for social change from a distance.

John Wesley recognized the importance of intentionally forming relationships that crossed boundaries. He noticed that when people were in contact with their poor neighbors, they could better understand their situation and could respond more effectively. When we dislocate ourselves from our usual places of work, school, worship, and residence, we can participate in self-giving and loving service to others.

Expressions of hospitality are to be exercised in a particular spirit or attitude of the heart. John Chrysostom was sensitive to the fragility of recipients of hospitality that resulted from their dependence on others. In various homilies, he exhorted his congregation to show "excessive

10. Ibid., chap. 1.
11. Ibid., 62.

joy" in order to avoid shaming recipients. He stressed the importance of respect and humility when offering hospitality.[12] The spirit of hospitality is joy, and Romans 12:8 encourages givers to be generous. Hospitality sprouts into compassion and, as with all the other gifts, is to be exercised in order to build up or edify the body.

In Greek, one of the words for edify is *katartizō*, which is a word used to signify the resetting and healing of a bone that has been broken and has healed improperly. The theological/biblical vision for multiculturalism is that of edification, the healing of wrong arrangements in relationships. It is a ministry of reconciliation.

Hospitality in the classroom depends on the teacher's initiative, since the teacher has the power to structure the learning environment. Hospitality in this context includes such factors as student-teacher interaction, understanding how culture results in various logic styles, and understanding worldviews.[13] When attempting to understand worldviews, it is vital to understand perspectives regarding time, family, competition, and orientation toward time.

A study on teaching in cross-cultural settings found that the most effective professors not only tried to understand the cultures of their students but also took time to make themselves known to their students. They shared their own customs, interests, preferences, and worldviews.[14] Hospitality encourages mutuality.

Self-awareness is vital for teachers who wish to express behavior that values the views of people from all backgrounds. Often, the differential treatment that occurs in interaction with students is inadvertent. Teachers need to develop pedagogical skills that meet the affective and cognitive needs of all students. A willingness to make curriculum modifications and provide academic support is necessary. Methods of teaching should provide equal access to learning in the classroom.

As a person from a culture in which the affective domain is as important for learning as the cognitive, I create syllabi that include a variety of learning activities. These activities require students to be engaged with communities outside the classroom. For example, students in a class on Christian education and the family had to work with three to seven families with the purpose of understanding their issues and find-

12. John Chrysostom, Homily 45 on Acts NPNFL, vol. II. p. 276, quoted in ibid., 269.
13. For further discussion on these factors as they relate to dominant culture professors and minority student learning, see Carol A. Jenkins and Deborah L. Bainer, "Common Instructional Problems in the Multicultural Classroom," *Journal on Excellence in College Teaching* 2 (1991): 77–88.
14. See R. Scollon, *Teacher's Questions about Alaska Native Education* (Fairbanks, Alaska: University of Alaska Center for Cross Cultural Studies, 1981).

ing ways to address them through creative means of Christian education in the home or as a group of families or as a congregation. Interaction with the families was a text along with the required readings. In
like manner, students in a course on education across the lifespan had
to focus on a particular age group for a final project. Students were expected to work with the group in a church or community setting during
the course of the semester. The students who learn well in this way are
very engaged in these, while the students who are accustomed to the
more traditional Western ways of learning are panic-stricken. I have
learned to support all students in this type of learning and to spend
more time explaining the educational value of these activities.

The goal of hospitality in the classroom is to create a learning setting
in which one can appreciate individual uniqueness, the complexity of
group identities (including intra-group differences), and the common
human characteristics we share cross-culturally. Educator Peter Frederick identifies ways of doing this. They include exposing students to powerful, evocative quotations about cultural identity and using evocative
visuals (cartoons, photographs, and videos) that reinforce issues about
cultural identity. After students make descriptive observations about the
images, they are asked to make descriptive observations about cultural
identity and to reflect on self definition in hyphenated words such as
Ukrainian-Slovakian or New York-American. One can also look for common themes, patterns, and issues that emerge in the observations and
the discussion.[15]

Another way to create hospitality is to allow for different learning
styles in the learning process. Data, experiences, practical knowledge,
and projects are valued by different types of learners. Sometimes these
tendencies grow out of the ways of learning in different cultural contexts. Such contexts relate to culture, as in Vietnamese or Samoan, as
well as gender and class.

One way to become aware of the different ways students learn is by
asking them to remember a time when they did the most learning. The
students then describe how their learning took place by speaking about
the steps involved and the forms that facilitated it. They should also talk
about the feelings they had along the way. Emotions are important in
the process of learning, for they reveal the places of resistance and empowerment. Emotions need to be treated as an integrated part of the
process rather than as a disturbance in the learning setting.

Hospitality can also take the form of mediating a transition in the
learning of students. Critical thinking is a rite of passage from inno-

15. See Peter Frederick, "Walking on Eggs? Mastering the Dreaded Diversity Discussion," *College Teaching* 43, no. 3 (summer 1995): 83, 92.

cence to awareness. We need rituals rich with symbols that help people come to places of conversion. In the same way that some traditions have a ritual of making a decision for Christ, such as lifting one's hand, so too we must acknowledge the moments of conversion in our classroom. This helps all involved to affirm the new places where they now stand.

In one undergraduate class, we look at passages in Scripture that relate to relationships between men and women. We also look at how these passages affect the understandings we have about men and women in ministry. New awareness is frightening to both the men and the women in the class. I usually allow students to speak about what they are feeling, and we have times of reflection outside of class to discuss the new places we feel ourselves going. We also have a time of meditation and journaling. There is a small altar in the front of the classroom, and students decorate it with symbols that are meaningful to them. On some occasions, they place pictures on the altar that represent their new understandings.

In a class with graduate students preparing for the ministry, we deal with issues of prejudice. Students often come to powerful moments of repentance, at which time they write their prejudices on pieces of paper and place them at the altar. They can then burn these papers in a litany of confession and forgiveness.

A welcoming spirit in the learning setting also allows for mutual negotiation and evaluation of the educational process. I may start the process by listing options in the syllabus. A quarter of the way into the course, I ask students to assess what has been the most and the least helpful (readings, small groups, lectures, simulations, fieldwork, research). I then make adjustments that will give shape to a more accessible learning process for all. Three-quarters of the way into the semester, we talk about the best form for the final requirements of the course. I base the decision on the goals I have set for the course and the individual goals of the students.

It is important to understand power dynamics in the classroom. Teachers have much power (the power of the grade) and authority. The institution where I teach invests certain power in me. Authority is earned and may be based on expertise. We are the decision makers. We decide on content, method, and criteria for evaluation. We also control the environment and ethos of the classroom—when breaks are given, who speaks and when, and who is affirmed. Students also have power. It begins with the power of their wills, their will to learn or to disobey, to contradict, harass, submit, or resist. Judith and Sherwood Lingenfelter point out that "through the engagement of will, teachers and students create an emotional climate."[16] They also remind us that the power issues of a classroom become more complex when there are cultural differences involved. This is because an understanding of authority and power is culturally bound. Our culture is the lens through which we see the world. Culture also determines how we relate to one another and therefore what arrangement of power dynamics is acceptable in different situations. While it clarifies things for us and makes us comfortable, culture also has its blinders and keeps us from seeing beyond it. It is through culture that we look at behavior, criteria, and feedback. Culture is our medium of interpretation.

To review, hospitality in the teaching/learning setting involves:

- being open to the voice and message of the stranger
- allowing the space to consider something new and different
- listening to the point at which even our own view is re-informed or expanded
- giving all students the right to learn
- creating a banquet table from which none are excluded

Encounter

Who knows one culture, knows no culture. We come to self knowledge on the boundary.[17]

An encounter is where we risk. It is a place for the collision of two worlds—for the multiplicity of views. It is where various streams meet. It is the bringing together of a variety of sources that might not often be placed together. This is the borderland. In these spaces, hybrid significations are created, requiring the practice of cultural translations and negotiations. It is here that we transcend dualistic modes of thinking and come to understand how opposing ideas can interact with one another. This place is called *mestizo/a* consciousness. Gloria Anzaldúa describes this term as a continual walking out of one culture and into another.[18] It is the transfer of the cultural and spiritual values of one group to another. It is straddling cultures. It is hearing multiple voices, at

16. Judith E. Lingenfelter and Sherwood G. Lingenfelter, *Teaching Cross-Culturally: An Incarnational Model for Learning and Teaching* (Grand Rapids: Baker, 2003), 19.

17. David W. Augsburger, *Conflict Mediation across Cultures: Pathways and Patterns* (Louisville: Westminster John Knox, 1992), 9.

18. Gloria Anzaldúa, *Borderlands/La Frontera: The New Mestizo* (San Francisco: Aunt Lute Books, 1999), 99.

times with conflicting messages. It is what Asian theologian Jung Young Lee calls marginality or being "on-both," which restores the balance between the two poles and creates harmony.[19]

The tolerance for ambiguity and for keeping opposites in tension is seen by James Fowler as a stage of faith.[20] In this stage, we are able to enter into cross-cultural and interfaith dialogue because we can deal with paradoxes. We believe that the Holy Spirit grants us the grace to remain flexible so that we can stretch the psyche horizontally and vertically. This is the gift of encounters.

When Moses was living in the desert, many people were living as slaves in Egypt. When God revealed their reality to Moses, Moses included their world in his world. Through hearing their story, the faceless, surface "others" whom he did not know were revealed to him. This revelation or encounter showed him the connections between the everyday life of his neighbor (slavery) and his own life. Now, the historical events of his time, which had no meaning for him, entered into his world with new meaning. Moses was faced with pangs of conscience.

God revealed to Moses the people invisible to Moses but visible to God. To open himself to them was to open himself to God. To shut out the slave was to shut out God. Storytelling, then, is a medium for the revelation of God. Moses' life was changed upon appropriating the story not as an event or a memory but as a moment of conversion. He internalized God by internalizing the slaves in Egypt. Moses, God, and the enslaved peoples became intertwined in a story of liberation. The way that Moses understood the meaning of life changed. The stranger, the "other," became his neighbor. Furthermore, Moses would come to an understanding of God's love through the liberation of the people in bondage. This is the love that leads to justice. If Moses had not gone out to liberate this people, he would have been conscious of having committed sin.[21] Church historian Enrique Dussel expresses it this way:

> If I do not commit myself to the liberation of a fellow man [person], then I am an atheist. Not only do I not love God, I am actually fighting against God because I am affirming my own divinity. . . . To be like God is to pretend to be the one and only being; to refuse to open up to the Other.[22]

19. Jung Young Lee, *Marginality: The Key to Multicultural Theology* (Minneapolis: Fortress, 1995), chap. 2.

20. James Fowler, *Stages of Faith: The Psychology of Human Development and the Quest for Meaning* (San Francisco: Harper & Row, 1981).

21. Enrique Dussel, *History and the Theology of Liberation: A Latin American Perspective* (Maryknoll, N.Y.: Orbis, 1976), 6–7.

22. Ibid., 7.

Storytelling and Listening

An encounter with God leads to an encounter with our neighbors because the *imago Dei* is present in them. In our encounters, the telling of and listening to stories leads us to deeper relationships. For example, in a Bible study group composed of Latinos and Anglos, the members began to tell their faith stories to one another. As they did this, they found that they were reflecting on certain life events for the first time. This led to questioning and discussion that helped them come to deeper faith meanings. It also helped them to understand the structures of their cultures and how they had influenced their behaviors and understandings of faith. They also discovered the places they shared in common in their faith journeys. These moments provided an opportunity for all to come to deeper ethnic and Christian identities.

Through the act of storytelling we recognize that those in the dominant culture have constructed the church to fit their needs, and their voices have been heard from pulpits, theological classrooms, books, and denominational hierarchies. Now it is time for others to be heard as well. An encounter is the place for shared experience. This means letting the silenced stories be heard. This exercise repositions our perspectives by allowing other perspectives to be heard.

These encounters are experiences, and our experiences are usually woven into stories. Educators D. Jean Clandinin and F. Michael Connelly claim that family stories about the world are usually teaching stories that tell the generations listening to the accounts the ways of the world according to the experiences the elders have had.[23] In immigrant communities, intergenerational storytelling is necessary because many times the younger generations, not the elders, are learning and telling about the ways of a new world. In this manner, the stories also help to forge community identity. Telling the stories of encounters is a way of teaching new attitudes to the next generation.

It is in our stories that we find what James Loder defines as transforming moments or moments of faith transformation.[24] For Loder, these moments alter our ways of being in the world. A transforming moment is a convictional experience. It disrupts our assumptions by puncturing our ways of making meaning, and it discloses to us dimensions of being not previously attended to. This enables us to re-ground

---

23. D. Jean Clandinin and F. Michael Connelly, *Narrative Inquiry: Experience and Story in Qualitative Research* (San Francisco: Jossey-Bass, 2000), 113.

24. See James E. Loder, *The Transforming Moment: Understanding Convictional Experiences* (San Francisco: Harper & Row, 1981).

and realign our ways of seeing and being. These are the moments that are apparent in our stories.

Listening accompanies the telling of stories. Pastor Brian Parcel, whose church is in a changing neighborhood, led his Anglo congregation through a process of listening to the stories of their Latino neighbors at a cookout that the church offered its neighbors in a nearby park. He encourages us

> to listen to our soul where lies the common place we all share with one another. Somewhere deep within our soul underneath the layers of power, dominance and difference that we hear and see in this world, there is the common place—our humanity. If we listen from this place we can get beyond the impulses to protect ourselves from what we hear, to reject what we hear and to judge what we hear and then we can just listen to the story of the other person.[25]

An encounter begins at the surface. We approach with faith our initial way of seeing and understanding. We know there is something more that goes beyond what we now see. We have a sense that what we see we cannot fully understand. We do not have the proper tools for interpreting what we see. If we tried, we would only project our own culture on what we see. We can observe, but we cannot decode. We cannot make connections between the lived phrases (daily events and routines) of people's lives, and a reading is impossible to us.

In a classroom, I listen to the introductions of my students. I listen to the sounds of their names. I ask students to tell the story of their naming or to define what silence means to them. I listen, but it is too soon to do a reading of who they are. The purpose of these introductions is to help us begin the process of storytelling and of communicating different perspectives. Our ears perk up, and we realize that this is not as simple as it seems. Already questions arise. We become aware of different views and of the cloudiness of our own lenses, which makes others' realities unclear. There is something more, but we see through a glass dimly.

Eric H. F. Law defines invitation as a way of giving away power. "Accepting the invitation is a way to claim power."[26] A process I have found most helpful in facilitating storytelling and listening is Law's "mutual invitation."[27] I invite someone to share, and after that person has spo-

25. Brian Parcel, "A Multicultural Model for Religious Education," in *Multicultural Models for Religious Education*, ed. Elizabeth Conde-Frazier (Atlanta: SCP/Third World Literature Publishing House, 2001), 40–41.

26. Eric H. F. Law, *The Wolf Shall Dwell with the Lamb: A Spirituality for Leadership in a Multicultural Community* (St. Louis: Chalice Press, 1993), 81.

27. Ibid., 83, 113–14.

ken, he or she invites someone else to do the same. The person invited to speak has the option to pass and may then invite another to share. In some of my classes, only one-ninth of the students represent the dominant culture. I have learned that those from the South Pacific Islands speak only when they have wisdom to impart. Mutual invitation allows them to pass and honors their tradition. My students have also taught me to honor silence as part of storytelling and listening. I therefore intentionally build in moments of silence when students may reflect and draw their own connections. They may also choose to write emerging insights. I have found that the discussion following these silences is much richer. There is also greater participation and more respectful listening.

Brian Parcel encourages us to listen to stories without necessarily looking for a quick solution.[28] We should let the dissonance be played on the strings of our hearts, where our compassion and passion may emerge. Stories can be told through art, music, dance, and drama in order to transcend language barriers. They break down the master narrative of our society, and master paradigms begin to shift. This shifting may entail telling the difficult parts of our common history. Relaying the stories of discrimination and racism is difficult, but if we are to rearrange relationships, then we must deconstruct how the common story was put together. This is what has taken place in South Africa as victims have told their stories in the presence of their victimizers. The common story of their brokenness has been told. This has allowed both sides to imagine the possibilities of a different story passing between them.

Recently, in San Diego there was an exhibit of portraits and stories of participants in a national forum called the Arab-Jewish Dialogues. The forum brings together roughly 150 people who meet once a month to talk about their differences and their common fears. Jews and Arabs get to know one another and their long-held prejudices. Participants have confessed that they have learned to stop dehumanizing one another and have come to respect one another. Digesting one another's personal narratives has been key to this process.[29]

When the unspeakable is spoken, it can no longer be denied. Denial is wounding for us and leads to guilt and unresolved anger. Converting knowledge to acknowledgment involves confession as well as giving support to victims so that justice can flow.

---

28. Parcel, "Multicultural Model for Religious Education, 40.
29. Janet Saidi, "Art Shows Arabs, Jews Reaching Out," *Los Angeles Times*, 2 February 2003, 36.

Within our encounters, the Holy Spirit helps to birth new stories. Such was the case when Peter visited Cornelius (Acts 10). The vision Peter received of the cloth with all kinds of four-footed creatures, reptiles, and birds of the air on it, including those the law prohibited him to eat, expanded the realm of the possible for him. The journey began for him with great puzzlement (Acts 10:17). As Peter went to Cornelius's home and shared freely in the hospitality offered at this Gentile neighbor's home, the Holy Spirit opened him up to new directions. Peter preached, and while he was still speaking, the Holy Spirit fell upon all who heard the Word. Again, astonishment filled Peter and the circumcised believers who were with him when they saw the Holy Spirit poured out "even on the Gentiles" (Acts 10:45). The Holy Spirit took them beyond the cultural and religious interpretations that had alienated Jews and Gentiles from one another. Later, Paul conveyed a Christian story that included both Jews and Gentiles in a new relationship.

> He has abolished the law with its commandments and ordinances, that he might create in himself one new humanity in place of the two, thus making peace, and might reconcile both groups to God in one body through the cross, thus putting to death that hostility through it. . . . So then you are no longer strangers and aliens, but you are . . . members of the household of God.
>
> Ephesians 2:15–16, 19 NRSV

I wonder what new stories the Holy Spirit is birthing today as we visit with our neighbors across cultures and even across religious experiences? What new directions and possibilities is the Spirit opening up to us? We know from looking at the stories the Holy Spirit initiates that they are narratives of reconciliation. These narratives go beyond the cultural and religious barriers that keep us as strangers and aliens.

What should we listen for in the stories? We should listen for God's revelation, moments of conversion, commonalities between our worlds that point to common wounds and passions, and the call of God in our lives. In a class on multicultural Christian education, I had students read stories about their cultures. These stories were in the form of novels, histories, songs, and folktales. In each of the stories, we looked for a synthesis of the actions of God, including the different religious traditions that may have been a part of people's stories. This led to rich discussions about revelation and conversion. We also looked for the multifaceted ways in which Christian education was taking place. We found that the symbols in the stories were a powerful means of helping us define common ways of understanding the world, our experiences, our values, and God. They also helped us to name our passions for the world and the contributions we felt called to make in partnership with God as persons and as the church.

In this process, we immersed ourselves in one another's cultures and came to an appreciation and respect of one another's worlds.[30] We became more sensitive to the things we assume and the attitudes that inform our conversations. We also became aware of the way we shape our values and how these include and exclude others. As we listened to the readings, our images of one another's cultures were transformed. We saw the layers of prejudice, fear, and justifying myths that had influenced how we understand (or misunderstand) one another change. These layers had fashioned unjust relationships. We were unrighteous people.

Righteousness is an attribute of God. God expresses righteousness or justice by giving to all created beings their value or place in the universe.[31] Unjust relationships are those in which we do not act toward one another in ways that give humans dignity and value. To restore these relationships, both personal and institutional, to a place where all are valued is to act in a righteous way. It is to act in accordance with the likeness of God.

Teachers and students represent different worldviews that have been constructed by cultural understandings, ideas, behaviors, and values. Righteousness begins with self-awareness and an understanding of social locations and relations and how we participate in them. In the classroom, it includes the assumptions that are constructed by our social contexts and relations and how these influence teaching style and selection of content. The learning experiences of teachers and how they have informed their educational theories and practices are also a part of this self-knowledge. As teachers reflect on these, they can see how and why their teaching is accessible or inaccessible to students from different cultures. This reflection is necessary to create a learning environment that goes beyond tolerance to mutual understanding and the ability to engage constructively. Kathleen Talvacchia claims that in such an environment students can be "taken seriously, be understood in their social milieu and be respected in their uniqueness."[32] Knowledge is an integration of academic content, social context, and experience. It empowers all students to learn.

30. Culture was defined by this class to include race, gender, country or class differences, differences between generations in an immigrant community, and regional differences in the United States.

31. D. W. Diehl, "Righteousness," in *Evangelical Dictionary of Theology*, 953.

32. Kathleen Talvacchia, *Critical Minds and Discerning Hearts: A Spirituality of Multicultural Teaching* (St. Louis: Chalice Press, 2003), 16.

Students in my classes come from countries that were evangelized during the nineteenth and early twentieth centuries by missionaries. Their faith histories helped us understand the ways in which conversion to Christ was equated with conversion to Western culture. This understanding informed how we read theology. For immigrant groups, becoming aware of this dynamic helped them explore the areas that need to be addressed by their indigenous churches. For others of us, we comprehended how theology can be a part of the empire.[33] It challenged us to read theologies from non-Western perspectives. The Christian tradition, therefore, was deepened and expanded for all of us. As we listened to one another's stories, we saw God acting in them. The gospel story became more deeply a part of us.

In the story of Peter's visit to Cornelius's home, it would seem that the story is of the conversion of Cornelius's household. But the class also saw the conversion of Peter in the story as he realized that the Gentiles had indeed been accepted by Jesus. The Gentiles did not need to convert to the Judaic form of expressing their faith in Jesus. Instead, the Spirit of Jesus was affirming the culture of the Gentiles, allowing them freedom of expression in living out the gospel. There are great commonalities in the comprehension of salvation. The differences that arise need to be appreciated and respected.

In this journey through one another's stories, we became aware of how God is intimately a part of our personal history and human development. This sense of rootedness led to a sense of personal and cultural acceptance, which in turn brought us to a sense of God's acceptance of the totality of our lives. With this apprehension of God's presence in our lives, we gained a sense of vocation or our contribution to the world.

Christian education espouses action and behavioral change, but often the limitations of time constraints reduce our teaching methods to the cognitive realm. This produces a passive faith relegated to the life of the mind. As a community of faith, we are impoverished in the area of a dynamic faith that enables us to be cocreators with God in the world—ambassadors of reconciliation.

---

33. W. A. Dyrness points out that when Emperor Constantine converted to Christianity, the position of the church in the world changed. It was now possible for a particular civilization or culture to be identified with Christianity. The faith could now be viewed in an institutional way. Throughout the history of the church, this institutional nature of the church has been in tension with the need for God to reform individuals and communities, including their institutional structures. The church has become enmeshed with the agenda of the empire. For this reason, discernment and critical thinking are required of church leaders. See W. A. Dyrness, "Christianity and Culture," in *Evangelical Dictionary of Theology*, 213.

In a world of two-career households for some and the impossibilities of trying to make ends meet for others, survival is what fashions our values and patterns of behavior. In our religious life, we simply fulfill the canons of religious minimalism (attending church on Sunday or on special days). What causes us to fall out of sync with the cycle of survival is an encounter with another. This makes us see one another differently, and we rediscover a desire to respond to the call to Christian discipleship. This call empowers us to forgive, to care for the poor, to speak out in multiple forms against injustice, and to help create alongside others more just structures. These are spiritual gains that take us from isolation and alienation to greater connectedness. This is part of the journey toward reconciliation.

Listening as Attending

James Whitehead and Evelyn Eaton Whitehead call "attending" the initial stage of theological reflection.[34] At this point, one shifts from a hierarchical role to one of servant leadership, where one listens for the Lord's presence and assists others in their own attentive response to God's movement in their lives.[35] This is important in the process of conversion because it helps us to discern where God is calling us to change. Conversion as a process may be slow and subtle at times. When as teachers we structure time for reflection about the meaning of our dialogue with one another, with texts, and with our experiences, we are attending to God's movement in our lives. An effective way to do this is through an intellectual journal. Students reflect on the connections between their personal experiences, readings, and class discussions. Class discussions include lectures, group dynamics, drama, devotions, and rituals.

Attending begins with an attitude of openness that enables us to set aside our preoccupations in order to turn our attention to others. This is followed by a response. We may respond for the purpose of clarification or for checking the accuracy of what we have understood. A deeper response involves an awareness of what something means from the point of view of the one who shared it. Attending, therefore, includes the ability to listen accurately and to respond with accurate understanding.[36]

Not all communication is verbal. Each culture has a set of nonverbal forms of communication that may include eye contact, posture, ges-

---

34. Whitehead and Whitehead, *Method in Ministry*, 81–89.
35. Ibid., 82.
36. Ibid., 83.

tures, silences, pauses, and tone of voice. Some cultures use these forms of communication more frequently. We must learn to listen to these as well.

Prior interpretations or judgments must be suspended in the process of attending. The goal is to hear thoroughly. In listening to different cultural perceptions, we must listen until we understand from the viewpoint of the one who is sharing. We must go beyond the sense of something sounding foreign, which causes us to think it is wrong rather than simply different. When we think we know what the meaning is, our interpretations shape our listening. Whitehead and Whitehead posit that these prejudgments function as prejudice.[37]

In short, we must listen for content, feeling, and context. We must respond with empathy or understanding without evaluation or judgment. We can respond by paraphrasing, by restating what the other person said. This confirms that we are present and attending to that person. Attending enables us to stand with others in their circumstances and enhances our effectiveness in multicultural communication and interpersonal situations of ministry.[38]

Attending and Questioning

Listening and attending earn us trust and therefore the right to ask a different level of questions.[39] These questions lead us into an evaluative discussion about the values of another person's culture. After listening and understanding to the best of our ability, we might feel unsettled about the values reflected in something that has been shared. In the context of trust, we can now ask the opinion of the other person about the matter in question. Jesus asked this type of question of his hearers. "What do you think, Simon? . . . From whom do kings . . . collect duty and taxes?" (Matt. 17:25). On another occasion he asked those present, "Which is lawful on the Sabbath: to do good or to do evil, to save life or to kill?" (Mark 3:4). Jesus questioned a practice and the values that informed it as he invited the opinions of the hearers. When we do so, we assume that the person is able to look at a situation honestly and evaluate it and will not become defensive. In this dialogue, we may ask deeper questions about the authority that fashioned the values under discussion. These questions help to sharpen the meaning of what one is trying to bring out. For example, Jesus asked, "If you love those who

37. Ibid., 88.
38. Ibid., 85.
39. The questions that follow are gleaned from my reading of R. E. O. White, *Listening Carefully to Jesus* (Grand Rapids: Eerdmans, 2000), chap. 6.

love you, what reward will you get? Are not even tax collectors doing that?" (Matt. 5:46). He questioned the givens, the assumptions of the culture and of the religious practice. He challenged people to reevaluate and perhaps admit the need for reform.

Along this same line are the questions that evoke better discipleship. Our critique may evoke a need to change, but in the face of change there are always resistances. A question can nudge people beyond places of safety and complacency. For example, Jesus asked Peter, "Do you truly love me more than these?" (John 21:15). He asked Mary Magdalene, "Woman, . . . why are you crying? Who is it you are looking for?" (John 20:15). Other questions Jesus asked were: "What do you want me to do for you?" (Matt. 20:32) and "Can you drink the cup I am going to drink?" (Matt. 20:22).

In one of my classes, we knew we would be speaking about difficult issues such as racism, sexism, and xenophobia. The class, therefore, decided to create rules to guide their interactions. One phrase that helped them to withhold judgment was "tell me more." This phrase took the place of a first reaction against something and pushed us toward openness. We also discussed the forms of questioning dealt with above. Such questions guided us through the turbulent waters of conflict in our class discussions. They helped to disarm the initial energy of a conflict and to channel it toward further listening, respect, and appreciation.

Listening and Perspective Transformation

Perspective transformation requires critical insight, which is the ability to analyze, deconstruct, and reconstruct theological and sociological contexts.[40] It allows people to look at themselves and their contexts so that they may come to new understandings of both. The goal of this analysis is to look carefully at our received cultural and theological constructions and the ways they inform the fashioning of our relationships with one another. For example, if my cultural understandings define the poor as lazy people and my theological constructs define poverty as an inevitable consequence of idolatry, then my view of the poor will be negative. I will blame the poor for their state of poverty. Critical insight helps us to examine our assumptions, allowing us to come to new perceptions. These new perceptions give us the opportunity to change our attitudes, behaviors, and the power dynamics in our relationships. Through critical insight we can reveal the assumptions that

---

40. Susan E. Davies, "Critical Insight: Enhancing Experiential Knowledge in Theological Education," *Union Seminary Quarterly Review* 47, nos. 3–4 (1993): 54. Davies describes her use of this process in her course at Bangor Seminary.

maintain the classist, sexist, and ableist views considered normative in our culture and theology.[41]

Educator Stephen Brookfield has designed exercises for assumption analysis.[42] These include exploring the actions of hypothetical characters, reflecting on the assumptions involved in crisis decision making, and examining why we admire or dislike our heroes and villains. As a part of coming to critical insight, participants name a time in their life when they identified the ideological cocoons in which they had been raised. They also name the social influences (family, work, church, school, media, global events) that encouraged or discouraged this realization.[43] If the participants are sufficiently acquainted with one another, they can talk about these in small groups. I have also used this form in a marriage and family class dealing with issues of gender roles. We examined the roles that significant males and females played in their families of origin and the cultural and theological makeup of these roles. Students reflected on their learning and wrote about whether they were moved to new considerations for their lives.

Jack Mezirow points out that such new considerations require support from others in order to become pursued realities in a person's life. I encourage participants to speak to at least two people close to them about their new goals. Spiritual support is needed if we are to embark on a journey of transformation. We must find a way of inviting God into our efforts.

Even when we verbalize our reflections, there is still room for us to mask our true habits of mind. Drama and simulation can be helpful in this area. On one occasion, I led a workshop on ministry with Hispanic immigrants for a group of dominant culture pastors. As I asked people why they had come to the workshop, I realized that their motive was to learn how to control what they perceived to be the negative social behaviors of their immigrant neighbors. We conducted an exercise in which the pastors were divided into simulated immigrant families. Their task was to resettle themselves in a country in which they did not have legal status and could not speak the language. I set up the social and governmental agencies they needed to approach and controlled the information to which they had access, the policies, procedures, and op-

41. Ibid., 51.

42. See Stephen Brookfield, "Using Critical Incidents to Explore Learners' Assumptions," in *Fostering Critical Reflection in Adulthood*, ed. Jack Mezirow and associates (San Francisco: Jossey-Bass, 1990); and Stephen Brookfield, *Developing Critical Thinkers: Challenging Adults to Explore Alternative Ways of Thinking and Acting* (San Francisco: Jossey-Bass, 1987).

43. Davies, "Critical Insight," 58. Brookfield calls these experiences critical incidents.

portunities. At lunchtime, only those who had successfully secured jobs were given tickets to enter the cafeteria.

Later in the day, we talked about their experiences. Some of the things the pastors had earlier called negative social behavior they now called strategies for survival. They were exhausted from the frustration, anger, and demoralization they had experienced. Some had felt marginalized, rejected, and silenced. The group then broke into small groups to work on creative ministries for partnering with their "brothers and sisters" (their words) in the community.

Teaching in this manner provides all of us with tools for listening to one another more deeply. It helps us remove some of the barriers that could produce conflict. We are enabled to see more clearly that what we considered "normative" perspectives are not normative but rather cultural constructions. We can also see who in our cultural contexts may be marginalized. Such encounters bring about transformations.

This stage of encounter perhaps requires the most from teachers. It requires that we be knowledgeable about our subject, the complexity of intercultural communication, and the plurality of viewpoints in our teaching settings. Our character needs to be grounded in the spirit of Jesus, which is a spirit of humility (Phil. 2:5–9). This is the foundation of incarnational teaching. It is with humility that we approach what is possible in this complicated task, what we are capable of, and what our limitations are. Robert Pazmiño reminds us that it is the indwelling Spirit who fosters the processes of learning so that our spirits are transformed along with our minds, souls, hearts, and bodies.[44]

Encounter and Conflict

Conflict is an inevitable part of our encounters. The fear of conflict is what keeps many from attempting to engage others at deeper levels. Yet the sources, causes, and processes of conflicts can be turned from life-destroying to life-building ends. We should not eradicate conflict. Instead, we should channel its energies toward life.

Conflict takes place when multiple realities need to be negotiated to create one common reality. Our realities have been constructed by our different stories. When we encounter one another in a common space, we, with our differing stories, must create a shared story in which we all have a role. This is, according to David Augsburger, the bottom line of conflict.[45] Constructive conflict involves focusing on the issues in

44. Robert W. Pazmiño, *God Our Teacher: Theological Basics in Christian Education* (Grand Rapids: Baker, 2001), 87.
45. Augsburger, *Conflict Mediation across Cultures*, 11.

question, not introducing secondary issues, making the goal of the conflict cooperative problem solving, controlling competition, and placing emphasis on mutually satisfactory outcomes.

Competition stresses the urgency of a victory (win-lose). Anxiety, therefore, fuels the argument, bringing misconceptions as well as faulty communication. Competition uses either/or attitudes and actions and focuses on what will bring victory for oneself and defeat for one's opponent. One's power is enhanced, and the opponent's power is minimized. The attitudes that emerge are hostility, suspicion, and defensiveness. These lead to unilateral actions. Cooperation, on the other hand, focuses on trust, open communication, perceived similarity, concern for the other, and an emphasis on mutual interests.[46] It is a both/and process in which tolerance and integration create mutual understandings. The actions that follow are actions of negotiation, interaction, and integration.[47] Honest communication allows underlying assumptions to surface so that misperceptions can be clarified and joint definitions achieved. It is also possible to see the legitimacy of something that at first may have seemed simply wrong. The positions taken by all parties and their rationales are better understood.[48]

Exploration is another way to channel the energy of conflict. Rather than focusing on what is objectionable in another, we focus on what is most excellent. This affirms the strengths of each position. It decreases rigidity and entrenchment so that other options may be explored by all. In exploration, one does not spend time dismantling arguments but engaging in constructive investigation. Augsburger shows that "when a creative alternative emerges, a choice can be made on the basis of values."[49] It is a process that synthesizes or combines. It is inventive collaboration. In short, exploration suspends fault finding, thus reducing defensiveness. It places emphasis on joint participation, ownership, and decision making. Defensiveness is perhaps one of the most difficult hurdles to jump. In exploration, energy is spent on collaborative change rather than on defensive behavior.

Conflict and Multicultural Teaching

Sustained reflection on who we are and what motivates our actions, attitudes, and values as we seek to develop relationships with people who are different from us is necessary. We need to look into ourselves

46. Ibid., 50.
47. Ibid., 51.
48. Ibid.
49. Ibid., 59.

to determine where we are coming from. To do so, we need tools for self-reflection. One such tool is what scholar-activist Eleanor Haney calls ecosocial location.[50] This is the awareness of the many influences in our life contexts that have shaped us. She reminds us that "we are shaped by our participation in racial/ethnic, gender, sexual, age, national, ability and biological groups and geographical settings."[51] This formation enriches and limits our understandings of ourselves, others, the world, and God. M. Elizabeth Blissman, director for service learning at Oberlin College, explains that this type of reflection can help "those in the dominant culture resist the temptation to participate unconsciously in the racist and individualist legacies of the United States."[52] This self-understanding is key when forming relationships associated with doing the work of God's reign. It helps us to look at how oppression and privilege are contoured. It helps us to clarify our implicit and explicit agendas, seeing how they fit or do not fit with those of others. Insights from such clarifications may help us to see directions for change. Ultimately, sustained commitments are the goal of such reflection. These commitments permit us to share our passions, pain, experiences, anger, fears, and visions for engaging in a collective action toward shalom. This type of reflection is a conceptual tool because it refocuses our vision and reshapes the criteria with which we think, judge, and act.

Multicultural issues always hold potential hot spots. Passionate emotions may trigger fear and anger. As an educator, Peter Frederick has taught multicultural issues for twenty years. He suggests that teachers include guidelines in the syllabus for acceptable behavior during conflictive moments. Such guidelines should articulate the values to be maintained and the spirit and final goal of any discussion. These include mutual respect and the search for truth, openness, and honesty. During class, teachers should acknowledge the difficulty of certain feelings to diminish their force.

If the tension becomes so disruptive that a discussion cannot go on, Frederick recommends calling a time-out during which students may reflect on the content and process of what took place. They may discuss this in small groups, after which the large group discussion may con-

50. See Eleanor H. Haney, *The Great Commandment* (Cleveland: Pilgrim Press, 1998).
51. Ibid., 7.
52. M. Elizabeth Blissman, "Expanding the Horizon of Engagement: Pioneering Work at the University of Denver," in *From Cloister to Commons: Concepts and Models for Service Learning in Religious Studies*, ed. Richard Devine, Joseph A. Farazza, and F. Michael McLain (Washington, D.C.: American Association for Higher Education, 2002), 79.

tinue.[53] Teachers should avoid doing this out of panic. I have found that I can usually trust students to work out the tension with honesty and civility. Nonetheless, there are times when an inflammatory and inappropriate comment or remark is made. Frederick suggests repeating back the words very slowly with "an invitational inflection supported by a hand gesture that makes it clear the person has another opportunity to speak."[54] Echoing a student's words can be a gentle invitation for him or her to look in the mirror. When a student simply repeats the same remark and perhaps with more energy, one can be honest and say, "That comment offends me; I'd like you to think about it."[55]

One of the things to remember is that change is most likely to come out of the listening process rather than a debate or argument. Io Imlay and Jerry Howard point out that "when people feel safe, they challenge themselves. When you give people a chance to open up, they really examine their beliefs and sometimes they reinvent them."[56]

Compassion

The word *compassion* comes from the words *cum patior*, which mean "to suffer with," "to undergo with." It connotes solidarity. Compassion, therefore, works from a place of mutuality. It involves participating in the sufferings of another with a strength born of an awareness of shared weakness.[57] It is this sense of shared weakness that distinguishes compassion from pity. Pity is felt at a distance from the one suffering, and the one suffering is seen as weak or inferior. With pity, there is less participation in the suffering of another.

Compassion and joy are linked. In Romans 12, Paul is helping his readers to come to an understanding of ministry done in mutuality and not competition. He uses the metaphor of the body to help them see their connections to one another. Each member of the body is encouraged to use his or her gifts according to the grace given. Each gift, then, is coupled with its grace. In verse 8, the grace of compassion is cheerfulness. Jesus' compassion was at times expressed in joy. Such times included when the disciples returned from doing the work he

53. Frederick, "Walking on Eggs," 90–91.
54. Ibid., 91.
55. Ibid.
56. Io Imlay and Jerry Howard, "Listening for a Change," *New Age Journal* (November/December, 1993): 50.
57. Matthew Fox, *A Spirituality Named Compassion and the Healing of the Global Village, Humpty Dumpty, and Us* (Minneapolis: Winston Press, 1979), 2.

had sent them out to do (Luke 10:21). In compassion as well as in celebration, togetherness is empowering. We share our sufferings and our joys. Compassion is passion with. Matthew Fox points out that celebration and compassion are a forgetting in order to remember. We forget or let go of ego and concerns in order to remember the common base that makes another's suffering ours. Then together we imagine a relief or solution for that suffering.[58] In celebration, we also let go of ego and concerns in order to share in the joy of a relief brought about.

Compassion involves imagination and action. The story of the good Samaritan speaks of the Samaritan's works of mercy. These works make it clear that compassion is not about sentimentalism. Works of mercy are described by the prophets (Isa. 58:6–7; Micah 6:6–8) and in the Johannine literature, where we are exhorted to love in truth and action (1 John 3:18). This action is described as laying down one's life for another and helping those in need (1 John 3:16–17). The Book of James creates a dialectic between faith and works (James 2:14–22), inviting us to be both hearers and doers of the Word (James 1:22). In the Gospels, Jesus shows us what works of mercy look like. Matthew's Gospel tells the story of the separation of the sheep and the goats according to whether they had tended to the needs of the hungry, thirsty, naked, sick, the stranger, or those in prison. In his acts of healing and miracles, we see Jesus moved to compassion. The power for healing and doing miracles is the power of compassion.

In the Latino community, a great number of people lack health insurance. Health care is a luxury; thus, prayers for healing are common. One of the names ascribed to Jesus in the Latino community is most excellent doctor *(el médico por excelencia)*. Healing services do not involve the drama portrayed by televangelists. Rather, they are about the compassionate poor pooling together their faith on behalf of a loved one. In one such community, a man in a wheelchair sat in the front at every service. One evening, the invited preacher was overwhelmed by weeping during the sermon and could not finish it. He moved with compassion toward the wheelchair and uttered a humble whispered prayer for the man sitting in it. The congregation prayed with him, although his words could not be heard. At the end of the prayer, a closing hymn was sung, during which the man in the wheelchair stood up and danced with tears of joy.

On other occasions, compassion takes the form of doing justice. Marcion created a dualism between the good God and the just God, cre-

---

58. Ibid., 4.

ating a polarity between mercy and justice.[59] This separated justice and love. In the United States, before the civil rights movement, churches could speak of love but could not articulate what that love looked like. During the movement, Martin Luther King Jr. equated justice with love. He said, "Justice is love correcting that which would work against love."[60] Before this statement and the actions of the civil rights movement, the relationship between theology and politics in the life of the church was bifurcated. There were few who claimed that the two could mix successfully and chose silence instead. Others advocated a form of gradualism that naturally denounced more radical expressions such as sit-ins and boycotts. These political, nonviolent strategies were the works of mercy or compassion. In this religious and theological context, Martin Luther King Jr. and other church people began to relate the Christian gospel to the struggle for justice in the United States. They called desegregation the expression or action of love. As King's own understanding of justice was amplified, he linked justice with the need to alleviate poverty for all citizens and later with the need for peace in the world, naming militarism an evil. When compassion's link with justice is made clear, so too is its expression of anger.

Anger has not been considered a positive emotion.[61] Like conflict, it has traditionally been considered a spiritual impediment. Anger in Spanish is *coraje*, which also means courage. Aristotle defined anger as an energy that enables people to face difficulty. Thomas Aquinas integrated Aristotle's view into Christian thinking and offered an expanded and more positive view of anger. Anger is a gift from God and also an emotion that God displays. It brings out resistance rather than helplessness. A person with a healthy sense of self, when hurt in any way, will be aroused to protest. This expression of protest is anger. It is a necessary part of our survival. Beyond survival, anger also serves social transformation.[62] We must combine our anger with the spiritual discipline of

59. For further discussion, see Hans Jonas, *The Gnostic Religion* (Boston: Beacon, 1963).

60. Martin Luther King Jr., "Address to the Initial Mass Meeting of the Montgomery Improvement Association," Hold Street Baptist Church, 5 December 1955. The tape and printed copy of this address are located in the Martin Luther King Jr. Papers, Center for Non-Violent Social Change, Atlanta, Ga.

61. The following passage is adapted from Elizabeth Conde-Frazier, "Hispanic Protestant Spirituality," in *Teología en Conjunto: A Collaborative Hispanic Protestant Theology*, ed. José David Rodríguez and Loida I. Martell Otero (Louisville: Westminster John Knox, 1997), 143.

62. James D. Whitehead and Evelyn Eaton Whitehead, *Shadows of the Heart: A Spirituality of the Negative Emotions* (New York: Crossroad, 1994), 46.

temperance so that it can be cooled to a productive level and can bear the spiritual fruits of justice, love, hope, and peace.[63]

Hesed is the Hebrew word often translated "compassion" or "mercy." Yet scholars agree that no one English word is an adequate translation of *hesed*. Perhaps this is why the dimension of action that the Hebrew word implies is missed. *Hesed* is something that one does with someone. It implies the doing of deliverance that justice is about.[64] Compassion moves us out of our egocentricity, which is a state of ego defense and the very stuff of which prejudices are made. Compassion is transcendence of the self. This transcendence is reflected in the first epistle of John: "No one has ever seen God; but if we love one another, God lives in us" (1 John 4:12) and also, "Everyone who loves has been born of God and knows God . . . because God is love" (1 John 4:7–8).

What keeps us from the expression of compassion is a guarded and cautious heart. We learn these behaviors as we experience rejection, exploitation, mistreatment, or oppression. As we experience difficulty in believing we are loved and valued, our hearts become guarded and the range of our emotions is reduced. The negative energy of our destructive emotions causes distrust, negative self-images, anger, relational conflicts, and communication difficulties. Such things affect our spirituality. Spirituality encompasses the ways in which we interact in relationship with God, others, and creation. Daniel Groody says it is "the force that humanizes and brings forth life."[65] Affective transformation is needed to help us move toward openness, positive self-identity, and forgiveness. Hidden beauty can then emerge from behind our guard. The following things facilitate this transformation: continuous expressions of acceptance, gifts of unconditional love, and challenges to our stories that help us reflect on our lives.

Compassion, as part of the journey of conversion, brings us from indifference to care. It also helps us redefine our inner parameters so that we can move from blood ties or ties with family and culture to ties with the created family. Compassion involves internalizing others so that we no longer feel displaced or dislocated when interacting outside our culture. Instead, we have a sense of our common humanity, which joins us to those who had previously been strangers, and a new understanding of who we are and who others are to us. By showing compassion we connect with others, allowing them to pervade us until they become significant in our lives.

---

63. Ibid., 47.
64. Fox, *Spirituality Named Compassion*, 11.
65. Daniel G. Groody, *Border of Death, Valley of Life: An Immigrant Journey of Heart and Spirit* (Lanham, Md.: Rowan & Littlefield, 2003), 8.

As these connections take place, we learn empathy. Empathy makes us aware of the world of our neighbor in the way that our neighbor experiences it. Heinz Kohut of South Africa says that empathy is the essential ingredient for human life. Through empathy we validate and confirm the experience of another, and in turn, our experiences are also validated. Empathy allows us to step back from our own feelings, while not disavowing them, to put ourselves in the place of another by vicariously grasping that person's emotional experience.[66] When we have compassion, we are able to listen empathetically and to confront or contradict misinformation or injustice because we are seeking the well-being of our neighbor based on our capacity to grasp his or her experience.

It is from this new perspective of self and neighbor that true compassion can be birthed. It is a perspective that comes through the lens of humility. Humility offers a balanced understanding of self-worth; it is not self-debasement but self-acceptance. Those who exhibit humility do not see themselves as greater than others. Therefore, they do not usurp the place of others. This sense of self and neighbor allows us to relate to one another not according to the social and economic statuses of our cultures but according to our true human worth. Compassion allows for equal partnerships and does not create dependency or false love. Those who pity others see them as unable to do things for themselves. They see themselves in a position of power to bring change to the unfortunate circumstances of others' lives. Pity, therefore, is birthed from a hidden sense of pride. Compassion, however, does not strip others of their dignity and power to act on their own behalf. Those with compassion partner with others, complementing their gifts and efforts toward humanization.

When considering how to educate for compassion, it is necessary to define Christian education in such a way that it includes all dimensions of life, not only eternal life. The word *educate* means "to lead out," "to bring forth." To bring forth into what? If the Christian gospel is about life in all its forms, then Christian education is the process of bringing forth into life. Compassion, in relation to this definition of Christian education, is "a process of waking up to life."[67] Life holds connections between all created beings. We need to wake up to our interdependence with all beings, and therefore, we need to wake up to all that threatens life. Teaching for compassion makes us aware of the thief who comes

66. Leonard M. Hummel, "Heinz Kohut and Empathy: A Perspective from a Theology of the Cross," *Word and World: Theology for Christian Ministry* (winter 2001): 64–74.

67. Mary Richards, *Centering* (Middletown, Conn.: Wesleyan University Press, 1964), 15.

to steal, kill, and destroy (John 10:10) as well as the ways of life that solve problems, create alternatives to death, and thus celebrate life.

An epistemology that informs teaching for compassion focuses on the understanding that biblical knowledge is relational. Knowledge in the Hebrew Scripture is to know in the practical sense rather than the abstract, referring to persons and things with which we are familiar. To know in this way implies a personal relationship between the knower and the person known. It is to know from experience; for example, to know afflictions, loss of children, disease, or grief. *Yada*, "to know," in Hebrew can also be used to designate sexual intercourse. To know, therefore, implies a degree of intimacy and intensity in a relationship in which an individual stands with the one who is known.

Knowledge is an activity in which the totality of one's being is engaged, not only the mind. Knowledge, therefore, is always accompanied by an emotional response. Full comprehension is manifested in action that corresponds to the relationship apprehended. In the prophetic writings, Israel's lack of knowledge is not theoretical ignorance but the failure to practice the filial or devoted relationship in which they stood with God.[68]

The initial encounter with the one to be known does not yield immediate full and true knowledge. To know God comes from knowing him in the historical events in which he has shown himself. It is knowing God in the biblical text as well as in the everyday events of life. Hispanic theologians call this everyday reality of life *lo cotidiano*. It is the experience of the transcendent in the immanent. "It allows us to see how God's grace, justice, presence and love manifest themselves in everyday occurrences."[69] Theologian Loida Martell Otero points out that *"lo cotidiano* allows the voiceless to tell their stories, and to cry out to the heavens for justice and peace."[70]

We come to know God through the witness of others. This witness then urges or inspires us to seek God for ourselves. Teaching can guide people in seeking to know God. It can lead them to knowledge that makes them ready to live the kind of lives that allow God to teach them and search them. Teaching takes the experiences through which we must pass and makes us aware of God in them.

Finally, knowledge of God implies a knowledge of ourselves in relation to God. In Scripture, "to know" frequently means to know God's

68. Insights gathered from O. A. Piper, "Knowledge," in *The Interpreter's Dictionary of the Bible*, ed. George A. Buttrick (Nashville: Abingdon, 1962), 43.

69. Loida I. Martell Otero, "Finding God in the Spaces of the Everyday," unpublished paper, 4.

70. Ibid.

ways or precepts, not just to know God (Pss. 25:4, 12; 119:104). We need to know the experience of the reality of God, not just the propositions concerning God.

In the New Testament, the realization of God's redemptive work modifies what it is to know God, thus bringing it to new levels. The subject matter of knowledge is the mystery of the kingdom of God. To know God is to know the will of God through God's redemptive purpose. This knowledge leads to a harmony of wills. In Johannine literature, to know God is to love one's neighbor. Notice that Scripture does not limit the "other" to persons in our midst. The gospel message makes it clear that the "other," the Samaritan, the Syrophoenician woman, the centurion, the leper, is a neighbor. Today, the Latina, the African-American, the gay and the lesbian, the Vietnamese, the Muslim, and the illegal alien are our neighbors. To know God is to love our neighbors. Teaching, therefore, should bring us to the knowledge of God through the knowledge of our neighbors. This teaching has the purpose of constructing or building up the community. It is teaching for neighbor consciousness, and this consciousness leads us to compassion in all its expressions, including social justice, and is an integral dimension of the spiritual life. "The Holy Spirit empowers humanity into the fullness of relational life."[71] This relational understanding of knowledge serves as the epistemology for teaching that cultivates compassion.

A. Boal's work on the different ways of knowing and learning has implications for the affective (emotions, sensations, and thoughts) dimensions of knowing.[72] The creative way of knowing is the capacity to remember and imagine. Memory and imagination ("the premonition of reality") are complementary parts of the same psychic/creative process.[73] The heartfelt way of knowing is the capacity to feel. Emotions affect the quality of a person's interaction and work so that emotions influence learning. Emotions help us to recognize contradictions and confusions and to gain clarity about relationships. This heart knowledge is necessary for learning and working compassionately. A wisdom that comes from this type of knowing is necessary for multicultural living. It allows one to tell when there is misunderstanding or hidden conflict that can obstruct communication. One can comprehend beyond words.

Compassion entails our emotions as well as those of others. To become a compassionate person, one must learn to be at home with one's

71. Frank Rogers, "Dancing with Grace: Toward a Spirit-Centered Education," *Religious Education* 89, no. 3 (summer 1994): 386.

72. See A. Boal, *A Rainbow of Desire* (London: Routledge, 1995).

73. Ibid., 21.

feelings and not run from them. Compassion involves feeling the very deep emotions of others and extending one's own feelings. It involves the knowledge of interconnections in order to foster, maintain, and transmit life. Heart knowledge works in tandem with rational knowledge. It connects the subject with the object, the abstraction with the action. Heart knowledge trains us for community and interdependence, the unity of the new creation. It teaches us to intercede.

Experiential methods seek to bring together these same elements. They rely on the life experiences of students. They involve some self-disclosure. They bring together theory, research, personal experience, and practice in ways that are educational and empowering to students. They make use of personal experiences to help students make sense of new information.[74] Experiential learning moves one from detached or objective knowledge to engaged and subjective knowledge.

As a Christian educator, I realize that transformational teaching needs to make use of personal experience. This is because transformation entails bringing together affective and cognitive dimensions. It requires reflection on everyday experience. This is how we become aware of patterns of behavior. In multicultural Christian education, transformational learning not only gives us personal insight but also helps us create common bonds and foster understanding across cultures.

Experiential learning includes a variety of learning and teaching strategies. These may be apprenticeships, field projects, field trips, simulations, or games. Notice that this wide range of learning strategies allows for a greater latitude in the exercise of various intelligences. John Dewey brought our attention to the link between education and experience during the early part of the twentieth century. For Dewey, experience is both personal and social. Experiences are also continuous—one experience grows out of other experiences and leads to additional experiences. They are the building blocks of perception formation and change that fashion worldviews.[75]

The two main elements of experiential learning are doing and reflecting on the action. Experience without reflection is a happening, and no learning can be reaped from it. One should begin with concrete experience followed by reflective observation. These observations are the building blocks for constructing new perceptions that reshape one's understanding of the world and how to be in the world. These perceptions

---

74. Elizabeth Graverholz and Stacey Copenhaver, "When the Personal Becomes Problematic: The Ethics of Using Experiential Teaching Methods," *Teaching Sociology* 22 (1994): 319. This article gives a definition of this type of method and discusses the benefits and problems of using it.

75. See John Dewey, *Experience and Education* (New York: Collier Books, 1938).

can serve as guides to behavior and feelings. One uses these insights to renew one's actions.[76] Any form of experiential learning can facilitate a constructed experience that when followed by thoughtful group or personal reflection designed by the teacher can bring students to points of decision and change in their personal lives and ministries. This is teaching for change. Judith and Sherwood Lingenfelter claim that "whenever the habits and practices of our social and economic relationships become obstacles to the fundamental values and goals we hold as people, we must teach for change."[77] On the personal level, we are changing into the likeness of Christ. Institutionally, the goal of change is to bring about kingdom values. When constructing an experiential learning activity, teachers need to have a sense of the point at which students find themselves in relationship to the subject being taught and how far they might move along the continuum of change. The continuum of change may look as follows:

Original perception: Information shaped by our communities.

A new experience: New information or a trigger event may lead to discomfort or dissonance. This is the initial connection with the issue.

Appraisal: Self-examination, identification, or clarification of the concern. What is going on here (with this situation and inside of me)? How were views or beliefs about this issue constructed? This is a place of deeper encounter with the issue.

Exploration: Exploring new and old assumptions. Where might this lead me? Testing the veracity of the new.

Support: Dialogue with others to develop a sense of security and confidence within the new. Seeking the encouragement of family and friends. Feedback is sought as one expresses new ideas and asks for comments. As one comes to new understandings, one also needs new symbols.

Continuous questions and challenges: At this point, one begins to see with new eyes, encounters new stories, and engages in deeper dialogue. One acts according to one's new understandings, views, and beliefs.

An example of how this may look is as follows:

76. These are the steps to David Kolb's model of the creation of knowledge. See David Kolb, *Experiential Learning* (Englewood Cliffs, N.J.: Prentice Hall, 1984).
77. Lingenfelter and Lingenfelter, *Teaching Cross-Culturally,* 89.

Original perception: The poor are poor because they wish to be poor.

A new experience: A field trip facilitates an experience of seeing the poor and hearing them speak on a panel.

Appraisal: Some poor work very hard, but their jobs don't pay enough to make ends meet.

Exploration: Readings, lectures, and discussions facilitate social analysis. Why do these jobs not pay more? Why can't the poor move to better paying jobs?

Support: A guest speaker constructs a simulation in which the class tries to help someone get a better job. The experience is discussed. Possible new understandings may include: The poor are poor because there are many obstacles before them. There are no places for training. There is no time to train because survival takes up all their time.

New action: The person becomes an advocate for the poor in relation to training resources.

Much planning and foresight must go into experiential learning. Students must be given options about assignments and asked to reflect on personal experiences. Teachers must carefully consider how to grade such assignments. For example, I ask students to keep journals that integrate course readings, class discussions, personal experiences, and theological reflection. Because personal disclosure is involved, students have the option of folding over pages of the journal they wish to keep confidential. As a teacher, I hold much power over students. Personal disclosure makes them even more vulnerable.

I also grade such assignments as check and check plus or minus depending on the quality of integration. Letter grades are not assigned. This brings down the level of stress for students who may already feel vulnerable. Students who feel especially vulnerable may discuss an alternative suggestion for reflection. On other occasions, I use movies, biographies, novels, or ethnographies as alternative means for achieving similar goals. These are vehicles for tapping into our understandings of the connections that other cultures and worlds have with our own at personal and sociopolitical levels.

Passion

Compassion is passionate. The compassionate God is a passionate God. Compassion is about being moved. It is a movement.[78] Because we

---

78. Fox, *Spirituality Named Compassion,* 20.

have in some way entered into the pain of our neighbor, shared it and tasted it insofar as that is possible, we are moved. Just as deep calls unto deep, compassion invites passion. After listening to one another's stories and getting to know our diverse gifts, we are connected by a common wound in the place where our worlds have encountered one another. Passion is derived from the Latin word *patior*, meaning "to suffer" or "to take on." To stand with Jesus is to share his passion.

When Jesus irrupts into our history, he announces that the time has been fulfilled and God's reign is at hand (Mark 1:9–14). The National Conference of Catholic Bishops, in their pastoral letter on social teachings, sees this proclamation as a "summons to acknowledge God as creator and covenant partner."[79] This can be done only when our commitment to God is enacted through love of our neighbor. This enactment of the Word is truth taking form in us. That form is devotion. Devotion is the act or condition of giving oneself up for another person, purpose, or service. It is setting ourselves apart for deep, steady affection. It entails grasping that which is not normally accessible, apprehending the way of God and the meaning of our times. Devotion helps us see the invisible God and the people visible to God but made invisible by injustices. In liberation theologies, the face of God is seen in those who suffer injustices. Devotion is a sacred and reverent expression of the totality of our person. The fruit of such worship is solidarity.[80]

This solidarity is what characterizes our priesthood, which brings with it the privilege of being broken. It is the privilege of the cross. It is the privileges of losses, grief, and tears, but let us remember that Jesus also wept. It was his compassion that caused the power of healing and of resurrection to be released on behalf of others. In his book *Who Comes in the Name of the Lord?* Harold Recinos reminds us that the cup symbolizes Jesus' suffering witness before the powerful. Drinking from it means entering into radical solidarity with the way of the cross.[81]

Empathy stirs our souls, and in this stirring the Spirit impassions us. This passion comes from reflection on and participation in the divine *pathos*, where God is involved in the life of the community. Passion is intimacy and sympathy with God and humanity. It is divine consciousness engaging us. When we see the places in need of the Spirit's gifts of

79. National Conference of Catholic Bishops, *Economic Justice for All: Pastoral Letter on Catholic Social Teaching and the United States Economy* (Washington, D.C.: United States Catholic Conference, 1986), 41.

80. *Solidarity* is a term derived from the Latin *solidare*, which means "to join together firmly."

81. Harold J. Recinos, *Who Comes in the Name of the Lord? Jesus at the Margins* (Nashville: Abingdon, 1997), 71.

wholeness, faith, hope, and love, we are empowered to bring life-giving fruit and wisdom to the struggles of our communities. This is a practice of love or an entering into the world of our neighbor. This caring disposition moves us to interact with and on behalf of those we love. It is a common passion that now unites us. Those things that break our hearts and make us angry and that we therefore wish to change are the things we now hold in common.

Passion asks, What is the nature of suffering? What is faith? What does it mean to "walk humbly with God?"[82] What would it be like to lead a life that is whole and integrated? Passion involves seeking and finding meaning in life. It invites us to commitment to relationship and community. Passion is the making of a disciple. It involves the integration of knowledge with values and vocation precisely because it is grounded in relationship with others. Keith Morton borrows from Parker Palmer's language to speak of service learning as "an opportunity to 'dance' between objective and subjective ways of knowing."[83] Passion gives us the courage to take risks in order to pursue what we believe gives life meaning. Through it, we become people who have vibrant spiritual lives.

Cultivating Passion through Teaching

One way to get at passion in the classroom is through service learning. Julie Hatcher and Robert Bringle define service learning as

> a type of experiential education in which students participate in service to the community and reflect on their involvement in such a way as to gain further understanding of course and content and of the discipline and its relation to social needs and an enhanced sense of civic responsibility.[84]

There are two dimensions to our service. One is the depth and continuity of relationships, and the other is a commitment to get at the root causes of a problem. A deep level of commitment to these two aspects gives service its quality. If our commitment is superficial, then we are

---

82. Keith Morton, "Making Meaning: Reflections on Community Service and Learning," in *From Cloister to Commons*, 45.

83. Ibid., 49.

84. Julie A. Hatcher and Robert G. Bringle, "Reflections: Bridging the Gap between Service and Learning," *College Teaching* 45, no. 4 (fall 1997): 153. For reading on how service learning can be used to achieve course objectives, see Thomas G. McGowan, "Toward an Assessment-Based Approach to Service-Learning Course Design," in *From Cloister to Commons*, 83–91.

giving charity. In 1889, Jane Addams founded the Hull House, a settlement in Chicago, in an attempt to deal with large-scale urban poverty. She argued that charity was contrary to democracy in that it created inequality.[85] Bart Shaha, the director of the Bangladesh YMCA, took the argument further by claiming that charity is minimal commitment to service and that project approaches show halfway commitment. These types of commitment do not necessarily look at policy questions and therefore do not bring about true change. True commitment leads to a process of true change. This process of change must make use of critical insight and social analysis. It needs to be a mutual and participatory process.[86]

Participatory action research is one such process. It is an umbrella term that includes several traditions of theory and practice. Participation recognizes the value of including practitioners, community members, citizens, employees, and volunteers. It sees them as essential in providing useful knowledge regarding social, political, economic, technical, cultural, and organizational problems. The knowledge comes from the people. Action indicates that the research contributes directly to efforts for change. Research indicates a systematic effort to generate knowledge. It may include historical, literary, theological, as well as scientific forms. The major thrust is to focus the knowledge generated on changes that better the quality of living of the participants. It is research that is attached to the humanization of persons in communities. Unattached research tends to create policies that continue to oppress.

For example, suppose there is a problematic situation in a specific community. That community, in collaboration with trained researchers, collects and analyzes information and in taking action improves or solves the problem situation. This is collaborative research and practice.[87] It allows the very people affected by the problem to have a responsibility in the changes needed, while those outside the community who wish to collaborate bring particular skills that are perhaps not found in the community. The process toward change is directed mainly by the participants and not by the outside experts. In this way, the participants

85. See Jane Addams, "The Subtle Problems of Charity," *Atlantic Monthly*, 83, 496 (1899): 163–79.

86. The story of Bart Shaha can be found in Morton, "Making Meaning," 45–46.

87. For an example of participatory action research in a Christian community and with theological reflection, see Mary Ann Hinsdale, Helen M. Lewis, and S. Maxine Waller, *It Comes from the People: Community Development and Local Theology* (Philadelphia: Temple University Press, 1995). Also, for those who wish a beginner's understanding, see Susan E. Smith and Dennis G. Williams with Nancy A. Johnson, eds., *Nurtured by Knowledge: Learning to Do Participatory Action Research* (New York: Apex Press, 1997).

have power over their own situation. The ultimate goal is political action for transformation.

As Shaha has suggested, such a process requires a deep level of commitment. Students of religious education who decide to work in communities, sometimes their own communities, understand that they are making a long-term commitment that may extend beyond the life of the course or of their doctoral project. Theological readings and reflection are a part of the course, as are readings on a variety of research and community organizing and educational methods. Such integrative education makes use of a variety of knowledge and skills. Students in the religious education doctoral program of Claremont School of Theology as well as some master's of divinity students have worked on projects with incarcerated women, church structures, different immigrant groups, and Bible institutes among others.[88]

Teaching for Passion: An Epistemology

The epistemology that guides teaching for passion is what Mary Field Belenky and her associates have called connected knowing.[89] This type of knowing flows from empathy. It encourages relationship and fosters collaboration among people. It fosters dialogue and solidarity through genuine reciprocity in the exchange of ideas. It revitalizes the recognition of the interdependence of all creation and calls for continuous forms of experiencing others so that the self is enlarged, reinforcing a need to be connected. Being open to others makes us aware that our stories are not the only stories. Connecting with one another helps us create a new story together and to imagine stories of cocreation with God in partnership with one another. This is the praxis of learning that nurtures connected knowing. We will call it connected learning. When people are disconnected, spaces are created where oppression can set in. Policies created without the knowledge of the people they are supposed to serve and evaluations of programs without the input of the communities they are assisting are examples of how disconnection can result in oppression.

Connected learning requires imagination. Mary Richards speaks of moral imagination and explains that we can behave imaginatively, "en-

88. For an example of how the University of Delaware carried out such a program with professors and students in collaboration and the involvement of some of the churches in the community, see Karen A. Curtis, "Help from Within: Participatory Research in a Low-Income Neighborhood," *Urban Anthropology* 18, no. 2 (1989): 202–17.

89. Mary Field Belenky, Blythe McVicker Clinchy, Nancy Rule Goldberger, and Jill Mattuck Tarule, *Women's Ways of Knowing: The Development of Self, Voice, and Mind* (New York: Basic Books, 1986), 431–46.

visioning and eventually creating what is not yet present. . . . In one's citizenship, or the act of politics, it is a part of one's skill to imagine other ways of living than one's own."[90] We see this vividly in Martin Luther King Jr.'s speech "I Have a Dream." In it, he describes a society whose values and behaviors are more appropriately aligned with kingdom values. Such an imaginative ability can grow into a capacity for connected passion. This is passion that emerges from being in relationship with those who live under injustices rather than from a "cause."

Education that nurtures passion as part of discipleship and the Christian lifestyle begins with the following theological assumptions: (1) Christian discipleship includes social action; (2) the reign of God is a social reality; and (3) God is uniquely present in the faces of those who suffer. All education occurs within a social context and is therefore political in that it either works to transform society or perpetuates social forms.[91] Education, therefore, is enhanced when it taps into the passions of the participants. These passions may come from personal wounds or from anger over the woundedness in the world. They may come from hopes and dreams for a healed and just world. Ultimately, they come from the very heart and will of God in us. Passions engage our compassion and social consciousness and compel us to be involved in social and political engagement at various levels. Out of this involvement emerge new opportunities for conversion or personal transformation.

In this justice-centered model of education, the curricular starting points are the wounds of a community, particularly those that people are passionate about. The teacher is an animator and committed learner along with the students. As an animator, the teacher helps to draw forth the passions of the students and facilitates a process of reflection and action that engages the participants in liberating actions in their communities. The teacher is thus an empowering comrade for justice.

The action-reflection-action method entails generating themes based on discussions about students' passions. The common themes of the group are then engaged. The group analyzes what factors contribute to a problem by looking at economic, social, political, and cultural dimensions. This may entail doing research outside the traditional classroom setting. Theological reflection involves asking, Where is God in this problem, and how does God's Word invite us to respond to these realities? After this discernment process, students consider ways to re-

90. Richards, *Centering*, 92, 115.
91. For further discussion of these educational themes, see Paulo Freire, *Pedagogy of the Oppressed* (New York: Continuum, 1983).

spond. They may want to respond to immediate needs through acts of care, or they may want to respond to the causes of the problem through acts of justice. After each cycle of action and reflection, discernment begins again.[92] The setting for this model of teaching may be a college or seminary classroom; a Bible study or Sunday school class; a mission trip or service project; or small groups such as cell groups, base communities, or social action groups.

When our love for those who suffer and the love of the heart of God for those who are in need of justice come together in us, we enter a borderland between God and humanity. Our initial connection with one another has now matured and facilitates the building of shalom together.

Shalom

Shalom is a concept that cannot be captured by a single word, for it includes many dimensions: love, loyalty, truth, grace, salvation, justice, blessing, and righteousness. It is a biblical vision in which all of creation is one, every creature living in community and harmony with every other for the joy and well-being of all. Shalom is therefore a vision of connectedness for an entire community: young, elderly, rich, poor, Latino, Anglo, Native American, Asian, African-American, powerful, and dependent. Shalom includes the process of denouncing, announcing, and making persons and structures responsible for responding to all with equity and compassion.

Shalom is not about shifting power from one center to another. Rather, it involves distributing power among all equally. Because equity and reconciliation are our final goal, we cannot hold metaphors or visions of the center. In other words, we cannot believe that one perception is correct or that one group possesses the central vision, which everyone else must accept. Asian theologian Jung Young Lee speaks of a multicultural theology. He refers to marginality as that which overcomes our need for centrality. He states that centrality is based on hierarchical value, is interested in dominance, and vies for control, while marginality is based on egalitarian principles, is interested in service, and seeks cooperation.[93] Lee invites us all to the margin rather than to the center. He posits that when everyone becomes marginal, there is no

92. This is a brief description of the justice-centered education model. It is one of six educational paradigms that my colleague Frank Rogers and I use in our introductory course for Christian education.
93. Lee, *Marginality*, 151.

centrality that can marginalize anyone. Marginality, therefore, is overcome by marginality.[94]

Latino theologian Orlando Costas also invites us to the margins by reminding us that Christ died outside the gate, implying a new place of salvation. The temple had been the central place of salvation and had been confined to the walls of the city. But Jesus died outside, at the margins. He displaced salvation from the center to the margins.[95]

The journey from hospitality to shalom is one of new spiritual practices that free us from the inclination to dominate and control. They teach us to be servants to all people so that all are served equally as brothers and sisters. It is this spirit that makes us multicultural people.

The Hope of Reconciliation

As a journey of conversion, experiencing God's love brings us to love others in like fashion. This means appreciating ourselves and others in a way so radical that it turns all previous knowledge and criteria of judgment inside out. Our old perceptions of neighbor die, and we can discover new life. Radical love of our neighbor allows us to enter the reality and worldview of that neighbor and to live with compassion and passion in a journey toward shalom. Through this radical love and the understanding that emerges from it, we experience *metanoia* (a journey of changes). In this love and renewed understanding, we discover new attitudes that release a new spirit.[96]

The five steps of this spiritual journey of transformation use different means of relational teaching, including narrative, simulation, experiential learning, service learning, and participatory action research. Relational teaching makes use of the imagination and facilitates connections. This is important for developing the cross-cultural understanding and social critique necessary to perceive the world of our neighbors.

The theological assumptions of relational teaching are:

- God is revealing to the world his creative-responsive love with the purpose of reconciling us in Jesus Christ.

---

94. Ibid.

95. See Orlando E. Costas, *Christ outside the Gate: Mission beyond Christendom* (Grand Rapids: Eerdmans, 1986).

96. Insights taken from Virgilio Elizondo, "A Bicultural Approach to Religious Education," in *Beyond Borders: Writings of Virgilio Elizondo and Friends*, ed. Timothy Matovina (Maryknoll, N.Y.: Orbis, 2000), 65.

- God reveals himself to us in Scripture and in the person of Jesus Christ through the work of the Holy Spirit in the world.
- Jesus is incarnate in everyday reality *(lo cotidiano):* We study/listen to this reality to find Jesus.
- The Holy Spirit guides us to new truth about ourselves and our neighbors in relation to the will of God (the reign of God) as we interpret this reality.
- As we seek to know the work of God through the Holy Spirit in our daily reality, the Word of God is more fully illumined.
- The fuller illumination of the Word takes us in new directions based on a fuller and affirmed understanding of the truth of God's work of reconciliation through the redemptive work of Jesus Christ.

Such teaching is open to what is revealed of God in the world. It explores God's presence in the world. Because God is a relational God, such teaching also seeks to facilitate the engagement of persons. We look at stories together, the biblical story as well as the stories that bear witness to God in our midst today. In the Latino community, we call these stories *testimonios.* They are both the articulation and the internalization of our theology and faith. This witness gives insight into God's work in our midst.

Virgilio Elizondo suggests that the role of the teacher in multicultural education is that of a prophet speaking out against the idols of our time by illumining the blindness of social sin.[97] Elizondo cautions that "once sin has been established as part of the normative worldview, it cannot discern the status quo. When this happens, sin has disintegrated to the level of becoming an idol."[98] Our prejudices reflect our idols.

Shalom extends the narrative of God's redemptive relationship with creation in a comprehensive manner. It makes us a part of the narrative by inviting us to be a part of the conciliatory ways of educating and living. As teachers, we are ambassadors of reconciliation (2 Cor. 5:20).

Cultures contain the values that shape human character and govern ethical action.[99] Character is formed by a habitual way of life. This chapter began by looking at the nature of prejudice as defined by sociologists. Our habits of prejudice shape the nature of our cultural stories and determine our values and ethical actions. Conversion entails a journey of intentional efforts to change the narrative of our lives from sin

---

97. Elizondo, "Bicultural Approach to Religious Education," 63.
98. Ibid.
99. Bruce Bradshaw, *Change across Cultures: A Narrative Approach to Social Transformation* (Grand Rapids: Baker, 2002), 17.

to living the will of God. God's redemptive story in Scripture needs to be internalized as opposed to our narratives of prejudice.

Forming habits of hospitality, encounter, compassion, passion, and shalom engages us in efforts to express the dignity of life. The hope of this journey is to transform our cultural narratives into the biblical narrative, which can free us to realize the potential of all living beings so they can become all they were created to be. Shalom is the result of God's reconciling work through Christ. God's reconciling work embraces social, cultural, political, and economic structures.

Narratives are symbols of our values. The Lord's Table is a powerful Christian symbol of Christ's redemptive work. It is the place where people from every social strata come together, creating a mosaic of humanity. The clearest images of shalom often involve the sharing of a meal. Around meals Jesus created a sense of community. The image of the banqueting table is one of inclusivity in which people are liberated from the cultural barriers that alienate them from one another. A meal creates a setting in which people can relate to one another at the level at which they recognize their common humanity. Eating together is a ritual that brings a sense of unity (Luke 14:13–14).[100]

Another powerful symbol is the feeding of the five thousand. Bruce Bradshaw points out that the crowd included people who were ethnically, religiously, and politically diverse. They lived in a culture in which a person's identity was shaped by whom he or she ate with. It was a culture in which people were concerned about associating with people who were clean or unclean. Cleanliness of food was paramount, as was clean company.[101] This crowd would have included Pharisees, who were too clean to eat with anyone else; tax collectors and others who earned their living through sin; some Gentiles; and even Samaritans. But the story suggests that as they ate together they overcame the cultural barriers and defied the symbols of cleanliness that governed their lives. The experience of eating together was Jesus' teaching method. He organized them into small groups in which they encountered one another face-to-face, and they recognized one another's humanity as they participated in the prayer that Jesus led.[102] By inviting them to eat together, Jesus reconciled them to one another, empowered them to affirm one another's humanity, and thus transformed the elements of the worldview that governed their lives, including the religious, ethnic, political, social, and economic structures that separated them.[103]

100. Ibid., 209.
101. Ibid., 208.
102. Ibid., 209.
103. Ibid.

Table fellowship symbolizes unity, and this symbol can empower people to bear witness to the same story or narrative. The banqueting table expresses a new reality that those who sit at it have grasped: shalom.[104] The old narrative of prejudice needs to be transformed. It cannot deliver the hope of a better future. Shalom, however, affirms that people have the capacity to invest their gifts and efforts in the construction of a society that benefits themselves and everyone else. This is the hope of multicultural living, teaching, and ministry.

104. Ibid., 238.

Conclusion

Living the Biblical Vision

ELIZABETH CONDE-FRAZIER, S. STEVE KANG,
AND GARY A. PARRETT

The Way or Not-the-Way: A Final Word from Gary

When my wife, daughter, and I moved to the north shore of Massachusetts nearly seven years ago, we had much to learn about life in New England. Learning the rules of the road was particularly interesting and challenging. The road signs in New England are not like they are in Washington State or in New York and New Jersey. In those places, when a driver approaches an intersection, there are signs for both the road one is crossing and the road one is presently on. In Massachusetts, this is not the case. There are signs marking the roads one is crossing, but there are very few that tell the driver which road he or she is currently on. I suppose the logic is that one surely knows which road he or she is on. Of course, as newcomers in the area, we often found ourselves on roads we did not know. When that happened, we could drive for miles before solving the mystery. We discovered that the local saying is, "If you don't know where you're at, you don't belong here!" I am confident this is but a friendly joke.

Even more striking was the discovery of rotaries. In other places, these are called roundabouts. Upon entering a rotary, the driver is presented with numerous exit options, usually at least three (four if we include the option of simply going full circle and reversing one's tracks). Adventurous drivers seem to love rotaries, as they can offer a sensation, at least briefly, of being a NASCAR driver. More cautious drivers, like my wife, are generally very intimidated by these circular intersections.

In figure 3 below, I use the rotary as a symbol of the choices that confront us in regard to the issues of multiethnicity raised in this book. I have even provided street signs, although it is entirely possible that at a given time we may not be consciously aware of which road we are currently on.

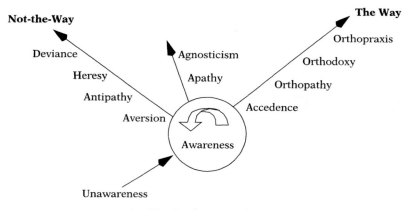

Fig. 3. Choosing the Way

The rotary represents a new level of awareness about the truth. We enter the rotary from a starting place of relative unawareness. How did this progress occur? Perhaps we were confronted by Scripture and began to see that things are not as we thought they were. Perhaps we picked up a book—a biography or a history text—and suddenly found that our prior knowledge of the matter was insufficient. Maybe we heard the story of a person with whom we had begun to form a new relationship. A television show, a news item, a movie, or a play may have provoked new ways of seeing things. Perhaps, whether we were ready or not, a teacher or preacher thrust this new awareness upon us.

In any case, we are now here, in the rotary of a new degree of awareness. But no rotary is a final destination. It is simply an intersection, a major junction, and it forces us to keep moving, to make a choice. There are, from this one rotary, multiple ways for us to go. Which will we choose?

Some may bypass the road that presents itself first. They choose, instead, a course called apathy. The whole thing, after all, seems "much ado about nothing" to them. Staying the course, however, may reveal that the road soon changes names and becomes agnosticism. Apathy about the truth can harden into a settled form of agnosticism. It is different from the original unawareness, for it is a choice to not know or to pretend that one cannot really know. "Oh, the whole thing is so complicated. Who can possibly know what to do about these things?"

Others choose the path of aversion. They simply do not like what they have heard and seen, and so they turn away. This road is soon marked with various signs: antipathy, heresy, and deviance. Those on this course have a *pathos* that is opposed to that of Christ, who knew suffering for our sakes and ministered with particular care among the poor, the *xenoi,* and the crushed. They fix in their minds an understanding of things that are contrary to God's revealed truth and thus become heretics. And since they have departed from the way, they are, in terms of their choices and actions, deviants (from the Latin *de,* "from" + *via,* "way").

There is, however, the first path, the one most obviously in keeping with what God has revealed in Scripture and in the life of his Son. It is marked at first with a sign called accedence, for to accede is to assent to the truth. This path, too, has multiple names, but they are all similar: orthopathy,[1] orthodoxy, orthopraxis. Travelers on this course are resolved to align their *pathos,* their doctrine, and their lifestyles with those of Jesus, who is the Life, the Truth, and the Way.

When travelers have ventured out a little distance from the rotary, the true names of the roads they have chosen appear. One path is called simply the Way. Both of the others and, indeed, whatsoever other road there is or could ever be bear the name not-the-way.[2] There are, in the end, only these two paths to choose from: It is either the Way or not-the-way.

I pray that God has allowed some measure of the truth about his heart for the nations and for the *xenos,* about his kingdom plans and the possibilities of shalom to be revealed through this volume. May God embolden and equip us to respond wisely and faithfully to his will, whatever new awareness we may have.

I will instruct you and teach you in the way you should go; I will counsel you and watch over you.

Psalm 32:8

1. For a discussion of the meaning of *pathos,* refer to footnote 35 in chapter 6.
2. E. Stanley Jones used the phrase "not-the-way" to describe the only real alternative to walking in the Way in a devotional book titled *The Way* (Nashville: Abingdon, 1991).

Kingdom Citizens: A Final Word from Steve

The kingdom of God is one of the most prominent motifs in the teaching of Jesus Christ, as depicted in the synoptic Gospels.[3] However, while scholars of wide-ranging traditions and ideologies all agree that it is undoubtedly a central feature of Jesus' message and ministry, the meaning of the kingdom of God is not entirely clear or agreed upon.[4] The kingdom of God should not be reduced to a concept or idea, with a single identifiable referent that adequately expresses its scope and meaning. Instead, it should be construed as a symbol, a "tensive" symbol, that generates a wide range of ideas and active obedience that dialogically stem from the deep belief that God is the king.[5] One thing is certain: The kingdom of God should not be understood in territorial or churchly terms. Jesus Christ discloses that the Triune God is the King of kings and the Lord of lords. While Jesus' ministry appeared to end in disaster on the cross, the Triune God was exercising God's kingly rule even in Jesus' death. Through the resurrection of Jesus Christ, the victory over sin and death has been accomplished, and it serves as a foretaste of the final triumph of God's kingly rule. The paradox, then, continues in that the kingdom of God is here and now but also not yet, in that it is not fully in force.

A permanent quandary remains: How do we make sense of the kingdom of God past (in the ministry of Jesus or in the notion of the kingdom of heaven in the Old Testament), present (in human history, with the church as the sign and messenger of it), and future (in the context of the ongoing life of the world)?[6] Throughout Christian history, the church, as the people of God, has had a strong tendency "to support the current status quo as an adequate expression of God's will," convincing itself that "whatever defects it has, any likely alternative would be worse, or even disastrous."[7] Thus, the kingdom of God has been largely understood as the future coming of the kingdom of God, which is based on the work of Jesus Christ in the past. Such an understanding has been coupled with a misappropriation of God's sovereignty and the abdication of a responsible human response to God's grace. Thus, the kingdom of God is seen as entirely the work of God. It is not too difficult to witness in recent Christian history in the United States how such a mis-

---

3. George Beasley-Murray, *Jesus and the Kingdom of God* (Exeter: Paternoster, 1986).

4. Alister McGrath, ed., *Modern Christian Thought* (Oxford: Blackwell, 1993), 301.

5. Norman Perrin, *Jesus and the Language of the Kingdom* (Philadelphia: Fortress, 1976), 31.

6. McGrath, *Modern Christian Thought*, 304–9.

7. Ibid., 305.

appropriation and abdication have led the church to acquiesce its responsibility of proclaiming God's shalom in the church and society, rendering itself useless and irrelevant.[8]

Instead, the church of Jesus Christ is called to live out the covenant with God and with one another as the eschatological community, realizing or showing forth in the present the communal life of the eternal kingdom of God. It is to cultivate the *habitus* of the life with the Triune God as a sign of the eternal kingdom that has been inaugurated by the incarnation, death, and resurrection of our Lord Jesus Christ. For this reason, the church must strive to proclaim in word and deed the fabric of the eternal kingdom—love, justice, righteousness, and peace.[9]

The church has already received, through the gift of faith, the oneness of the church. It is God who has declared us one in Jesus Christ. The church is not called to work toward creating a multicultural community merely for the sake of being in step with the world. Instead, the church is to declare to the world, through an authentic and persistent *habitus*, that the immanently Triune God has graciously and decisively acted in history through divine economy.

The kingdom *habitus* takes its cues from the disciples at Pentecost as opposed to the power builders at Babel. The disciples allowed the kingdom of God to take them by storm instead of trying to storm the ramparts of heaven. The disciples had no less zeal than did the power builders, but their obedience stemmed not from ambition but from utter dependence on the Holy Spirit, with gratitude and joy.[10]

The church is made up of those who are made vulnerable to God's history of forgiveness. They are those who have been given a new history, a new story, rather than the world's story. That is why we quite literally receive at baptism a new self and name. Baptism is but a reminder that we need the *entire* church to help us understand the ongoing task of unlearning the old self and learning to appropriate our new life.[11]

As a significant aspect of such a trajectory, the church of Jesus Christ must remember the terror Christians have perpetrated on one another.

8. Rodney Clapp, *A Peculiar People: The Church as Culture in a Post-Christian Society* (Downers Grove, Ill.: InterVarsity, 1996). For instance, race relations in America are depicted this way in Michael Emerson and Christian Smith, *Divided by Faith: Evangelical Religion and the Problem of Race in America* (Oxford: Oxford University Press, 2000).

9. Stanley Grenz, "The Community of God: A Vision of the Church in the Postmodern Age," *Crux* 28, no. 2 (June 1992): 24.

10. William Coffin, "Fires of Sin and Flames of Creativity," *Christian Ministry* 17, no. 3 (May 1986): 30.

11. Stanley Hauerwas, *A Better Hope: Resources for a Church Confronting Capitalism, Democracy, and Postmodernity* (Grand Rapids: Brazos Press, 2000), 151.

We as Christians are obliged to confess and remember our sins, but we are also "required to remember the sins of those who have sinned against us. Any reconciliation that does not require such a remembering cannot be the reconciliation made possible by the cross of Christ."[12] God's shalom does not ignore human suffering but takes it up and vindicates it. Jesus Christ is not a victorious, uncrucified god. He is the God "who achieves victory through suffering, and liberation through oppression. Ours is a God who, having known oppression, shares with the oppressed in their suffering" so that all Christians can also share in God's shalom.[13] The fulfillment of God's shalom on earth, however, is a drawn-out and messy task for the church. Yet the recognition of and commitment to realizing the kingdom of God is the spark that provides hope and commences shalom in the church and the world through the grace of the Triune God.

> Peace I leave with you; my peace I give you. I do not give to you as the world gives. Do not let your hearts be troubled and do not be afraid.
>
> John 14:27

> The light shines in the darkness, but the darkness has not understood it.
>
> John 1:5

The Power That Subverts All Powers: A Final Word from Elizabeth

Multicultural living, teaching, and ministry involve understanding power dynamics. At a recent conference on urban multicultural congregations, this was the main topic of discussion.[14] This book began with our personal journeys. In them we can see moments of powerlessness, such as shame, a lack of confidence, marginalization, different forms of victimization, fear, silence, discrimination, and alienation. These give birth to depression and hopelessness. Where we find powerlessness, we also find its counterpart, power over. This is the type of power we most

12. Ibid., 140–41.
13. Justo González, *Mañana: Christian Theology from a Hispanic Perspective* (Nashville: Abingdon, 1990), 93.
14. The conference was called "Multicultural Congregational Journey: Negotiating Power Dynamics." It was organized by Partners in Urban Transformation and held at the William Carey International University, Pasadena, California, in March and May 2003. For further information, see www.partnersinurbantransformation.org.

often find in our society. In industrialized societies, oppressive power is taken for granted. We have learned to live with it.

Power over is based on domination and authority. One person or group can determine the behavior of another person or group. It makes use of economic or social punishment or its possibility as a means of control. We need only read about labor disputes or news related to our corporate culture to see the many forms it may take. One example of this in our institutions is the body of knowledge that constitutes our curricula. That body of knowledge usually represents Western culture and excludes the value of other bodies of information to the detriment of a generation of leaders who must prepare for a global reality.

Power over affects the sphere of relationships. It fragments our connections and results in the disruption of relationships with others and with nature, as can be seen when corporate interests disrupt the ecology of an area. Power over is power that bankrupts. This is the type of power that we wish to see transformed through the ministry of reconciliation.

Our journeys also reflect power from within. This is power that arises from the building of connections and bonding with other persons and the environment. It is power that awakens a person's abilities and potential. This is the type of power we strive for in our teaching and ministries. It is felt in acts of creation, such as planting, writing, preaching, outreach, healthy parenting, healing, cleaning, singing, worshiping, building, envisioning, and making love—the acts that care for the soul. To treat others with dignity and worth, to honor their language and culture, to provide opportunity and support, to help others name their own realities and make meaning of their lives, to validate a person's anger or other feelings over an injustice are all expressions of power from within. We can see in Jesus' preaching, teaching, and signs the many ways that he denounced power over and facilitated power from within (Matt. 5:1–11; 12:1–14; Luke 6:27–36; 7:36–50; 10:38–42; 18:15–17).

The theological conversation of this work emphasized the incarnation and the place of marginality rather than centrality. This shows how powerlessness is the power of the cross. This is foolishness to the world but the wisdom and power of God (1 Cor. 1:18). We do well to reflect on this point as we end. The church has mistaken the power of the resurrection for triumphalism. This has yielded the fruit of power over in the history of the church and has obscured the truth of the gospel. In some places, it has polluted the very symbol of the cross so that it has come to mean oppression instead of salvation.[15]

15. This is true in Kazakhstan. Kazaks do not use the symbol of the cross in their churches because all the peoples who waged war on them and oppressed them came bearing the cross.

The incarnation, the death of Jesus, his resurrection, and Pentecost are the four main events of Christianity. In the incarnation, we come to understand humility, which is that which heals us from our identity crisis—inferiority and superiority. Some suffer from an identity crisis because of power over, while others suffer because of subjugation. Humility helps us to understand who we are and who we are not so that we do not usurp the place of others and can be hospitable. The death of Jesus points us to self-denial as a corrective to our narcissism and a way toward solidarity. The resurrection is victory through identification with suffering. It is the power that can bring liberation where there is oppression. Finally, Pentecost focuses us on the initiative of the Holy Spirit to bring about unity and equality.

Together, these point us toward a pneumatological cultural *kenōsis,* or a spirituality of cultural emptying that leads us to power with.[16] This is the type of social power shared among people who value one another as equals. Power with includes respectful caring, mutual influence, and shared power. It is fragile and fluid and requires disciplined listening, patience, and openness. It validates the history, experiences, and aspirations of neighbors who are invisible in our society. Acknowledging their presence ushers in love, justice, righteousness, and peace. Power with refers to human beings living in harmony with God, self, and all forms of life. It is when I most feel at peace with God and myself that I am most able to connect with others, being sensitive to their uniqueness. As a teacher, I am then able to facilitate a process of empowerment.

Spirituality is attentiveness to the Holy Spirit and participation in his initiatives. The kingdom of God is a communal initiative of the Spirit. It emphasizes the corporate nature of our lives of faith. Covenanting, the knitting together of those lives, is needed for forming and equipping a community whose character makes visible the gospel. Covenanting as faith partners or friends makes possible formation of character, values, habits, and a vision of a community that chooses to be in tune with the Holy Spirit and to be displaced from the power dynamics of society.

In the theological interpretations of this book, we root ourselves in the biblical story, which is an alternative story to that of our dominant cultures and which begs to be embodied in our relational and organizational practices, whether at church or in our institutions of learning. On our spiritual journey, we face the question, What kind of people do we need to be for this to make sense? This is different from the question,

16. This term was used by the participants at a regional conference of scholars of the Hispanic Theological Initiative when speaking about these matters (Boston College, Boston, 15 March 2003).

Does this make sense? This different question allows us not only to read Scripture but also to let Scripture read us.[17]

Gary invites us to choose the path that aligns us with Jesus and is called the way. Steve encourages us to become kingdom citizens. I would suggest that the Spirit summons us to begin this journey by being of the same mind that was in Christ Jesus. This mind-set calls us toward an emptying and toward taking on the form of servants. It invites us to be humble and reminds us that this may take the form of suffering (Phil. 2:5–8). This is the incarnation. The incarnation is the power that subverts all other powers. It is the place of surrendering to the Spirit. It is the place of confrontation, compassion, and suffering with. It is in this position of weakness that Christ's power is made perfect (2 Cor. 12:9). Let us choose this way of witnessing to the lordship of Jesus, our servant Lord!

17. For further discussion about how Scripture reads us, see Justo L. González, *Santa Biblia: The Bible through Hispanic Eyes* (Nashville: Abingdon, 1996). See also Pablo A. Jimenez, "The Bible: A Hispanic Reading," in *Teología en Conjunto: A Collaborative Hispanic Protestant Theology,* ed. José David Rodríguez and Loida I. Martell Otero (Louisville: Westminster John Knox, 1997), 66–79.

Index